Janet De Neefe has had a passion for cooking from an early age. The youngest of three children, she spent most of her pre-school days in the kitchen, watching her mother cook hearty casseroles, old-fashioned puddings and assorted cakes.

Trips with her Maltese grandmother to the market were sensory adventures, where assorted pungent cheeses, piles of shiny fish of all shapes and sizes and fleshy meats revealed a world of exotic ingredients and interesting ethnic peoples. A family holiday to Bali when she was a teenager awakened her tastebuds to a new, vibrant and exciting Southeast Asian cuisine and culture.

After Janet gained a BEd in Arts and Crafts at Burwood State College in Melbourne, she decided to take a break from formal education to work in restaurants. She returned to Bali in July 1984 and met her future husband, Ketut, on the second day of her holiday. One chapter of her life closed and another opened.

In the following years, Janet returned to teaching in Australia, in between spending time in Bali. She taught Balinese cooking at the Council of Adult Education in Melbourne for a brief time, giving up this work to open her first restaurant, Lilies, in Ubud, in the foothills of Bali's volcanic mountain range.

By 1989, Janet and Ketut were married. The next year they established the Honeymoon Bakery and Guesthouse, the name reflecting this happy time for them. In the following years, they opened two more restaurants, Casa Luna and Indus, as well as the Casa Lina Homewares shop and, most recently, an emporium selling Indonesian antiques and textiles.

Janet and Ketut live with their four children at the Guesthouse. It is also from here that Janet runs her classes on Balinese cooking, which are attended by visitors from all over the world.

fragrant rice

JANET DE NEEFE

flamingo
An imprint of HarperCollins*Publishers*

Quotes from *Parthayana, The Journeying of Partha,* translated and edited by
Helen Creese, are reproduced courtesy of KITLV Press.

Excerpts from *The Painted Alphabet* by Diana Darling are reproduced courtesy of
the publisher, Periplus Editions (HK) Ltd.

Flamingo
An imprint of HarperCollins*Publishers*, Australia

First published in Australia in 2003
Reprinted in 2003 (twice)
by HarperCollins*Publishers* Pty Limited
ABN 36 009 913 517
A member of the HarperCollins*Publishers* (Australia) Pty Limited Group
www.harpercollins.com.au

HarperCollins*Publishers*
25 Ryde Road, Pymble, Sydney, NSW 2073, Australia
31 View Road, Glenfield, Auckland 10, New Zealand
77-85 Fulham Palace Road, London W6 8JB, United Kingdom
2 Bloor Street East, 20th floor, Toronto, Ontario M4W 1A8, Canada
10 East 53rd Street, New York NY 10022, USA

National Library of Australia Cataloguing-in-Publication data:

De Neefe, Janet.
  Fragrant rice: my continuing love affair with Bali: a tale of passion, marriage and food.
  Bibliography.
  ISBN 0 7322 7612 8.
  1. De Neefe, Janet. 2. Restaurateurs – Indonesia – Bali Island – Biography.
  3. Bali Island (Indonesia) – Description and travel. 4. Bali Island (Indonesia)
  – Social life and customs. I. Title.
959.86

Cover and internal design by Kate Mitchell Design
Cover photographs: Window onto rice paddies by Petrina Tinslay; inset food shot, front cover, and
              back cover photographs by Tim De Neefe
Internal photographs: Tim De Neefe
Typeset in 11/14 Sabon by HarperCollins Design Studio
Printed and bound in Australia by Griffin Press on 80gsm Bulky Book Ivory

6 5 4   04 05 06

To my husband, Ketut,
and my precious children,
Dewi, Krishna, Laksmi and Arjuna.

Contents

Author's note

The Balinese way of life is very different from how we live in the West. In my early years in Bali, I remember walking through villages and experiencing the most extraordinary sensation of feeling totally separated from what I was seeing. It was as if the Balinese were behind glass, or I was watching an old movie on a huge screen. They were so absorbed in their daily activities that it gave me the impression I was invisible, and in a way maybe I was. Their detachment from passers-by and complete focus on their own routine was so different from anything I'd known in my own life. I imagine that most tourists must feel something similar.

The local people's lifestyle is largely inaccessible for visitors to Bali and remains a mystery on many levels. Usually, in a different country, going to a restaurant or bar is a good way to get to know the local people, but in Bali the only other people likely to be in such places will be foreigners. The Balinese prefer to eat at home, or maybe at a *warung*, a food stall. There are not many occasions when a tourist can socialise with the Balinese, unless they are staying in a traditional compound. One of my main reasons for writing this book, therefore, was to reveal a little of the character of these lovely gentle people and to explain something of how they live and eat.

I have found gathering recipes from the Balinese as much of a challenge as getting recipes from my grandmother. If I asked Grandma how to make her fluffy vanilla-scented pikelets, she would reply vaguely that she added a handful of this and a little bit of that. She never had anything written down, and neither do people here. The importance of measuring and weighing ingredients is alien to the Balinese way of doing things; everything is learnt from the old folk in the compound or by chatting with friends and neighbours. I've often heard the women discussing how to make certain dishes while preparing offerings at the temple. Many a time, when I was trying to write down a recipe while watching my sister-in-law cook, I had to stop in frustration when it was clear that a large knob of turmeric, tamarind or galangal had been added without my realising. Because of my determination to record every detail accurately, I'd have to patiently wait until another day and then ask shyly if we could make the dish again.

The way we eat here is also different from how meals are presented in the West. The Balinese principle of sharing applies at mealtimes too: several dishes are prepared and eaten together with a mound of steamed rice. There are no starters; the meal is presented buffet-style, with each person helping himself or herself to the selection. In general, at least four dishes are prepared, along with a spicy sambal, and the rice holds centre stage. In our household, the selection might include a spicy soupy dish of vegetables with legumes, leafy greens with roasted coconut, fried fish, tofu or eggs and a sambal.

The recipes in *Fragrant Rice* are in keeping with this style of eating. One dish could provide a hearty feed for two people, or a generous spoonful to be eaten with a number of other dishes for up to six to eight people, depending on their appetite. If you are planning a dinner party for eight, you'll probably find that three to five recipes with a sambal should be sufficient, plus rice of course. If you're cooking just for one, halve the spices and ingredients in the recipe, or cook the whole dish and freeze the remainder. Leftovers are never a problem as the flavours of simmered spices are more exciting the next day. Spice pastes can be stored in the fridge for up to two weeks, with a smear of oil on top.

Nowadays, the search for Asian ingredients does not have to comprise an all-day trek to a remote suburb. Many supermarkets are stocking their shelves with exotic seasonings as more

Australians embrace the cuisine of their closest neighbours. In my home city of Melbourne, Box Hill, Springvale, Abbotsford and the Victoria Market are a wonderful source for the ingredients used in this book, as well as providing an exciting cultural excursion. When I need to buy fresh galangal, Chinese greens or lime leaves, I jump in the car with the children and tell them we're off to 'Vietnam' — my favourite haunt in Victoria Street, Abbotsford. I'm sure our children will grow up thinking that Vietnam is only a ten-minute drive from our house in East Kew.

I hope you enjoy my story of life in Bali as much as I have enjoyed writing it, and that you take the time to nurture your soul with the wholesome recipes in this book. My enriching experience of this peaceful island paradise, spanning nearly twenty years, has allowed me to see the world in a whole new light, where love and respect are the key principles. It's been a joy to share my journey with you. And when you close the pages of this book, remember to carry the blessings with you into everyday life.

Preface

THE BOMB THAT SHOOK
THE WORLD

On Sunday, 13 October 2002, the gentle touch of my daughter Dewi shook me out of my early morning dreams as she whispered there had been a bomb in Kuta. I can still hear her words clearly in my head and recall the expression of nervous concern on her face at the first news of the event that would rock her innocent world during the coming weeks. Together we watched the television with disbelief. The devastation caused by the bomb that destroyed the Sari Club and Paddy's Bar in Kuta was massive; none of us will ever forget those tragic scenes of injured bodies and charred corpses.

Many Balinese friends gathered at our house that morning and my husband's eyes were moist as he discussed plans to help the victims. 'Your daddy's very upset,' I told Dewi. 'Yes, I know, Mummy,' she said. 'I think he's going to cry.'

For Ketut, one of the greatest sadnesses was that the tourists had died on Balinese soil and that the Balinese people had not been able to protect them. They had lost their lives in a foreign land, a tropical paradise that has embraced travellers for so many years. He reminded his friends that they have a great responsibility to keep visitors safe from harm, and now, in return, they must help to save lives. We also realised that this tragedy would have far-reaching consequences that would only spell further hardship for the people of Bali.

We gathered at Casa Luna with a large group of expatriate friends and made plans to help in whatever way we could. Ketut set up an extra phone line at the front of the restaurant and began contacting nearby hotels and restaurants for donations of food. In the kitchen, we began to make hundreds of sandwiches and rice meals and collected drinks and other necessities for victims and helpers. The first team of volunteers headed off to Sanglah Hospital in Denpasar. The car was loaded with people, food, refreshments, towels and other bits and pieces that had been gathered within an hour or two. I stayed at Casa Luna to help manage the relief efforts. I secretly knew I wouldn't be strong enough to deal with the inevitable death and sadness at the hospital.

A 'Donations Needed' sign was placed on a table opposite the piles of freshly baked bread, chocolate yoghurt cake and apple crumble. The Casa Luna relief centre was well on its way by early afternoon. Ketut and his friends helped organise a blood donors' unit at a nearby clinic and a handful of expatriate volunteers sat there with Indonesians to translate. I remember being on the phone for most of the day, coordinating transport and relaying vital information back and forth, alongside a host of helpers who assisted from morning until night. We existed on the edge of our emotions all week and fought back the tears by immersing ourselves in necessary duties.

Volunteers from all walks of life spent day after day at Sanglah Hospital, counselling parents who had lost their children, answering desperate phone calls enquiring after missing persons, attending to the injured and organising bodies in the morgue. Their only skills for dealing with the crisis were a compassionate heart and a determination to help as many sufferers as possible. I remember hearing the story of a volunteer who sat with a badly burnt Indonesian woman. The Indonesian woman did not speak English and the volunteer could not speak Indonesian. She wanted to whisper words of comfort to ease the woman's pain, but did not know how. In the end, she took the woman by the hand and sang simple gentle songs that rocked her to sleep. When the Indonesian woman woke, she asked the staff to find the tourist who had sat by her bed and sung so sweetly. This story, and others like it, will stay in our hearts for ever.

As an Australian, I was deeply saddened to hear of so many Australian lives lost. I helped in every way possible, as a statement of Western solidarity and sympathy. I imagined the shock our people would be experiencing, in a land that we claim has 'no worries'. I also felt deeply sad for the Balinese. I saw my niece a few days after the bombing and she looked at me with misty eyes. 'I wanted to call you when I heard about the tragedy, but I just didn't know what to say,' she said. The Balinese were full of sorrow and also suddenly concerned for the safety of their precious island.

I remember Ketut saying that Bali belongs to the world, and this has never been more apparent, for the world shared this disaster. People from many countries expressed their love for Bali and we received countless heartfelt letters of sympathy. But the Balinese love Bali more than anyone. Destruction of their land and their property sinks deep into their hearts. In a country where a dream of a burning building is a certain omen of death, the Kuta bomb was the ultimate tragedy.

After the bombing, the Balinese made offerings to apologise to God. If they had made a mistake, they were now asking for forgiveness. They searched for possible reasons why the bomb had happened, and repented for their perceived errors. Several months earlier, a large ceremony had taken place south of Kuta during which a giant old turtle had been slaughtered. The turtle had been used purely as an offering and the flesh had not been eaten. In that ceremony, a man in a trance predicted something bad would happen in Bali. The Balinese now claimed the bomb was the manifestation of this premonition. Perhaps they were being punished for slaying this old beast, perhaps it was karma for their ill-chosen deeds, or perhaps a sentence from a previous life.

'Do you think we are being punished?' a driver asked a Western friend of mine. She was astonished by the fact that the Balinese people could internalise this tragedy as part of their fate, their karma. Who could ever expect to be dealt such a blow?

The tragedy spoke to the Balinese of another issue too: the balance between man and his environment. Was this a message that there has been too much development on this picturesque island? Has the government overlooked building codes and security, and have the Balinese been too complacent about tourism? Ketut is deeply concerned about such matters, and spoke about Bali in the future and the hope that it could become a better place.

Mystical stories started to filter through, as if carried on the air, as would only happen in Bali. We heard that at Paddy's Bar, none of the staff were killed. They somehow escaped blindly through the back of the property and maintained they were led by God. The shrine at the entrance to Paddy's Bar stands unscathed as a statement of divine power.

On the Friday after the bombing, under a waxing moon, sprays of fragrant tears fell to the ground from the leaves of a huge shady tree within the inner courtyard of the Ubud palace. Word spread throughout the town and by 10 p.m. the small area that had received the droplets of water was crowded with Balinese throwing their arms up to receive blessings. The atmosphere within this royal sanctuary was charged with happiness and hope. 'Could this be a miracle?' I heard a Westerner ask.

The following day the shower persisted. By midday the priests had arrived and began chanting sacred mantras to the anxious crowd. More Balinese arrived to gather water and take it home to their shrines. People lined up for blessings. The holy men who channel the spirits were called upon to communicate with God and ask for an explanation. The message finally spread around town that the ancestors of the palace were responsible for the water. The collective team of deified spirits was showering the people of Ubud with holy water to protect them from further troubles and to purify the village. The impact of this single event gave all of us great hope that peace would prevail. A snake seen rising from the main road and soaring towards heaven was viewed as another good omen.

Prior to the bombing, our economy had just started to get back on its feet. Poor Bali has suffered countless blows from neighbouring islands: over the years, we have had to withstand the troubles in Java, Aceh and Timor. I've often wished we could lift the anchor and float to another part of the world where the neighbours are more settled, but perhaps there is no such place. The acts of terrorism in the United States the year before had brought economic hardship to Bali, and the Kuta tragedy was a further blow. After the 11 September events, we had cheerfully claimed that Bali was safe. Perhaps now we were being punished for our arrogance.

In an attempt to brighten the spirits of the local people, a team of young Ubud residents formed a committee to host a peace gathering which they hoped would strengthen mutual understanding and cooperation amongst all members of the community. It was called a Tribute to Peace and Unity and a total of 81 *banjars* representing more than 58,000 people were invited to participate in the grand event, along with the local Moslem, Christian and expatriate community. The idea gathered momentum and the original plan of a procession expanded into a weekend of activities.

In the nearby village of Peliatan, thousands of people gathered under the shade of the banyan trees. Mothers, children, students and men represented the different communities. They included Balinese dancers, marching girls, Catholic priests, *barongs*, *gamelans*, artists and people from all corners of the world. Some wore traditional clothing or national costume, others wore white T-shirts printed with the words 'Bali, Peace and Unity'. Students in white suits led the procession, carrying the Indonesian red and white flag of truth and bravery. A team of enthusiastic young men followed them, supporting a large decorated monument of peace on a bamboo frame with a white dove perched on top. Other groups followed with banners, flags and flowers. It was a unified message of peace, goodwill and love.

As I walked with the people of Ubud to the soccer field, my heart swelled with pride. I am so lucky to live in such a wonderful community. The gentle tinkle of the *gamelan* and chorus of bamboo flutes floated along the road, creating a magical feeling of warmth. I looked at the faces of the people lining the street and saw shades of hope in every colour. Sun-beaten farmers and old grandmas looked in admiration at the Indonesian flag. Moslems sat beside Balinese Hindus, chatting and laughing. Children on bicycles decorated with white feathers streamed past like doves on wheels. Balinese men wearing sarongs in the sacred black and white check talked happily about the next ceremony, their attire representing the opposing forces of good and evil carrying a stronger message. Balinese dancers wrapped in bright cloth, wearing their gold headdresses, weathered the intense heat with grace. Young girls drifted by carrying roses, others held peace signs and candles. The world had come together in the little town of Ubud and I was a part of it. I wished everyone everywhere could be here to enjoy the positively charged atmosphere. The veil of sadness that had settled over Ubud dissolved in a shimmer of gold decorations, white banners, flowers and love. Would it be any other way in this tropical haven?

But a week later, Ubud had become a ghost town. I watched the deserted streets from Casa Luna and thought about the old days, when life was simpler. Businesses came to a halt and our restaurants and the guesthouse were empty. Stories of rising unemployment started to brush past our ears. Other workers had had their hours cut, were on half pay. More people spent time sitting on their steps watching the traffic go past or simply staring into space. Temple ceremonies were held with the same enthusiasm but there were no crowds of visitors to watch the displays. We were on our own. The stark reality that our economy relies solely on tourism and the tourist dollar hit me full on. I remember lying in bed, tears falling on my pillow, as I thought of all the plans I had made for the coming months, plans I now had to abandon. And I was only one amongst thousands.

*   *   *

The cleansing ceremony for the victims of the Kuta bombing was held on Friday 15 November, forty-two days after the tragedy. On the Thursday afternoon I travelled down to this former beachside paradise with some friends to join the ceremony the following day. The streets were so quiet it felt like a long weekend, but then every day was beginning to feel like a long weekend.

I had mixed emotions about visiting Kuta, and my children were very frightened to see me go. 'Don't worry, I'll be OK,' I cried as we drove off down the road. During the sad weeks since the bombing, my children had been very anxious. Arjuna, my four-year-old son, asked me if all the tourists had gone home because of the terrorists. His Balinese-Indonesian-English vocabulary now includes that evil word that scares the entire world and I was stunned to hear this question coming from such a small person. Dewi and Krishna were fearful there would be a bomb in Ubud and didn't want to walk home from school or leave the family compound once they got home. When my father was talking to Krishna about meteorites and asked if we had any in Bali, Krishna replied, 'No, Grandpa, we have only bombs.'

The children asked endless questions about why the bombing had happened and who had created such evil. They watched every television report with terror and gazed at the ghastly images in the papers. At night they dreamt of ghosts and disturbed souls flying through the villages. They heard stories about the security guards at ground zero in Kuta, who heard screaming voices in the dark silent hours after midnight.

Weeks later, when I intended to drive past the site with the children, Dewi was almost hysterical in her refusal. 'We can't drive past today. It's a dark moon and we haven't brought any offerings to place there,' she cried.

When we arrived in Kuta, the first hotel we looked at was almost empty. A few Australians checked in ahead of us and were quietly shown to their rooms. The Indonesian girl at the front desk whispered that the teenage girl had lost her mother in the tragedy and had returned to see the ceremony. 'I feel so sorry for her,' she said with genuine sadness. Her words struck a chord deep down inside as I imagined how heartbreaking it must be for these people to return to the place where their loved ones had passed away. I greatly admired this young girl and her father for joining in the prayers at their time of need.

We ended up finding a small hotel closer to the site and checked in. Within minutes, Dewi had called me to see if I was OK and, more importantly, to ask whether there were any ghosts in the room. I assured her that the coast was clear and that I would let her know immediately if I saw anything unusual. Since the tragedy, my children have been plagued with fears about ghosts at the site, for a soul that is not cremated properly can wreak havoc.

We wandered along the deserted streets of Kuta. The atmosphere of this worldly playground was deflated; the feeling was not necessarily one of sadness, but rather of quietened spirits and concern for the future. A deep silence filled the air, the kind of silence that is born from tragedy. The streets were empty and the beach was almost deserted. At sunset, we sat in a restaurant by the sea and I stared at the fringed palm trees alongside the road and thought about Bali in the early seventies, when Legian, the next village along from Kuta, consisted of coconut groves and fishermen's huts. Who could have dreamt this terrible thing would happen?

The next morning the phone stirred me out of sleep at about 6 a.m. 'Did you see any *hantus* [ghosts], Mum?' Dewi whispered. I told her that it was surprisingly quiet in the hotel, but didn't let her know that I'd had a very disturbed night's sleep. I assured her that the cleansing ceremony would release the spirits and she wouldn't have to worry about them any more.

We set off for the ceremony at 8.30 a.m. I hadn't been to Jalan Legian yet and hoped I wouldn't be too overwhelmed. We walked up the side streets and entered the main road just beyond Poppies. In the fresh morning air, Jalan Legian looked very pretty. It was a welcome relief to step out of the hot laneway into this cool shady street. There was no chaotic traffic zooming past and the breeze rustled through the leafy trees lining the road. In fact, I was suddenly seeing it all with fresh eyes. I hadn't remembered that there was so much greenery in this famous street and had never realised just how narrow the main thoroughfare is. The Balinese security men in their checked sarongs sat on the edge of the footpath chatting away. Young men and women walked ahead of us carrying fresh flowers for praying. There was a wonderful feeling of solidarity in the air. The Balinese smiled at us with heartfelt warmth, their hopes hinged on the power of this massive ceremony to cleanse all evil.

We eventually entered a covered area that led to another covered area, over which white cloth was suspended: the road to God. We knew the site was near. From here, we could see shrines and temple paraphernalia sparkling in the sun, surrounded by Balinese umbrellas and crowds of people. And the devastation of the bomb site unfolded before me. To the right was the rubble of Paddy's Bar, and on the left the devastation of the Sari Club. But what struck me most was that so many of the surrounding buildings had also been destroyed. I stared at the ruins and wondered what kind of people would do this. The Legian side of the Sari Club was blocked off for families of the victims. The face of an older Australian woman sitting there plagued me: I knew I'd met her before, perhaps in a cooking class, and I wondered who she had lost in this tragedy.

A pavilion had been constructed outside the Sari Club and it was there that twelve high priests sat, chanting and ringing small brass bells. They had been invited from all over the island and I was thrilled to see that my favourite priest from Padang Tegal was present. The *gamelan* played soft music outside and special performances were held. Young girls dressed in yellow and white danced the *rejeng*, a traditional temple dance, and a mask dance followed. Standing amidst the Balinese in their glorious ceremonial costumes were soldiers in their tight khaki uniforms, looking a little baffled, and journalists, looking perhaps even more baffled. One sweaty reporter was ready to explode when he was stopped from barging into the prayer area; luckily his companion calmed him down. I didn't think he was very wise to argue with a uniformed man with a huge gun strapped to his back, and wondered what sort of article he would write. Curious tourists in skimpy halterneck tops and thin rayon sarongs wandered around. 'Well, at least they're not wearing their bathers,' I thought. Other, more sensitive, tourists wore a full ceremonial outfit or a peace T-shirt and sarong.

We eventually sat down near Paddy's Bar and it was then I noticed the small shrine outside the destroyed building. Amidst such destruction, this one silent shrine, the guardian of the bar, stood unscathed, the black and gold cloth still wrapped around it. It had been showered with offerings, and small bottles of holy water were perched on the ledge. Things like that always happen in Bali.

We have had many cleansing ceremonies over the years in Ubud. The purpose of these ceremonies, known as *Pacaruan* or *Mecaru*, is to balance all aspects of the universe to maintain peace and harmony on the planet. The October tragedy was of such magnitude that the sacred texts were consulted. The basic principles of life, known as *Tri Hita Karana*, had been violated and only ritual and prayer could restore these. The *Tri Hita Karana* outline the three most important relationships for the Balinese: their relationship with God, with fellow humans and with the world around them. When these are out of balance, the universe suffers.

When the priests had finished chanting, certain areas were blessed and then we were called to pray. There must have been at least three thousand people there, in an area stretching from the Sari Club to the *bemo* corner, all waiting in silence. All those along the footpaths and side streets were instructed to sit down. From where I sat, there was an ocean of people as far as the eye could see.

The prayers started with the *Trisandya* or *Mantram Gayatri*, which is a little like the Lord's Prayer. This famous Hindu creed is from the ancient *Vedas*. It begins with *Aum*, the resonating sound from which it is said the universe manifested. I held my hands to my heart and lowered my head in preparation. The whole area was charged with an extraordinary power as thousands of people joined in this mystical chant and my hands began to shake with the intensity of the prayer. The smell of sandalwood and jasmine incense sat on the moist air. We then followed the priest's instruction by praying with flowers. We prayed to bless the departed souls on their journey to eternity, for forgiveness of our careless deeds that created such tragedy, for the recovery of the wounded victims, for the tormented survivors of the disaster, and for the blinded criminals so that they might repent and see the evil of their ways. We also prayed for restored balance between the macrocosmos and microcosmos, man and the universe and the *Tri Hita Karana*. And finally we prayed for Bali, the island of the gods, this tiny land that has touched the heart of so many. May this gentle paradise recover from sadness and return once more to a life of peace and harmony.

When the prayers were finished, crowds of Balinese made their way to the main shrine to collect holy water that had been gathered from sacred sites in Bali and Java especially for this occasion. My companions and I slowly walked back to the hotel in the scorching midday sun. Later that afternoon, as we sat at a roadside café near Kuta Square, a beautiful procession passed by. It included Balinese girls in shimmering gold and white, a Moslem dance ensemble, a Chinese dragon, a Balinese *barong*, *gamelan* players, *baris* dancers, Christians and many more. It was the same message of peace and unity embodied by hundreds of people from all over Indonesia. Here in Bali, we continue to live harmoniously together and that cannot be changed.

Now, almost a year later, businesses remain deserted and the streets are still quiet. There's an atmosphere of peace and calm, but beneath the Balinese smile lies a deep concern. The future looks grim. Will the months to come continue as quiet as it is now? Unemployment is rising and shops are slowly being vacated. The ceremonies are still lavish in a land that enjoys opulent celebrations, but will they continue this way? Drivers sit in groups on the edge of the pavement, staring at the road, waiting for the next job. Every person on this idyllic island is suffering the consequences of this massive tragedy and it doesn't seem to be getting better. There's a feeling of being abandoned by the rest of the world.

The older folk must be baffled by world events. I often wonder what the Balinese grandmas or the farmer in the rice fields thought of the Kuta tragedy. I watch the women who work on our building site and realise that life is a day-to-day existence and the future goes no further than the next big ceremony.

I remember praying in the temple a few days after the bombing. There was an enormous cloud of silence in the air that held the shock and sadness of all those present. When people spoke, they did so in whispers. The prince gave a speech at the temple; his heartfelt emotions were obvious in the tears on his cheeks and his delicate words. He asked for God's forgiveness. There was no talk of blame, and together we prayed for Bali and the universe.

Many tragedies have been experienced in Bali but it has risen from the ashes every time. On the island of the gods, the people fight terrorism with peace, prayer and ceremony. The restoration of balance of the *Tri Hita Karana* is now a priority. During this time of reflection, the people wait patiently; patience is surely one of their greatest virtues. This terrible event has created a positive time of deep introspection and spirituality, a time to examine the seen and unseen elements of mystical life. It has reminded the Balinese who they are. Joking amongst friends still continues, although the laughter is subdued. And at the end of the day, the allegiance to family and friends is the light that illuminates their lives. *Takwa Masi* is the Hindu belief of brotherhood, which states simply that all people of the universe belong to each other and together share the triumphs and tragedies of the world. The Balinese are optimistic that time will heal the wounds of misfortune and that tourism will return to Bali. Their prayers may take many full moons to be answered, but we all know that good things come to those who wait. God bless the Balinese.

Stepping into a garden paradise

MY STORY BEGINS

They looked like an ocean of blossoming flowers
In their brilliant festival attire,
And it was especially the lovely women who created
this beautiful scene,
With the movement of their eyebrows as sharp as slivers of gravel . . .
PARTHAYANA, THE JOURNEYING OF PARTHA

My love affair with Bali began in 1974, with my first visit on a family holiday when I was fifteen. I remember landing on the shores of a garden paradise, surrounded by waves and nodding palm trees. When the plane doors were flung open, the warm heavy air, redolent with fragrant frangipani and the sweet smell of clove cigarettes, embraced me like a long-lost friend.

My memories of that first step onto the soft hot tarmac are still very clear. The heat was overwhelming. The bright sun beat on our backs as we made our way towards the airport terminal. Rivers of sweat trickled through my hair, down my arms, my legs, and collected at the back of my knees. Even the thick jungle of palm trees in the distance seemed to be melting. We were directed towards the two-storey arrivals building; it reminded me of a school with its yellow walls and cement details. The sound of the plane's engines charged our surroundings. As we walked towards the old frangipani trees that still edge the tarmac, the alluring scent of these moist white blossoms saturated the air. You can still smell them today with that first breath of Bali. Huge tufts of dark green leaves and a thousand small flowers hid the gnarled silvery trunks that arched over us as we walked by. The gentle patches of dappled shade offered a welcome relief from the intense sun.

We stood in line at customs for what seemed an eternity. Small carefully groomed men in tight khaki-coloured uniforms examined our passports and slammed them heavily with large stamps the size of their hands. We eyed each other with curiosity. The sound of a different language and voices of a different pitch rang in my ears. The clammy stifling air reminded me of my grandpa's house, which smelt mouldy and mildewy. We wandered out to collect our bags into an ocean of clove tobacco, dark bodies and sweat. There were people everywhere. Some of them grabbed our bags enthusiastically and waved to their friends for more assistance, calling out and smiling cheerfully.

Our young driver was waiting for us outside. He was dressed in neat polyester flares that swam around his skinny legs and a pale blue batik shirt patterned with Indonesian motifs. A layer of sweet coconut oil kept his thick black hair in place so it framed his smooth round caramel-coloured face. He could have been anywhere between eighteen and thirty years old. A single frangipani blossom was tucked behind his ear. With a warm smile that revealed large perfectly even white teeth he politely introduced himself as Wayan.

'Nice to meet you, Wayne,' replied my father, shaking his hand eagerly.

We piled into the sparkling white Holden, our bodies gleaming with sweat.

The drive from the airport to Ubud took us along busy bumpy narrow streets lined with the tallest trees I'd ever seen, which formed a distant canopy overhead. I had to crane my neck to see a patch of sky. Gracious Balinese people dressed in faded sarongs sauntered alongside, at arm's length from the car window. Part of me wanted to touch them as we drove slowly by, just to make sure they were real. We passed mud-brick grass-roofed cottages half-hidden behind ancient-looking stone gates, rows of gnarled frangipani trees studded with yellow-white blossoms, papaya trees with huge cut-out leaves, red hibiscus hedges, robust roosters and barking dogs. Giant shocking-pink bougainvilleas climbing over old mango trees laden with green fruit, enormous ferns bathed in sunlight under fringed palm trees, and small roadside food stalls drifted past. The tiny visible patch of cloudy sky was framed by a riot of pink, red and green. And in between the tropical growth we glimpsed stretches of bright green rice fields, massive banyan trees, moss-covered shrines, black and white checked umbrellas and piles of small sun-bleached offerings. Men and women washed in the shaded deep gutters that lined the streets, oblivious to passers-by. Children waved, smiled and called out 'hello' as we drove past. The scent of fragrant flowers, coconut oil, smoky incense and rotting vegetation filled my head. It was a moving kaleidoscope of life and colour.

I was immediately enchanted by this ornate culture, where the vivid colours of the tropical vegetation were matched only by the graciousness of the Balinese. In fact, I thought they were the most handsome people I had ever seen. I was charmed by their gentleness and warmth. This fragrant paradise was saturated with sensuality and beauty and I will never forget the impact of my first visit. There's something about Bali that gets into your blood, into your heart. I was already in a dream world, already besotted.

Our holiday began when we arrived at the Hotel Tjampuhan in Ubud. Nestled into the slope above the Tjampuhan river, this cosy network of rustic grass-roofed bungalows with wide cool verandahs was our first experience of a tropical paradise. Tjampuhan means 'meeting place' and is the name of the sacred river that meets Ubud's East Woz and West Woz rivers, which wind lazily through either side of Bukit Gunung Lebah valley, near the Tjampuhan bridge. Each night, summoned by the call of the *kul-kul*, the traditional wooden gong with the male-like appendage, we gathered in the open-air restaurant overlooking a sprawling garden of brilliant flowers, flamboyan trees and ginger plants. The scent of coconut candles infused the air and provided a gentle light as we mingled with the guests. Balinese bamboo music drifted around us and tinkled down to the river. Mealtimes were like a temple procession of the senses. Young Balinese men and women wearing traditional shirts and patterned tea-coloured sarongs, each adorned with a single brilliant red hibiscus flower, brought exotic colourful platters of Indonesian food to each seated guest. I remember being spellbound by their beauty. Frogs' legs, spicy pink fried rice, green leaves tossed in peanut sauce, a variety of satay, fruits poached in palm sugar and other unknown dishes were part of the foreign menu. It was the most aromatic food I had ever tasted.

One day, my family and I walked west of the hotel as far as Sanggingan, the next village. This narrow pot-holed road now bustles with traffic and runs past our restaurant, Indus. Back then, we strolled past hundreds of busy ducks quacking in the rice fields, tended by sturdy, bare-chested farmers dressed in cotton sarongs tied between the legs like a baby's nappy. They waved and smiled as we passed. Small joyful children greeted us with 'hello, hello' and then followed us as we happily wandered up the hill. Bright-eyed and bubbly, they laughed and sang as we made our way to the next village. Years later I was to learn that 'hello' is the name children give to tourists.

Sometimes on our walks we took the other direction into town, crossing over the small bridge that no longer exists. The sacred Tjampuhan river that flows below was the communal bathing ground in the mornings and afternoons. If you peered down, you could see young women scrubbing clothes on the smooth grey rocks that line the water's edge. Tropical vines suspended over the cool water provided outdoor sport for athletic young boys, and men and women flirted from their designated swimming areas (women upstream, men downstream). The sound of splashing and laughter could be heard from the road and it was hard not to peek at the glistening wet bodies having so much fun.

The Tjampuhan river was also a hive of building activity at that time as the Tjampuhan bridge was under construction. Women effortlessly transported rocks the size of wheelbarrows on their heads, carrying them from the river bed to the road. My dad took countless photographs of this amazing feat. I cringed every time he asked one of them to hold a pose and smile under a thirty-kilo weight of stone.

At night, we watched spellbinding performances by delicate dreamy girls wearing brilliant pink, green, purple and gold-patterned costumes and crowns of white frangipani flowers. To the accompaniment of traditional *gamelan* music, they danced with curved fingers, flashing eyes and movements reminiscent of swaying palm trees. Every day I'd practise the sliding eye movements; I still wish I could have been a Balinese dancer. Other times, we would sit and watch the fireflies after dinner, sipping on sweet rice wine and enjoying the balmy fragrant evening air and the pulsating sounds of crickets.

My second visit to Bali, in 1984, was the turning point of my life. On the second day of my holiday, I met my future husband, Ketut, and from then on slowly started to absorb the culture that had so spellbound me ten years previously.

Ketut and I first met at the Hotel Tjampuhan, to where I had returned with my friend Jo from college. With great excitement, we had escaped Melbourne's chilly winter and were looking forward to a tropical adventure. I was longing to relive some of my early teenage memories of exotic flavours, fragrances and pervading beauty. I wanted to wake up in a grass-roofed bungalow to see the mist drifting across the Tjampuhan valley early in the morning, behold the small bowl of pink and red hibiscus lovingly placed on our table before each breakfast, listen to birds chirping all day and smell the sweet scent of Bali. Even the waxy Blue Band margarine they served with toast had grown more appealing. My first visit to Ubud had had such a dramatic impact on me that, in the years that followed, through secondary school and college, part of me felt as if I was filling in time until I could return, like a Balinese national waiting to come home.

After dinner at the hotel on the second night of our stay, Jo and I relaxed in the lofty grass-roofed restaurant. Very little had changed during my absence. Meals were buffet-style now, but the magic still lingered. The walls held the same memories and the air held the same scent of frangipani and lush foliage. The Balinese still flashed the same heart-warming smiles and laughed without a care in the world. We sipped on Cointreau with lashings of ice and relished the tranquil atmosphere. The frogs in the nearby pond were singing erratically and we could hear the glorious, royal-blue-feathered pet peacock wandering through the garden, making a few persistent calls before sleep. I had noticed Ketut when we first walked into the hotel restaurant. He was sitting on a sofa near the bar, talking casually to the prince of Ubud, Tjokorda Gede Putra Sukawati. The smoke from their clove cigarettes framed them in a cosy mist. In the lamplight, I could make out the shape of a Balinese man wearing a traditional cotton sarong and a blue T-shirt with a huge koala on the front. In fact, I'm not sure if it was the koala that caught my attention or the adult wearing this cuddly symbol of Australia.

As Jo and I sipped our way through our duty-free alcohol, discussing the pleasures of good food, wine and liqueurs, Ketut wandered up to our table with a young friend. The restaurant was now nearly empty and the bamboo music had stopped. Ketut approached us with a steady, almost regal grace and gently asked if he could sit down. We giggled and replied, 'Of course.'

His inquisitive friend joined him. There are only a few things a Balinese man will do on his own and talking to foreign women is certainly not one of them. The Cointreau had taken its toll and our spirits were blurred with excitement. We offered our exotic companions a drink and started making light conversation in simple English.

'So, what are your names?' we asked loudly and slowly, assuming they couldn't understand us.

'My name is Ketut and this is my friend, Wayan.'

This seemed hilarious to us as every other waiter in the restaurant had the same name.

'So how do you tell who's who?' I asked, looking at our guests curiously.

Wayan explained that everyone has a nickname and that, for instance, Ketut's nickname was the Balinese word for the creamy-white seed of a young coconut.

'Why on earth would they call you that?' I asked, looking at his skin the colour of palm sugar and his arms like polished wood, and trying to make the connection.

'Because my complexion is so soft and fair,' he answered with a broad cheeky grin.

I enjoyed his poetic interpretation, but to this day I'm not sure if it's correct.

There was certainly something about Ketut that held my attention. He had an immense presence that made others appear insignificant, and his sharp wit and wisdom often left me speechless. From the time we met, it was as if we had always known each other. I remember smiling to myself and thinking, 'Here you are.' It was as if fate had brought us together in another land, which was as comfortable to me as the place where I was born.

We chatted casually at the table. Ketut sat across from me and watched the way I spoke and laughed. I watched him in return and observed his smooth glowing skin and beautiful hands, one of which was adorned with a heavy gold ring set with an unfamiliar creamy stone.

'Can I see that ring?' I asked cheekily.

'Of course,' replied Ketut. 'But, beware,' he added, and paused, 'anyone who tries on this ring will fall in love with me.'

I quickly looked at his friend to see if there was an 'I've heard him say that a hundred times before' look on his face.

'Oh, don't be ridiculous,' I replied defiantly. 'Pass it to me.'

I had studied jewellery-making at college and was intrigued by this ancient-looking talisman. Ketut told me his mother had given him the ring several years ago, and I could see it was a symbol of her love for him, a gift to cherish always.

He slowly edged the ring off his elegant finger and placed it in the palm of my hand. I examined the stone, marvelling at its silent power and the craftsmanship in the setting. The gold held a rosy tinge and the creamy opaque stone was an organic oval shape. It looked as if it had been poured into the giant claws of its setting and seemed almost to breathe with life, a heart beating with molten love.

I slid the ring onto my finger and gazed at it as if it were a crystal ball. At that moment, I closed the final pages of the book that spanned twenty-five years of happiness and sadness, of growing pains and childhood antics. My new life had begun. Five years later Ketut and I were married.

The ring remained on Ketut's finger until the first anniversary of his mother's death. On that day, we were in Paris, on our way to catch the night train to Germany. While we were dragging our bags along a small cobblestoned street in the sixteenth arrondissement, Ketut stopped abruptly and started playing with the ring.

'There's something wrong with it,' he said anxiously. He prised it off his finger and the stone virtually jumped out and disappeared. We both cried out and fell down on our hands and knees, but couldn't find the creamy stone anywhere. We looked in the gutters, on the road and all along the pavement. People passing by helped us in our cause but the stone was lost for ever. Only then did we realise that Ketut's mother had died twelve months ago to the day and we'd forgotten to light incense, make offerings or pray to her soul. The shell of the ring still sits sadly in our cupboard.

Three weeks after that first meeting, I returned to Melbourne with the thrill of new romance burning in my heart. Ketut and I wrote words of tenderness and devotion to each other every week. In the meantime, I searched the shelves of Melbourne's bookstores looking for information on Balinese cooking. I longed to fill the house with the aroma of ginger and lemongrass and taste the flavours of paradise once again. But my efforts met with no success.

By January 1985, six months later, I was back in Bali with a mission to write a Balinese cookbook and introduce the world to the food I had grown to love. I moved into Nani House, a small guesthouse owned by my future sister-in-law, Kasi, in Monkey Forest Road, Ubud. There I watched with a keen eye as she slowly introduced me to a magical cuisine. I jotted down recipes, methods and cooking techniques while she created an array of lively mouth-watering dishes. I remember waking in the early hours of the morning to be greeted with a freshly brewed cup of Balinese coffee as the vibrant rays of sun started to bathe the fragrant flowers with their warmth. The smell of steaming rice would call me to the kitchen and I would almost fall out of bed in anticipation of what breakfast might bring. But I was also aware of hiding my overflow of excitement in a culture where extremes of behaviour are not considered appropriate. In fact, I still wonder if the Balinese think my passion for their food is somewhat over-zealous.

Kasi is a great cook, the only sister in a family of ten brothers, many of whom are also talented cooks. Warm and jovial, she always makes you feel at home, filling you with freshly cooked curries, cakes and ginger tea on even the shortest visit. Ketut Ngetis, my late father-in-law, was the head of the culinary team and had a history of cooking for famous people, including the German artist Walter Spies and Dutch officials during the Dutch occupation. Ketut always claimed that his father made the best jackfruit curry and was the authority on Balinese cooking in the whole extended family.

Back then, I'd sometimes go with Kasi to the market and follow her obediently through the network of small stalls and powerful smells while she carefully selected the finest fresh silvery fish, plump shiny vegetables, glossy green leaves or glistening chunks of pork. I would cringe as she haggled passionately over the prices. It would be the same argument every time as she bellowed, 'Is that your best price? Last week it was cheaper!' Sometimes she seemed to be furious with the stallholder and her shrill voice would rise several octaves as she quarrelled over a few rupiah. In the months that followed, I came to realise that this was normal bargaining behaviour.

With our bags overflowing with fresh tomatoes, bright red chillies, dark green leaves, slimy brown elvers, tiny fish and brick-red shrimp paste, I'd balance the goods on my knees and sit side-saddle on her motorbike as she rode home to cook breakfast. One of my favourite dishes was sardines simmered with small sweet golden-brown potatoes, tomatoes and chilli. The texture of the soft potatoes and gentle fish perfectly balanced the luscious tomatoes and sweet chilli. In fact, I loved all the many ways Kasi cooked fish: steamed in banana leaves, marinated and grilled, or deep-fried until crisp and crunchy. Tuna, mackerel and whitebait were always so delicious with fresh chilli sauce and freshly steamed rice. Some sort of curry was also common fare, or maybe sweet fried tempe (fermented soya bean cake). All kinds of boiled dark green leaves mixed with coconut and eggs in various spicy sauces were a regular feature on the morning's menu.

Every day after our hearty breakfast, I would fill my bag with my large notebook, my favourite black felt-tipped pen for jotting down recipes, coloured pencils for drawing spices and my weather-beaten camera for action shots of food, and then make my way by public transport to the Pantheon, Ketut's wood-carving gallery in Mas. Mas is about a twenty-minute ride from Ubud and is the famed woodcarving centre of Bali. There were only open-backed vans or *bemos* to get around then; very few people owned a car. After a sweaty journey, alongside friendly toothless grandmas with betel-stained lips, bundles of anxious chickens tied at the feet, sacks of rice and vegetables piled high on the floor, and small bright-eyed little girls slurping on pink drinks in plastic bags alongside their well-groomed perfumed mothers in polyester dresses, I would arrive at the gallery. It was here that I threw myself into learning as much as possible at what became for me a kind of culinary/cultural college. My husband and his team of jolly young workers spent hours giving me an insight into all aspects of Balinese life. I learnt how to greet friends with a subtle flick of the eyebrows and a tilt of the chin, and how to beckon friends with a nonchalant downward cupping of the hand. I also learnt the Balinese art of sitting with family and friends, hardly speaking a word, for what seemed like an eternity.

Silence is just another way of communicating feelings, a space for words and thoughts to gather. Western people are not comfortable with this and fumble uneasily at silence. This was perhaps the most difficult skill to master.

I was motivated by an insatiable desire to fit into this charming culture. I spent every day recording, tasting, smelling, drawing and photographing every piece of food that found its way into the kitchen, while at the same time observing body language, clothing styles, customs and etiquette. At times I felt frustrated because I was so ignorant of the more subtle cultural differences. I remember Ketut and his friends roaring with laughter at me because I chose to carry a bright pink plastic market bag as a handbag. I thought it was charming and was deeply hurt by their energetic joking at my expense. For them, the bag was designed to carry vegetables and spices, nothing more. Ridicule and teasing is the Balinese way of showing you the rules. I stopped using that bag and bought myself a more acceptable leather one.

I was gently reprimanded for wearing sleeveless shirts that revealed my armpits or short summer dresses. When I wore my favourite hot-pink sarong through the streets of Ubud, the loud chatter and laughter from the Balinese grandmas had me cringing with embarrassment. I had wrapped the material around me and tied it at the front in what I thought was an exotic Dorothy Lamour style, but to the Balinese it looked as if I'd just stepped out of the shower and forgotten to get dressed. It was the equivalent of wearing a mere towel for clothing.

My mother-in-law, with her gentle kindness, tried to guide me in her own way. She teased me for not asking her enough questions, or for not asking my father-in-law where he was going, which, I was to learn, is the 'How are you?' of Bali. It's one of the essential polite greetings, usually followed by 'Have you already eaten?' and 'Have you already had a wash?' These were the first phrases I learnt in Indonesian. One day, when I incorrectly addressed my mother-in-law as 'you' instead of 'mother' when travelling to Denpasar with Ketut and his cousin, you could have cut the air with a knife. The words hung in the stifling confines of the small sedan as Ketut drove slowly along the main street. I could feel my face turning scarlet. Sensing my deep embarrassment, my mother-in-law gently tapped me on the hand and said quietly, 'You must never call me *kamu*, you must always call me *meme*.' There is a certain way to speak to elders and this was a basic rule of which I was totally unaware. We all breathed a sigh of relief after my small blunder, and the men resumed their noisy chatter in the front seat. I couldn't believe I'd put my foot in it again and was relieved that the punishment was so tender. I decided it was safer to look out the window and observe the stone carvings on sale at the side of the road instead.

I still remember those early days of learning with great fondness. When I look back, I can see I was being gently shaped like warm rice for offerings and all those experiences have changed me in many ways.

Ubud was a sleepy town in 1985. There were mainly Vespa motorbikes, a few Holden cars and old Dutch bicycles on the roads. Late in the day, the farmers would walk along the main street with their precious cows in tow or a herd of noisy ducks obediently following the farmer's white flag. Ketut's niece and the neighbouring children would walk to the Monkey Forest near our homestay to wash in the cool rock pool beneath the temple, carrying empty buckets on their heads. I loved to see them return, refreshed and laughing, with their buckets brimming with sun-drenched spring water for the next day's cooking.

I spent most of my mornings at the Pantheon, sitting on the slatted bamboo bench in the simple kitchen, writing notes and drawing diagrams, as the filtered sun cast lines of warm light across the floor. Surrounded by the haze and scent of steaming rice and smoky coconut oil, the girls chatted, laughed and cooked lunch. Piles of aromatic rhizomes smelling of earth and eucalyptus, sun-bleached fragrant seeds, creamy waxy nuts and dark shiny leaves were at first a mystery to me. But I slowly became familiar with these seductive spices, and my passion for learning this sensual cuisine still runs hot through my blood.

At other times, I would sit with Ketut's brothers while they noisily prepared food for the different life-cycle ceremonies. Watching the men making spicy *lawar*, pork stew and coconut satay, I felt as if I was unravelling the deep secrets of a cuisine embedded in ancient myths and magic. This sensation led me on with heightened devotion. Shy in nature, I wished I were more outgoing so that I could perhaps help with the preparations, or ask more questions. But, in hindsight, my mild-mannered approach was the more acceptable one, as questioning is not a part of the Balinese character.

Our afternoons were spent lazing in local restaurants on old-style bamboo chairs around small bamboo tables. We'd sip on freshly squeezed lime juice with loads of crushed ice, while Ketut entertained us with tales of Indian myths and Indonesian legends. He retold the romantic stories of Rama and Sita, Arjuna and the five Bharata brothers, Krishna with his words of wisdom. He also spoke about the terror of the 1960s in Indonesia. I remember sitting in the pavilion of Murni's Warung, one of my favourite eateries in Ubud, overlooking a cool tropical jungle of oversized ferns, leafy trees, red and green striped shrubs and pink hibiscus. The foliage seemed to grow before my eyes. As Ketut told the story of Ken Dedes, the Javanese prince, and his seven generations of karmic law, the sound of the sacred Tjampuhan river roared beneath us in a torrent that echoed those early days of love and happiness. Ketut said that if I wanted to learn about the Balinese character I should read the *Mahabarata* and *Ramayana*. I eagerly followed his advice and ploughed through pages of drama and unpronounceable names in an effort to understand the Eastern mind. In fact, I read anything on the subject of Bali to gain some insight.

And Ketut became my hero. In my dreams, he was a fearless prince, a charismatic leader whose fairness and wisdom could solve all the world's problems. Ketut was different from any other man I had met. His relaxed calm manner and solid frame inspired such confidence and his deep insight into all things spiritual fascinated me. Our souls seemed to link in a timeless bond.

Ketut had a natural humility that had grown from poverty and hard work, the sort of upbringing I could never imagine. He warmly recalled the early days in Bali, when life was very simple. There was no electricity or running water. Nights were spent telling stories around a kerosene lamp, afternoons were spent playing in the rice fields and village temples, and twilight was spent sitting by the road. Like all children then, he helped his mother carry spring water to the house every day for cooking, and the Tjampuhan river was the communal bathroom. He caught fireflies at night so he could have a spark of light beside the thin bamboo mat he slept on, and caught eels and frogs for dinner. His only possessions consisted of two sarongs, a couple of shirts and a pair of thongs, and from the beginning he was taught to share all of these and to help his family, friends and neighbours at all times.

Ketut's strength became my strength as I listened to his lessons of life, humanity and self-respect. At times, he was cruel in his kindness as he tried to break down the walls of guilt I kept building around him, something I was totally unaware I was doing. And the gentle fire that fuelled the silent sanctum of his heart was kindled by pure love, generosity and truth based on a fundamental belief that there are only three relationships that matter in life: your relationship with God, with nature and with mankind. That was the secret of his inner power, and I knew in our hearts we would always be together.

Ketut was the embodiment of Eastern spirituality and Balinese playfulness. His child-like sense of humour had us laughing every other minute of the day, usually at someone else's expense. A master of practical jokes, I saw him startle friends with trick cigarette lighters, cigarettes with matches hidden inside, food tinged with too much chilli and endless jokes. I watched how he calmly spoke to his peers and how they listened intently to every word, before he delivered the punchline that would have them doubling over with laughter. Happiness became a drug and I revelled in its life-warming properties.

Eight months later, it was time to go home. I wanted Ketut to come with me, to see my beloved home town of Melbourne and meet my family and friends. I felt that it would strengthen our relationship to step out of the cosy nest that Bali had provided, and I wanted him to catch a glimpse of the Australian culture, my birthplace. So, in 1987 we arrived together at Tullamarine airport with the blessings of scented holy water still warm on our skin. Our eyes were full of love and sweet innocence and our spirits were high. The first glimpse of rolling green hills, large dams, farmhouses and grazing woolly sheep revealed the quiet Australian landscape as the plane swooped over the misty fields before landing. There were no temples, no palm trees and very few people. In fact, compared to Bali, the whole place seemed deserted.

In Melbourne, our two cultures came abruptly face to face: the gentle East and superior West. I believe you can never fully understand your own culture until you become immersed in another.

The first thing Ketut had to do immediately on arriving was to find his orientation points of north and south; without this orientation his spirit could not be at ease. I had never thought about these directions before in Melbourne, but managed to work it out by remembering where the sun rose on frosty mornings. Once we had established these directions, certain adjustments had to be made in Ketut's new bedroom. The bed had to face north-east, which meant moving all the furniture around to accommodate the change. In Bali, they believe that if your feet face east, your life will become shorter, and if your feet face north, you're in even bigger trouble. North, where the mountains lie, is the place of Siwa and I don't know any Balinese brave enough to show the god of destruction his dirty soles. 'Siwa doesn't like feet in his face,' said Ketut as we pushed the heavy cast-iron bed to the other corner of the room. We were staying in my grandparents' old Californian-style bungalow with my sister and her husband. Grandma and Grandpa had both passed away and I hoped the furniture-moving wasn't arousing any bad feelings.

Every morning, Ketut would sweep the magnolia leaves that gathered in the driveway into small piles, just as he did at home. He couldn't understand why wealthy people in the suburbs didn't clean up their yards every day. In the afternoons, when the sun shared her gentle warmth, he'd sit on our white cement garden bench under the shade of the oak tree in the front yard and say hello to the passers-by. When I came home from teaching, I'd see him sitting there, chatting with various people of all ages. Old folk would sit beside him and tell stories of World War I. Others would tell of their migration to Australia. There was a constant stream of traffic — our old bench seat had never seen such a crowd. He became friends with my neighbour and spoke more to him in one week than I had in ten years.

Ketut was curious about Western life. 'Where are all the old people?' he asked one day. I reluctantly replied that many were in special homes for the elderly, trying to make it sound like a wonderful option. In Bali, one of your greatest life obligations is to care for your parents, so the thought of sending them away is very disturbing. Similarly, when Ketut found out that most babies' placentas were thrown away at the hospitals, I could see his mind spinning. It seemed to him that we were a generation of lost souls, with no connection to the earth. He started to wonder if the West really was a better place.

At night, we'd go to different restaurants with friends and sit and chat for what seemed like an eternity. Ketut found it difficult to understand the animated conversations and would often have to go for a walk to get a breath of fresh air. Balinese don't usually socialise over a meal and eating is done in relative silence. Our meals, on the contrary, were loud noisy affairs that lasted all night. The Western concept of punctuality was also confusing. In Bali, they call it *jam karet* or rubber-time, meaning you can arrive within a certain time frame — but it's something that really only applies to the priest. He can arrive when he's ready and finished with other ceremonies, but regular folk are supposed to arrive before his entourage. In school, the students must arrive before the teacher. Years later, when I arrived at the church for our Western wedding more than one hour late, Ketut was surprised at my audacity and apologised to the priest. He always tells me I'm more Balinese than the Balinese.

After a week or two, I decided to take Ketut to my parents' house in Bonnie Doon, near Eildon. I had to work during the week and he became lonely and melancholy in the suburbs on his own, so I thought Dad's constant company would cheer him up and that maybe Dad would even find a few odd jobs for him to do. When we arrived at the farm, Dad reported that it was sheep-drenching time. I wasn't sure how Ketut would handle this sort of work, but he stepped into overalls, RM Williams boots and the action started. He put on a brave face and helped as much as he could. His job was to direct the puzzled sheep into a steel compartment and then ram a steel nozzle loaded with worm medicine down their throats. Sometimes the sheep would wriggle free and Ketut, the boy from Bali, would have to run round the paddock, arms outstretched, trying to catch this bleating oversized bundle of wool.

Other times, he helped Dad to fix fences and slowly learnt about the Australian culture. He learnt that the size of a country town is determined by the number of pubs in the area, and that the pub is the meeting place for local people. He imagined a pub must be something like a temple, but soon found out it was an Australian watering hole. He had to learn how to ride up and down the steep rocky hills on a motorbike, and fell off a dozen times. Dad told him proudly about Ned Kelly and the bushrangers. The story wasn't quite as exotic as the princely Arjuna, dressed in gorgeous Indian robes with ornate gold headgear, surrounded by beautiful earth maidens while battling the Bharata family with a magic bow and arrow; Ned Kelly somehow carries a different message to that of spiritual enlightenment. But Ketut enjoyed the story all the same and the courage of both heroes is undeniable.

One night, Ketut went rabbit-shooting with my burly bushranger-lookalike uncle. They charged across the hills in the dark in the four-wheel drive, startling the animals with a huge spotlight. Uncle Phillip shot half a dozen rabbits in no time at all and brought them home in a bundle, tied at the ears. But when he skinned the furry grey bunnies on the kitchen floor, Ketut thought he was going to faint. The sight of their smooth pink bodies lined up on the lino reminded him of newly born babies and he had to leave the room. Ketut's mother delivered all her eleven children at home, so since he was little he had been around small babies. He has never eaten rabbit to this day.

There were certain parts of the property that made Ketut extremely nervous. He said they were haunted by ghosts, perhaps from gold-mining days or earlier. These ghosts disturbed his sleep: he had nightmares of little people pulling at his arms and legs and screaming in his ears. My dad also spent a few sleepless nights, wondering what on earth Ketut was dreaming about. At first, Ketut was a little shy about suggesting moving the furniture so he could sleep in the 'right direction', but after a few nights of disturbed sleep, he asked Dad to help in his dilemma. The farmhouse then was a small two-bedroomed fibro-cement cottage with a narrow verandah and tiny bathroom, and rearranging the furniture proved rather difficult in such a small space. The seagrass matting buckled under the pressure of shifting old cupboards and stubborn farmhouse beds. But after a few hours, the room had a new glow and Ketut (and Dad) breathed a sigh of relief.

In keeping with Australian Friday night tradition, Dad often took Ketut to the Bonnie Doon pub to meet the locals. After one bourbon and coke, Ketut would already be blurry-eyed and feeling queasy, while the smell of his clove cigarettes convinced the regulars that he was smoking something illegal. In keeping with Balinese tradition, Ketut washed Dad's car nearly every day and then had to watch the layers of fine red dust settle back into the same places the moment the car was taken out again. He still finds the state of cars in the West puzzling. In Bali, our cars are washed every morning and sparkle inside and out.

You can imagine the initial reaction of my father, a farmer from Bonnie Doon, to this boy from Bali. For my father, a spade is a spade. In Bali, a spade is anything but a spade — it could be a magic *kris*, an evil demon or a beautiful goddess. But these men from two different worlds forged a friendship that still lasts to this day. Ketut felt secure in my dad's company and was happy to join him in his daily routine. Their respect for nature and their love of the land, albeit different landscapes, was their common bond.

*　　*　　*

Ketut returned to Bali at the end of the year, full of new experiences and new perceptions of Western life. I remained in Melbourne, working as a relief teacher and part-time waitress. I had somehow imagined that Ketut would eventually move to Australia, the land of golden opportunity, but was now faced with the reality that this would probably not be the case. During the months that followed, I thought seriously about our cross-cultural relationship. Ketut's visit to Melbourne had exposed differences between us that I was oblivious to in Bali, but I couldn't imagine life without him. If we lived together in Melbourne, the pressures of the West would see him wilt like a lotus flower, petals dropping one by one to reveal a parched soul. In Bali, he was the leader of the youth group, highly respected and well known in the community. He actively participated in temple festivals and ceremonies. Life in Melbourne would seem dull and empty by comparison.

I continued to visit Bali three times a year for a month or two at a time. And the fabric of our lives slowly merged together like the threads of a precious textile. An exotic pattern was unfolding and I was starting to realise that Bali was already my home.

In 1987, Ketut and I set up our first restaurant together. It was called Lilies, named after the glorious white Christmas lily which is one of my favourite flowers, but Western visitors thought it was named after me and it took a few years to shake off that misconception. It was purely accidental that Ketut and I became involved in this small establishment. The previous owner had gone bankrupt and was looking for new tenants. A friend of ours decided to give it a try and asked us to join in. I had dreamt of owning a restaurant in Ubud, but thought there were already too many in town, so this was an exciting opportunity. I had worked in restaurants and catering companies in Melbourne and was brimming with ideas. After a couple of weeks of minor renovations, we flung the doors open, ready for trade, and the rest is history.

Lilies was a quaint little restaurant. We were conveniently located near the soccer field, near several other famous cafés. We only had nine tables, of which two were long enough to seat eight people or more. One other table was permanently set up for chess, an Indonesian sport. I loved the sight of the young men draped over each other, silently watching their favourite players hour after hour. The long tables were a meeting ground for young enthusiastic travellers and I saw many romances and friendships blossom on those rickety bamboo seats. The walls were covered with golden-brown woven bamboo displaying local paintings, some of which were mine, and a huge pot of Christmas lilies sat on the bar. The kitchen was the size of a small bathroom and the wonderful food we produced from these tiny quarters amazed everyone. The single tiny Dutch oven that sat on a small kerosene burner outside the kitchen was the goddess overseeing the production of our delicious cakes and bread.

This was my first time as an employer of Balinese and I was a little nervous at seeming bossy and 'colonial' in my approach. So I followed my husband's leadership technique of joking at all costs and never raising my voice. To maintain high staff morale, we spent most of the time laughing about girlfriends, boyfriends and whoever walked past.

Lilies was popular from the minute we opened our small purple door. We were the first restaurant in Ubud to fuse Balinese and Western food and our influence can still be felt in restaurants all over Bali. Ketut and I quickly built a successful business that occupied all our time.

Years ago, Ketut's father had given him a piece of land behind the junior secondary school on the main road; Ketut decided now was the time to build on it. He commenced his first building project: a house for two in the rice fields. He affectionately called it the *pondok*, which means 'simple resting place in the rice fields'. And rice fields surrounded us on all sides, a sea of lush green that changed shades with the movement of the sun throughout the day, populated by soft brown ducks and edged with palm trees.

Three years later, around the time of our first wedding ceremony in Bali, the tiny kitchen Ketut built near the entrance of the compound became the Honeymoon Bakery. In 1991, the lease on Lilies expired and we closed the doors for ever. Ketut started building Casa Luna in Ubud's main road shortly afterwards, and the restaurant opened in 1992. In 1995, we built a new house at the bottom of the land to accommodate our growing family, and later acquired the property next door. Indus, our next restaurant, opened after Arjuna was born in 1998. In the meantime, the *pondok* grew into a village of children, guestrooms, animals and businesses. Our home is now known as the Honeymoon Guesthouse, but amongst Balinese family and friends is still called the *pondok*. And, after so many years, every day is always a honeymoon.

Three weddings, one union

MARRIAGE AND A NEW LIFE

In full view, the two went out and sat side by side on the verandah.
After they had bathed and put on their jewels and ornaments,
They looked as sweet as the conjoined beauty of the lotus and honey,
Bearing with fortitude the presence of the maids, all of whom were
beautiful and were wearing mandaga ornaments . . .

PARTHAYANA, THE JOURNEYING OF PARTHA

Five years after our first meeting, Ketut and I were married, first
on a freezing cold and wet Melbourne day in June, and again the
following year in Bali, during the wet season. We were showered
on for every ceremony — a sign of good luck, I was told.

Our Melbourne wedding — the first of three ceremonies — was
held in the small parish church around the corner from my family
home, which is where we went for the reception afterwards. This
was the way I had always envisaged my wedding. I love my family
home; it has a special charm. The large living spaces feature
leadlight windows (one portraying a kookaburra), wood
panelling painted ivory white, high ceilings, old-fashioned floral
carpet and picture rails that hold my grandfather's paintings.
French doors open onto a front garden blooming with pink
azaleas, soft purple lavender, fragrant white roses and blue salvia.

It's the perfect house for parties. However, for the wedding we set up a huge white marquee in the backyard and enjoyed a marvellous lunch together under its airy circus-like roof.

Ketut's brother, Koming, flew over from Bali to represent the family. He arrived on a frosty morning with two changes of clothes and only two packets of clove cigarettes, which he'd finished by the next day. Somehow he'd figured he could buy these in a local *warung* and we spent the next couple of days driving all over Melbourne trying to purchase these sweet-smelling *kretek*. The cigarettes kept him warm inside and provided comfort in this strange land, so we knew we had to find some for him. Virtually as soon as Koming arrived from the airport, he made straight for the broom leaning against the side of the house and swept all the dried magnolia leaves into a neat pile within minutes. They obviously bothered him as much as they'd bothered Ketut. Between the two brothers, the leaves didn't stand a chance.

The wedding took place on a bleak Saturday morning. Ketut was feeling queasy after eating mushrooms the night before, and I had hurt my leg falling off my push-bike when the tyres got caught in the tram lines near our house. We were a sorry pair. Nevertheless, Ketut especially enjoyed dressing up in a tuxedo for the big day. Ketut's good friends, Nyoman Suwitera and Ketut Yuliarsa, had flown down from Sydney to join the wedding party, and my sister Susan and my cousin Joanne were my bridesmaids. The men looked very handsome in their new outfits. Their golden-brown skin and blue-black hair was the perfect match for their tailored black suits set off with crisp white shirts and bow ties. However, Dad noticed that despite wearing jackets, the men were shivering and starting to turn blue. He also noticed that they were all wearing nice black shoes but no socks, so he went on an emergency errand to buy them thermal underwear and socks to battle the freezing cold.

My brother, Tim, and Dad read speeches during the service and my cousin Brigid sang that song about heroes with wind beneath their wings, just like something out of the *Mahabarata*. All went to plan, until the priest said to Ketut, 'You may now kiss the bride.'

Ketut looked at me anxiously. Balinese never kiss in public; in fact, never show any outward sign of affection to their husband or wife. Amorous acts are private and always take place behind closed doors. In all our years together, we had rarely held hands in public, as those sorts of gestures are reserved for friends and children. As the words echoed above our heads, I had to think quickly. I looked up and caught sight of the jewel-coloured stained-glass windows showing Jesus battling with the cross. All the guests were staring at us curiously and the priest was standing there waiting for some action.

'Congratulations, Ketut,' I blurted and held out my hand.

We shook hands joyfully and the audience cheered and clapped.

The reception that followed was full of joy and merriment. We toasted the Balinese for their charm and good spirits and my parents for putting up with both of us over the years. Together with my other grandpa we sang his favourite song, 'The More We Are Together, The Happier We'll Be', and danced and had a wonderful time. Grandpa Syd had figured out by then that the Balinese probably weren't going to invade Australia — by the sounds of it, they didn't have time with all the ceremonies they had to perform!

The wedding finished in perfect time for Ketut to watch the World Cup soccer on the television. Two weeks later, we returned to Bali with plans for a Balinese wedding.

Years later, one day when my daughter Dewi was watching Julie Andrews (my children always thought I looked like Mary Poppins) marry Christopher Plummer in *The Sound of Music*, she squealed with delight and called out to me, 'Mummy, Mummy, look. She's wearing a white wedding dress just like yours, except you didn't wear a mosquito net on your head!'

Our plans to have a Balinese wedding later that year came to a sudden halt with the death of Ketut's mother, who had been sick for some time. I was sad that she hadn't been able to witness our Balinese wedding, but relieved that at least she had seen us together legally as husband and wife. Having her son marry a Western girl was probably one of her greatest fears, but we had become good friends over the years. She was pleased that I was hard working and not an over-zealous beer-drinker.

In keeping with tradition, we had to wait for the period of death to pass before the priest could choose a date for the wedding. It was decided that our Balinese wedding ceremony would be held in February 1990, on a day deemed the most appropriate according to God. I pleaded with my husband to wait until the following month, when all my family could come over from Australia, but the priest insisted it had to be on that particular day. So the only alternative was to have another ceremony the following month, with my relatives.

The first wedding ceremony was a delightful and highly amusing occasion. It was held in the courtyard of Ketut's family home, under the shade of the frangipani trees on a crisp February morning. I was rather nervous, especially as I'd heard many different stories about what I should do and wear. Nevertheless, I carefully dressed in my favourite mauve and turquoise floral chiffon *kebaya* and an inky blue traditional-style hand-woven cotton sarong. I slicked my hair back in a ponytail and wrapped a gold sash around my waist. I knew I would be changing once at the house as a part of the ceremony and had bought a raspberry lace *kebaya* and rich-brown woven cotton sarong for the occasion.

The family and neighbours were crouched on the ground in the lane outside the gates to the compound, anxiously waiting for us. Dressed in white, the priest stood beside them, in front of a few simple offerings spread out on the ground. Ketut and I took our place behind him, facing the beautiful carved gates, and then the ceremony commenced. The priest, holding burning incense and a silver bowl of holy water in both hands, lowered his head and started chanting. I was in some sort of euphoric state and didn't notice the small chicken next to the offerings. Suddenly — wham — its head was chopped off, blood was spilt, and the evil spirits were left to eat the aftermath as we sailed into the family compound, taking God's blessings and good spirits with us.

The ceremony that followed was full of joking and ritual. We walked around the courtyard three times, amidst smouldering coconuts and bamboo that was set alight so it exploded with a noise like a gunshot. I was required to carry a basket on my head, containing a shaved coconut, a string of Chinese coins and an egg. Each time I completed a circuit of the courtyard, I had to sit on a shaved coconut and then stir rice porridge that was boiling in a terracotta pot on a makeshift oven on the ground. As I walked slowly around, Ketut walked behind me. Over his right shoulder he carried a wooden pole and in his left hand a small stick. From the back of the pole swayed some little rice packages, symbolising the husband as the farmer and provider for the family. Tied to the front of the pole was a sprouting coconut tree, which symbolised our married life together, which, hopefully, would grow straight, strong and ever bountiful like the tree itself. The pole, with its two weights, suggests that in life the man will receive twice as much as the woman, but his responsibilities are also twice as great. Ketut was instructed to hit my back gently with the small stick in his left hand, while the family laughed and made all sorts of jokes, as you might imagine.

We threw small offerings over our shoulders, walked through a piece of string tied between the branches of the sacred *dadap* tree to symbolise the crossing of a new threshold, and Ketut had to spear a small woven leaf mat with his mighty *kris*, or Indonesian knife. This was quite clearly a symbol of male strength and fertility. It was another hilarious part of the ceremony and I watched my in-laws roll around with laughter.

Ketut and I were then requested to proceed with the next part of the ceremony by washing together in the privacy of the family bathroom, as a rite of total purification. In the villages, the young couples wash in the river and the wife is supposed to wash the husband's clothes as a symbol of servitude. Ketut washed his own shirt and hung it in the sun. Cool and revitalised, I put on my new sarong and matching red *kebaya*, the colour of love and marriage. Usually a gift from the family, it symbolises the start of a new life together and the adoption of the husband's ancestors.

Together, Ketut and I prayed in the family temple and finished the ceremony by feeding each other roasted chicken and rice from the offerings in the eastern pavilion. I'll never forget the happiness and warm spirits of this day.

The basket I had carried on my head was carefully brought home, with all its contents, and placed under our bed. After a few weeks, I began to smell the odour of the rotting egg. I wondered how long the basket had to stay in its symbolic position underneath me as I slept. In the meantime, the ants started to form a confident trail across the bedroom floor to their target and the smell became more unbearable. I started to think the egg was defeating its purpose as a fertility offering, as sleeping in our bed was now becoming quite unpleasant. I even considered sleeping in one of our guest rooms to escape.

At that point, I shyly asked my husband if we could perhaps move the basket, or at least the offending egg. Ketut was very surprised by this, but nevertheless was anxious to please his new bride. He approached his father and awkwardly explained the situation. The discussions went on for days, or so he said. In hindsight, I think Ketut was just biding his time. A week later, the basket with all its contents was removed — just a few days short of the forty-two-day vigil period. Four children later, I can only imagine I was given a double-strength serve, just in case.

For the third wedding, we dressed up like a Balinese prince and princess, and the ceremony included all the trimmings of music, dancing and feasting. I wore an olive green and dusty pink checked silk sarong embellished with gold thread over a purple and gold cotton sarong. I was then zipped into a black Madonna-style corset and wrapped around with a bright gold-painted ribbon. Another piece of painted cloth was attached under my arms and trailed elegantly over my shoulder and down my back. My hair was pulled back tightly beneath a crown of white *cempaka* flowers and a million gold leaves skewered into place on thin bamboo sticks to form a towering mountain of fragrance and opulence. A special long golden-brown ponytail was attached to my bundle of hair and strung with *cempaka*. I had ordered the piece especially from a Belgian wig-maker as I figured the usual black hairpiece might look a little out of place. A brown line was drawn around my forehead to disguise my hairline and a layer of make-up was applied. I borrowed some traditional carved gold earrings, the size of twenty-cent coins with a funnel-shaped back, and thick bracelets to complete the picture. I felt like a fairy princess or goddess from a Busby Berkley film.

Ketut wore a thick crimson and gold silk sarong that was tied under his arms, and a silk *udang*, a headpiece. A *kris,* the traditional Balinese sword and weapon of magic and strength, was strapped to his back. He even wore a touch of rouge and red lipstick.

The wedding ceremony was solemn this time and held in the *bale* and temple of the family home. The priest said the same prayers and we followed the same routine of wafting the plume of incense towards us. Our hands were brushed with egg and coconut leaves and our wrists were tied with string, and a delicate and beautiful offering of a blade of grass and flower petals was tied around our heads. Several hours after the ceremony, we had a huge wedding reception at the family's new woodcarving gallery nearby, actually combining the opening of the gallery with our celebration. Hundreds of people arrived, bearing gifts of all sizes wrapped in bright shiny paper. My family from Australia joined in the celebrations, as well as a handful of expat friends. The gallery was the perfect venue. Shady *flamboyan* trees, mango trees and pink frangipani were surrounded by cascading bougainvillea and flowering gingers, all overlooking a large well-clipped lawn. In the centre of the grounds was a pavilion surrounded by a pond full of bright orange goldfish, where a *gamelan* orchestra played traditional music that tinkled sweetly across the garden.

After dinner, the guests were treated to a *joged* performance, which is a Balinese dance performed at family ceremonies, in particular, weddings. The *joged* is one of the most fascinating dances I've seen in Bali and certainly the most erotic. Frenetic music sets the pace and the beautiful young dancer appears with a sash and fan and claims a partner from the audience by lassoing him with the silky belt. This is where the fun begins, as the partner chases the young maiden around the dance floor in his attempt to kiss her. Often the chosen man is also a skilful dancer and the antics that go on have the crowd in fits of laughter. At our wedding reception, my dad and a few other Westerners were selected as dance partners and this had the Balinese roaring with delight. The *joged* dancers are intriguing to watch. The way they swing their hips and roll their pelvis back and forth is reminiscent of a Middle Eastern belly dancer. They twirl a fan, twisting it like a fluttering butterfly, while they move quickly across the stage. My friends were intrigued at this outwardly flirtatious concert and marvelled at the agility of the young girls. Several of the men managed to kiss the dancers and the girls beat them with their fans in return. The crowd was ecstatic.

In the meantime, I watched the presents mount into a haystack of colour and paper bows, more gifts than I had ever seen in my life. They were all shapes and sizes and I was so excited at the thought of what could be inside. I was eager to start opening them straight away, but Ketut insisted we return the next day as it was already late.

The following day, we returned to the gallery and saw an army of people happily cleaning up the previous day's mess. I had only one thing on my mind: the presents. Christmas had never been this exciting. I returned to the room where the precious treasures had been left and was shocked to see that the huge pile had shrunk to a mere twenty or so pieces.

'Where are all the presents?' I asked Ketut, almost shedding tears in my deep disappointment.

'You didn't think they were all for you, did you?' he answered, amazed at my response. 'They've been divided up amongst the families and all the people in the village who helped prepare the ceremony. They deserve them too.'

I suddenly felt embarrassed at my greed and didn't want to seem like a spoilt little girl, so I started to unwrap the remaining presents without a word. The most popular gift at that time was a set of creamy-coloured matching ceramic mugs, shaped like beer mugs, with Mama and Papa written in a deep brown cursive script on each one. I unwrapped one after another and lined up a whole army of these ugly drinking vessels. One or two sets of cheap imitation Delftware tea cups broke the monotony. I stared in disbelief at the unappealing bounty. How could I have known the whole community would share the presents?

Afterwards, I bumped into a few Western friends who had attended the wedding. 'So what did you think of our present? Was it suitable?' they asked.

'Oh yes,' I replied. 'Perfect! Thank you so much.' Of course, I had no idea what they'd given us.

A few days later, another friend came to the house. She explained that a mutual friend who had attended the wedding was a little confused as to why I hadn't thanked her for the special present her daughter had made us.

'What exactly did she give us?' I asked shyly.

The friend explained that the daughter had silk-screened a beautiful cotton bed sheet with her own design of an ocean goddess surrounded by waves, shells and starfish in my favourite shades of coral pinks, violet and turquoise. It sounded beautiful and I was touched by their generosity. I sadly confessed that I didn't have the present but would try to find it. Ketut spent the next day trying to track it down but to no avail. It had disappeared into the home of a happy villager, who probably still enjoys this wonderful piece of art to this day. And I was left with a cupboard full of mugs that I gave as wedding presents for months after that.

After all our weddings, we went on a four-month honeymoon to Europe and my mother came too. Ketut and Mum joined forces, so I soon became the odd one out as they shared all sorts of jokes at my expense. We travelled through Spain, France, Vienna and Italy and I watched Ketut develop a passion for architecture, sculpture and landscape. Building became his canvas, and you can see the evidence of this European experience in all that he creates today. When some friends recently asked us to visit them in Las

Vegas, I shuddered to think what impression the palatial casinos with their flashing lights and huge water features might have on Ketut. I don't think Ubud is ready for that yet.

When we returned to Bali from our European holiday, my education in Balinese culture really commenced. I became a member of the North Ubud *banjar*, or neighbourhood. In the years that followed, Ketut and I became the proud parents of four spirited happy children: Dewi, Krishna, Laksmi and Arjuna.

I am always grateful for the gentle guidance of my husband, Ketut, who is also my strength and spiritual teacher, but through my children, I have learnt a different aspect to Balinese life. I feel that without my Balinese husband and the children, I would have missed out on a whole layer of understanding. I am blessed with a wonderful life in Bali. I thank the people of Ubud for embracing me as their daughter, and rejoice in a community that offers such gracious warmth and protection. And my family and friends continue to nurture my Australian soul with frequent visits.

The fruits of our deeds

TALES OF FAMILY LIFE

My devotion to my parents is beyond words,
Truly it is as great as both the mountains,
Hima and Semeru.
But if I told you of my love for you,
It would be wider than the widest ocean.

PARTHAYANA, THE JOURNEYING OF PARTHA

Over the years, I have watched many of Ketut's nieces and nephews and our neighbours' children blossom into charming polite teenagers — and you don't have to be in Bali very long to work out that it must have something to do with the great love and reverence with which the Balinese treat their babies. It was for this reason that I decided to embrace Balinese customs in the raising of my children, starting with Dewi. During the day, she was cared for by a multitude of warm happy young men and women who were working with us at the time. I watched their skills and never-ending patience in distracting and entertaining our pride and joy and I started to employ the same techniques. They laughed with Dewi, sang to her, rocked her to sleep over their shoulder, carried her everywhere, fed her sweet bananas, rice porridge and eventually mild red chilli. They made a paste

44

of turmeric to spread over her cuts, homemade poultices to cool her warm skin, spread coconut oil on her mosquito bites or sandalwood paste over her bruises. When she fell over, Nyoman, her nanny, would rub the spot on the ground where she had fallen with her long black hair to smooth away evil spirits. When she couldn't sleep, they'd massage her legs or gently rub her back. I watched them tease her constantly by asking for her food, clothes or shoes and saw how this gradually taught her generosity and flexibility. In Bali, it is said that your children are your *karma*, the fruits of your deeds. Shower your children with love and respect and you will surely be blessed in this life and the next.

Beside the steps in front of our old house lie four small rocks that mark the place where our children's placentas, or *ari-ari*, are buried. The two on the right are the boys' placentas and the two on the left are the girls'. The Balinese believe that a baby is born with four brothers, *kanda empat*, who surround them in the cardinal directions. These are represented by the blood accompanying the foetus, the placenta, amniotic fluid and coating skin of the newborn. The placenta is the most tangible aspect of the four brothers, so great effort is made to ensure its well-being. After birth, the placenta is collected and gently washed, just like a newborn baby. It is placed inside a small golden coconut, wrapped in white cloth and buried in front of the parents' sleeping pavilion or *bale*. A rock is placed on top to mark the spot and a small bamboo altar is built over it to house the offerings. A spiky pandanus tree is always planted beside the rock to protect it from animals and evil spirits. I have seen this grow into a tall tree in many family compounds. Once buried, the four brothers bond with the earth and link with the ancestral soul of the land. The Balinese don't like to wander far from this sacred spot, perhaps explaining why they don't usually travel far from their birthplace. It represents their home, where their heart lies, a place that holds eternal significance.

The role of the four brothers is to guide and protect you in life, but as you might imagine, there are strings attached. They must be nurtured like a baby or a best friend. To keep the guardians happy, we feed them with offerings every day, placed on the smooth river rock that seals the spot. This ritual continues until the child loses his or her first tooth, or for roughly six years. Ketut tells me that if you're clever, you can call on your brothers to help you out in life. For example, you might get them to run a few errands at the market for you while you stay home and relax. Or you could have them create a bit of mischief on your behalf. It's a little like cosmic cloning or having a pet genie in a bottle. They can even learn to perform evil deeds of witchery and black magic, should you wish them to. Never underestimate the power of the placenta. It is said that a Balinese will never buy land that lies between members of the same family because the force of the placenta will strangle them.

With each new baby, I have watched the girls in our compound place small offerings of flower petals sprinkled with a few grains of rice and food on the rock that guards the placenta. Shaded by the spiky pandan leaves and enveloped in a constant haze of sweet burning incense, the rock is symbolically washed and fed like a baby. On certain powerful days, such as the full moon, the offerings are even more elaborate. They make a lovely sight sitting at the bottom of the steps of my and Ketut's old room, which is now occupied by tourists from all over the world.

Aside from burying the placenta, a multitude of offerings are also placed throughout the compound after a child's birth. These are for the deities, the ancestors in their carved shrines, good and evil spirits who reside on our property. They are the unseen tenants who can make life miserable if you don't care for them. Pity the man who chooses to move to the other side of the rice fields, for in this culture, you can't just put the For Sale sign out the front and leave. Generally in Bali, once you build, you stay. And the youngest son takes over the household duties, as will his youngest son, and on it goes.

Dewi

Truly, she was the origin of bounteous beauty,
The jewel of loveliness,
The soul of the whole world.

PARTHAYANA, THE JOURNEYING OF PARTHA

Our first child, named Dewi, meaning goddess, was born on a cold Melbourne morning in April 1991. As fate would have it, she was a breech birth and consequently delivered by Caesarean. With a divine name like Dewi, I guess there was only one way to appear.

Six weeks later we returned to Bali with this precious little girl with her flurry of black hair, huge melting eyes, soft pink lips and creamy olive skin. All the family came to visit as soon as we arrived and you can imagine how excited they were to see our first offspring. Inevitably, Dewi gave Ketut and me a new focus: there was another person in our lives now who required special love and attention. It also pushed me up a few rungs on the Balinese ladder of respectability, as mothers are highly regarded in this culture.

The day after we arrived from Australia, preparations began for the ceremonies we had not yet carried out. The *kumara* — a small ornate throne usually painted red and gold — had to be purchased at the market and placed beside our bed. We had made a special request at the hospital in Melbourne to keep Dewi's placenta and Ketut had taken it back to our East Kew home on the tram, sealed in a plastic ice-cream container. He bathed it like a baby, carefully wrapped it in white cloth and buried it under the sleepy beech tree in our inner-city backyard. He made offerings of flowers and said prayers under the musky spell of incense. For the next six weeks, Ketut nurtured this silent life force while I was nurturing Dewi. And when we returned to Bali, Dewi's placenta came with us.

For years, I'd watched loving Balinese mothers, aunts and grandmas massaging babies and decided this was a skill I had to acquire. So I asked my sister-in-law, Kasi, mother of three, to show me the ancient technique. Kasi is a very loving and cheerful sister-in-law who's always eager to advise me on Balinese ways. I was instructed to buy fresh coconut oil and to roast a handful of red shallots over a flame. With the tips of her fingers, Kasi carefully mixed the fragrant oil with the chopped grilled onion then rubbed it between her hands. Gently but firmly, she started to massage Dewi's tiny body with the luscious velvety concoction.

'She's terribly stiff,' she commented shortly after she had started. She firmly pulled Dewi's arms and legs, rubbing confidently into the joints and up and down the limbs. Then she massaged her tummy, pressing right in under the pelvis, slowly moving her hand in a clockwise direction. It was more like a deep-tissue massage than a gentle rub, but Dewi didn't protest. Kasi picked her up by her tiny fingers, let her head fall back, and swung her gently back and forth. 'Terribly stiff,' she kept saying, and at that point decided to swing her around like a Ferris wheel. As a new mother, I thought I was going to either faint or scream, but quickly calmed down by telling myself that Kasi must surely know what she was doing. Luckily, she gave up on the swinging idea and turned her attention to the baby's head. Dewi, in the meantime, seemed to be enjoying this new vigorous routine.

Kasi sat Dewi on her knee, supporting her head. 'Her head's terribly long,' she commented eventually, after careful examination.

'What's that?' I asked anxiously.

'Her head,' she said, 'it's far too long.'

Dewi was such a beautiful baby with what I thought was a perfectly rounded head. Even my friends had commented on its beautiful shape. Kasi tapped Dewi's head at the back and started massaging firmly, trying to push the lovely rounded part in at the back, to flatten it out. I was starting to break out into a cold sweat! At last she said, 'Too late,' and gave up. I felt very relieved! Years later, when I was comparing Bali baby stories with a Western friend, she told me that in the mountains, north of Ubud, where she first lived with her Balinese husband, her mother-in-law had insisted that her baby sleep on a tin pillow to flatten the head at the back.

*   *   *

About a week after our arrival home, my father-in-law visited one of the special priests who could determine Dewi's previous incarnation. An offering of flowers, holy water and incense was placed in a small bamboo basket, together with a tiny piece of umbilical cord wrapped in white cloth. On his return home, Ketut's father proudly announced that our dear little baby was his beloved late wife, Ni Ketut Mugleg. The word spread through the town and many members of the family appeared on our doorstep, looking at Dewi in a different light.

The next day, a trail of little Balinese grandmas came to our compound, anxious to see the return of their adored friend. They called Dewi by her previous incarnation's name, and giggled and chatted to her, staring at her to catch maybe a wink or some familiar gesture.

One morning, one of my late mother-in-law's best friends, Gung Biang, arrived on our doorstep. Gung Biang is one of Ubud's most gracious old women. She is of aristocratic blood and an air of refinement surrounds her like a gentle halo. She is the link to a past era and her presence in a room can change the entire mood. When Gung Biang appeared on our doorstep with her young assistant, we all became a little nervous. The kettle had to be boiled to make the appropriate cup of sweet fragrant tea, served in our finest tea cups, and suitable snacks had to be quickly purchased from down the road to serve with it.

Gung Biang asked to hold my baby. Taking Dewi firmly in her arms, she walked her around the courtyard, chatted about recent events and told Dewi how she had missed her over the past years. She asked her what she had been doing since she last saw her, and told her she was so happy to see her again as they had been such good friends. Dewi, calmed by the gentle chatter, fell asleep. I'll never forget the sight of the two of them together: Gung Biang slowly walking under the shade of the white frangipani tree in our garden with little Dewi dozing in her arms.

Before leaving, Gung Biang handed me a present, saying humbly that it was just a tiny gesture, of no great significance. This surprised me as the present was rather large and beautifully wrapped in pink scented paper with pink ribbons.

'Oh, that doesn't matter,' I replied, puzzled by her words.

'You said what to Gung Biang?' Ketut asked me later that night when I explained how the old lady had claimed her gift was an extremely modest gesture, but when I unwrapped it I'd found it to be a beautiful outfit made of fine cotton with matching booties and mittens.

I could see the dismay on Ketut's face. 'Balinese people always say that,' he said. 'You should have said thank you, or at least, I'm sure it's grand, or something like that, but you must never say, don't worry about it! Especially with someone as important as Gung Biang.'

I was so disappointed to have made yet another *faux pas* and wondered what the neighbours were saying about me this time. I was also a little anxious about the constant embarrassment I must have caused Ketut over the years.

When Dewi turned two, the girls who work at our house asked my father-in-law if Dewi was anything like his late wife. He replied, 'Funnily enough, exactly the same. My wife didn't like me and neither does Dewi!'

Dewi is the epitome of Balinese graciousness and, just like her namesake, the goddess, always elegant and calm. She already understands the meaning of duty and observes all ceremonies and family obligations. She has great aspirations and a determination that will help her achieve whatever her heart desires.

Krishna
My heart is true and has never been otherwise.
PARTHAYANA, THE JOURNEYING OF PARTHA

Krishna, named after the favourite of all Indian Hindu gods, was born unexpectedly in Bali, just four days before I was booked to fly to Melbourne in 1993. All the Balinese claimed that our first boy obviously wanted to be born in Bali, as opposed to Melbourne in winter (for which I couldn't blame him). Ketut and his family were ecstatic, as Krishna immediately became an Indonesian citizen and, thus, the inheritor of our home and assets.

During my pregnancy, I had decided to follow Balinese custom by binding my stomach with an eight-metre-long cotton sash. At first it was unbearably hot, but eventually I became used to the comforting support it gave. I could walk for hours without straining my stomach muscles, and I never had back pain as the sash prevented my back from arching under the heavy weight of the baby. I massaged my stomach every day with coconut oil scented with essential oils of ylang-ylang and sandalwood. In the later months, I drank tea made from the leaves of the white hibiscus, to aid childbirth. Other times I drank *dalumen*, the slimy green drink made from the *dalumen* leaf that pregnant women love, as well as green coconut juice, prized for its nutrients and cooling properties. I stopped eating mango and pineapple in the early months, as they are said to have the power to abort a small foetus, and rejoiced in a Balinese daily diet of fresh fish, green leafy vegetables and tropical fruits.

But even after a careful regime of diet and exercise, Krishna was another breech baby and delivered by Caesarean. As soon as he was born, Kasi, Ketut's diligent sister, brought a pile of offerings to the hospital and placed them beside my bed. She was full of spirit and added warmth and happiness to my little room. Ketut's father sat quietly with us, never taking his eyes off our small son. When I look back now, I think he was sending him prayers of strength.

Krishna was only 2.4 kilograms at birth and looked like a withered old man. His skin had a yellow pallor that remained for two months. He was bald with very little facial hair and his flimsy ears were tucked in like tightly curled rosebuds. The placenta was taken home and buried immediately after his birth and the first ceremony was performed that afternoon at our house.

Each day, one of my sisters-in-law appeared with fresh offerings and snacks of sweet cakes. Piles of coconut leaves, fruits, flowers and sweet-smelling incense replaced Western-style bouquets. I was encouraged to eat peanuts for creamier, more nutritious breast milk and advised to only eat mild chilli with my food.

At mealtimes, a variety of clear soups with tofu, stir-fried Asian greens, fish or chicken simmered with gentle spices and rice was served. In fact, in this simple Balinese hospital, I enjoyed the most delicious hospital food I have ever eaten. Afternoon tea ranged from mung-bean porridge to Indonesian-style sticky rice cakes and fresh tropical fruits. On reflection, serving mung-bean porridge was a very clever tactic by the hospital, as it is not only highly nutritious but assists in helping you recover after a Caesarean. The fine skin on the mung beans irritates your throat and forces you to cough. This helps clear the lungs of the drugs given during the operation. I remember sitting on my small white cast-iron bed, looking out through dusty venetian blinds onto the street life outside. As I slowly ate my porridge, I watched the local people buying soups and tofu from the food vendors outside the hospital. Other people were sleeping on the bench seats or crouched in groups on the ground discussing the day's events. They were waiting for their loved ones to get better. The olive green walls and smooth grey tiles of my room provided a cool retreat from the afternoon heat. As I ate my porridge, the nutty legumes irritated my throat causing me to cough and I had to hold my belly to ease the pain. Every time I eat mung-bean porridge now I think of Krishna.

One of my staff stayed with me day and night. If the baby whimpered or wet his nappy, they would attend to him straight away. Ketut also slept in the spare bed beside me. When you go to hospital in Bali, most of the family go with you, so you're never alone. In this small private clinic, I enjoyed seven days of complete relaxation. On the last day before we left the hospital, a small ceremony was performed. I was required to pat the bed three times with my hand, to make sure the spirit of my baby wasn't left behind.

We returned home with our fragile baby son. On arrival, I noticed the new stone next to Dewi's underneath the delicate bamboo altar. A week later, my father-in-law went back to the old priest who determines previous incarnations. It was discovered that Krishna is the reincarnation of a woman who lived in Ubud about four hundred years ago. Needless to say, we didn't have any visitors from her family to say hello.

I was so pre-occupied with Krishna's delicate condition, resulting from his premature birth, that I forgot certain customs. My main concern was to keep this tiny golden-skinned boy well fed. When one of the girls remarked on Krishna's restless spirit, I suddenly remembered the bathwater — I had forgotten to splash his special rock with his bathwater and had been pouring it carelessly down the drain, with all his bodily fluids and youthful spirit. The Balinese say that if you neglect the stone, the baby will suffer. I hoped that nobody had noticed. The next day, I observed the custom, heartily splashing the stone with the sweet-smelling bathwater. From that day on, Krishna seemed to grow stronger, or maybe I was more at peace.

Krishna, however, remained the most sensitive of all our children. For the first two months, I lay his delicate body on a towel facing the morning sun that filtered through our bedroom window. Even the whites of his eyes were the colour of weak jasmine tea. I never dressed him in the beautiful yellow baby clothes I'd received as presents — they went straight to the bottom of the drawer. About six weeks after his birth, in desperation we took him to see one of Bali's most famous doctors. I explained that I was worried Krishna had jaundice, because of his yellow skin tone. The old doctor looked at Krishna affectionately. He firmly pressed his hands into his liver and moved them around, tracing the outline of the organ.

'Nothing wrong with him,' he pronounced happily. 'He's in fine health.'

I'd never seen a doctor use only his fingers to diagnose an internal complaint. I was expecting to see sophisticated apparatus, but all he needed was his hands. After that, when Krishna was two months of age, I commenced the daily ritual of massage.

Krishna never travelled well, so if I had to go out on short trips, I left him at home in the care of the workers. But he needed to accompany me on longer journeys as he was still breastfeeding. On returning from a trip to East Bali one day, Krishna, who was about eight months old at the time, started to cry in a very unusual way. By the time we arrived home, he was howling uncontrollably. There was nothing I could do to stop him. The girls in our house were horrified to see his anguish and immediately gathered in the kitchen. Wayan, the nanny at the time, took charge. While I tried to settle the screaming Krishna, she quickly peeled a pile of red shallots. Seconds later, she appeared in front of me carrying these glossy purple-red seasonings. She promptly chewed some up and then energetically spat them at Krishna while he cried: one, two, three mouthfuls. The air was tinged with the sweet sharp smell of the tiny onions.

'I'm sorry. This is what we do in the village,' she exclaimed, almost out of breath.

I had no objection and encouraged her to continue. I was willing to try anything. I imagined that the girls thought an evil spirit had accompanied Krishna in the car back to Ubud. And red shallots are always used to protect small children from black magic and demons.

Wayan spurted forth with more fresh shallots. Krishna slowly stopped crying, appearing a little bewildered at the layer of pinkish vegetable matter covering his face. He was exhausted after his efforts and nestled down to a sturdy drink. I was amazed at this creative approach of using something so powerful to calm a frantic child. I've never seen it done since.

Everyone loves Krishna. He has the sweetest nature and easy-going spirit and is the eternal gentle giant, with a crowd of adoring friends always surrounding him. He's the one who cries when the films get too sad, while his older sister remains stoic.

Laksmi

You are the embodiment of honey, the goddess of flowers,
the splendour of asana blossoms,
the jewel of maidenhood.

PARTHAYANA, THE JOURNEYING OF PARTHA

Laksmi, named after the Hindu goddess of prosperity and general voluptuousness, was born a month early in January 1996, in

Melbourne. After two Caesareans, I had no choice in the delivery, so the celestial Laksmi was born the easy way.

Melbourne hospitals are not as stress-free as those in Bali. I had to attend to my baby's every whimper myself and longed for the help of the nannies in Bali. Across the room was a frantic mother who seemed too young to have children. She spent day after day crying as her attempts at breastfeeding failed, her body denying her baby that simple pleasure of life-giving sustenance and bonding. I felt so sorry for her in her anguish, which was only made worse by tired nurses. I wished I could help her with a Balinese tonic or perhaps a herbal poultice.

Where I lay, there was no view of passing life or food vendors selling spicy snacks. On waking in the morning, I had to roll slowly and painfully out of bed to wash Laksmi in the specially designed tub, using creamy non-allergenic baby soaps and no-tear shampoos. She had to be dried in a certain way and dressed in layers of well-worn clothes. It was all extremely organised and I felt I was failing the efficiency test, even though I'd already had two children. Women who'd had fast easy deliveries of big bouncing babies walked up and down the hallway, noisily chatting and laughing, wearing stretchy nylon pants. They seemed to think they were at a gymnasium. I hobbled around slowly, hugging my sore belly with my hands. I remember sitting in the empty television room, counting the days before I could escape back to Bali. As I watched Lawrence Olivier as Hamlet struggle frenziedly with evil on the screen, like the Balinese *barong* dance at the temple, I dreamt of my lush garden scented with frangipani, tropical magnolia and ylang-ylang. I longed to hear the call of our Indian mynah bird that says '*selamat pagi*' all day, the roosters that seem to never sleep and the cooing doves. Even the barking dogs seemed an attractive alternative. Mealtimes were dismal by comparison. There were no gentle tofu soups, Chinese greens or wok-fried noodles. Even the teddy-bear biscuits were stale.

I wanted to throw off Laksmi's clothes and let her kick her legs freely in the warmth of Bali's moist air. I wished I could snuggle into my own bed and gaze at the coconut trees through the soft white mosquito net. My body and soul was tinged with a misery

I will never forget. I had become so accustomed to a life full of chatter, with happy people around me, that the absence of this human element made me wilt like a hibiscus shadowed from sunlight. My only joy was my beautiful precious baby.

Laksmi looked like an angel from heaven, a delicate rosebud with her soft pink skin, sparkling eyes and cherubim lips. She was the perfect baby and remained so for about two years — or until she discovered her independence and powerful voice! When we finally returned to Bali, six weeks later, with precious baby number three, the necessary ceremonies had to be organised again.

Meanwhile, my expatriate friends in Bali had been doing a little cosmic research of their own. One friend had drawn up Laksmi's natal chart and another had done her numerology. When we all finally met over lunch, both friends proudly announced that my dear little baby was going to be very creative and artistic. Later that day, I told Ketut with great excitement about their predictions. Art has always been taken very seriously in our household, so this was great news for me.

'Well, of course,' he replied casually from behind the sports section of the *Bali Post* (one of his favourite hiding places).

I imagined Ketut was referring to my side of the family: my dear grandfather was an artist, and even I am quite accomplished in that field. I had chosen to study art at college and also taught it for a short time in one of Melbourne's finest private schools.

'Didn't you know that Laksmi's the reincarnation of an artist in our family who died about forty years ago? Of course she's going to be creative!' he continued, dispelling my theory instantly and returning to the comfort of the soccer pages.

It is said that the reincarnated person is always Balinese because the spirits can't cross the water, therefore my ancestors don't get a look in. To this day, Laksmi insists she wants to be an artist when she grows up. She spends hours colouring in, just as I did as a child. She used to make her mark on our soft pink walls with all sorts of scribbles and scrawls. When I'd crossly ask her if she'd drawn on my wall again, she'd throw up her hands theatrically and exclaim 'Yes!'

Laksmi is like a glass of bubbly pink champagne. She's an effervescent goddess who likes to wander round in my high heels, make-up and hair bows. Her teddy-bear is her feather boa, the softest security blanket imaginable.

Arjuna

They stared and stared at the extraordinary beauty of the Prince,
He encompassed the arrival of the God of Love, the seasons of flowers and
the sweetness of the season of honey at once.

PARTHAYANA, THE JOURNEYING OF PARTHA

The Balinese doctor who delivered Arjuna is probably still telling my remarkable story to his other patients. Even Ketut claimed that *karma pala*, or the fruits of my deeds, had held me in good stead after this extraordinary birth. After three Caesareans, Arjuna was born naturally and easily, something not usually possible. It happened purely by chance. Yet again, I went into labour early and we arrived at the hospital anticipating an operation. Ketut and Dewi were with me. While I lay on the bed, Dewi, then seven, massaged my back. But it happened that on that fine July morning, just one week after my own birthday, one operating theatre was full and the other was being renovated. Arjuna, the eternal athlete, was born in the delivery room within a few hours of our arrival.

Following the birth, a small bag of sand about the size of an envelope was placed on my stomach and tied down by a cotton girdle around my waist, to help remove excess air and return the uterus to its original size. I shyly asked the nurse if I could have a cup of tea. 'Certainly,' she replied, 'you can drink whatever you want.' After a Caesarean you have to wait twenty-four hours for any sort of refreshment so I was ecstatic. I couldn't believe my incredible fortune and thanked God for my blessings.

I wore the sandbag for a couple of days, after which I resumed wearing the black cotton sash, which had become almost like a security blanket during the pregnancy, around my stomach. Every night, after a gentle dinner, the nurses made my favourite drink of hot milk with honey and ginger to send me into short but deep slumber. I relished every comforting drop.

The children came to visit in the afternoon of the first day. I watched the bewilderment on little Laksmi's face at the new centre of attention. Four days later I returned home, still amazed at the remarkable birth.

Named after the princely hero of the *Mahabarata*, Arjuna was what you might call an accident, but was also the baby we had to have. After the birth, Ketut asked me what name I wanted to call our precious son. When I was pregnant I'd told him that it was Arjuna who was inside me. When the doctor asked me if I wanted to know the sex of the baby after an ultrasound, I told him I already knew it was a boy. Balinese usually name their children after the first six-week cleansing ceremony. However, with all the children, I had chosen their names and even bought clothes for them before they were conceived. My wardrobe was always full of beautiful outfits for the next child.

'Actually, we can't call him Arjuna,' Ketut said shyly after the baby was born. He had obviously been waiting for the right moment to break the news. 'Everyone here will laugh if you call him that.'

'Why? Everyone knows who Arjuna is,' I replied. That was the problem. The Balinese see Arjuna as the eternal playboy, something of a James Bond character, in fact. He's the one always surrounded by beautiful women, fast chariots and palm wine!

'He'll have to excel at sport, be highly intelligent and extremely handsome,' Ketut warned me.

I replied that this was not a problem, as I imagined our son would surely have all these qualities, especially as our other children were so beautiful.

'People will get used to the name,' I said in defiance. 'I can't change it because that's who he's been from conception — he's been Arjuna for nine months already.'

I knew I'd won, because the Balinese can be a little superstitious about names, and would never play around with someone's identity unless a priest was consulted first. I had already broken the rule with each of my children by naming them so early, so it was necessary to make this choice seem like divine intervention.

The next day, Wayan, one of my workers, came to visit me to see our new baby. 'So what will you call him?' she asked curiously.

'Arjuna,' I said proudly. 'His name is Arjuna.'

Wayan laughed as soon as I'd uttered his name. 'The playboy! That's hilarious,' she replied. She was still giggling when she left our room.

I was determined to stick to my decision. Nevertheless, when my next visitor asked my baby's name, I said I was still deciding.

Arjuna has become an adorable little boy. The longest eyelashes imaginable frame his huge brown cheerful eyes. His enormous smile is tinged with absolute mischief. I've seen flight attendants turn into cooing doves at the sight of him. In Japan, a girl squealed when she caught sight of him and then broke into animated chatter and gesticulation. I thought she'd seen a snake. Arjuna always surprises us with his clever wit and intelligence. I can only imagine he will do his name justice. Funnily enough, those around him call him Arjun — a slight concession to the king of romance.

Balinese law states that the youngest son in low-caste families inherits the family house. Thus, Arjuna has become the prince of our household. He is considered the spoilt member of the family who will eventually govern the whole property. In fact, he already knows that the swimming pool is his domain. But in return, his great obligation is to maintain and look after our property and, more importantly, his life duty is to help and look after his mum and dad. He has to replace Ketut in all village duties and his wife will be my stand-in. As I always say, 'No nursing home for me, I'm staying right here!' The thought of living in our garden paradise in my old age, attended by this happy landowner and surrounded by beautiful grandchildren, is very comforting. I only hope Arjuna's wife is as agreeable to the idea.

I recently went to visit a Balinese friend after the birth of her latest baby. Now the mother of three beautiful children, Wayan worked for me for many years and was one of my brightest and most dedicated staff members. During those years, I spent many an hour consoling her over her miserable situation at home. She was deeply in love with a boy named Made, who lived nearby, but Made's mother would not accept her. When she eventually married Made and moved into his compound, the mother-in-law set about making life unpleasant for her. She criticised her constantly and accused her of being lazy and self-centred. Even after Wayan gave birth to the twins, the situation did not improve. It only worsened. Eventually the mother stopped talking to her altogether and the young couple were forced to build a small separate kitchen next to their bedroom.

Sitting on Wayan's front porch, I looked around in admiration at the little house she had built with her husband. A blaze of hot-pink bougainvillea trailed across the small verandah. At the entrance was a small pond brimming with plump goldfish, softly sheltered by a white frangipani tree. Red hibiscus, flowering gingers and purple orchids grew alongside. The twins played contentedly in the garden and the new baby gurgled and squealed in his mother's arms.

Everyone seemed joyously happy. Even the grumpy mother-in-law was full of smiles when she greeted me warmly at the gate.

'Tell me, is your mother-in-law speaking to you now?' I asked Wayan. I was puzzled by the more pleasant dynamics of the household, but I love happy endings and, as I sat watching the twins playing, I thought that Wayan and Made deserved the best that life could offer. They'd worked so hard together and you could feel the warmth and kindness in their cosy little home.

'As a matter of fact, yes,' she replied.

'When did she start speaking to you again?'

'Funnily enough,' she said, 'it was when I had my new baby son, Komang.'

She was holding Komang tenderly in her arms and Made watched him proudly. Wayan then told me how Made, in accordance with Balinese custom, had gone to the special local priest to find out the baby's previous incarnation. To Made's delight, the baby was a reincarnation of his grandfather. 'So,

Made, go and tell your mother that your new son is actually her father!' exclaimed the priest.

When Made returned home he presented the good news to his mother. 'Mother, Mother, this is Grandpa, your dear father.'

From that day on, mother-in-law spoke to daughter-in-law, and peace and harmony was restored in the family compound.

Rujak
Chilli–tamarind fruit salad

This is my children's all-time favourite snack. In the afternoons, especially as the season becomes hotter and more humid, my children always eat *rujak*. One big bowl of the finely sliced fruit tossed with tamarind-chilli sauce can be slurped, munched and finished between friends in minutes. Krishna loves it with fresh mango and orange. Dewi loves it with green mango and nashi pear. Laksmi and Arjuna will eat it any old way, preferably with more palm sugar. *Rujak* is a spicy sweet and sour salad that refreshes the palate, clears the head and sharpens the mind. It gives you a shot of energy when you're starting to fade.

My sister-in-law told us the other day that her teenage daughter had lost her appetite and was finding it difficult to enjoy her food in the hot weather. But she'd found if she ate *rujak* as an appetiser, she could then proceed with rice and all the trimmings. *Rujak* stirs up the gastric juices and awakens the tastebuds.

1/2 teaspoon shrimp paste, roasted
1–2 large red chillies, trimmed (or use small red chillies for hotter flavour)
sea salt, to taste
3 tablespoons tamarind pulp
4 tablespoons palm sugar syrup (see recipe, page 181)
1 teaspoon lime juice (optional)

Sit the shrimp paste on a small square of aluminium foil and grill under a pre-heated griller until slightly toasted. This will take about 30 seconds.

In a mortar and pestle, grind the chilli, salt and shrimp paste. Mix in the tamarind pulp, including the seeds (if using a food processor, the seeds will need to be removed). Add palm sugar syrup. Add sea salt to taste and the lime juice, if using. It should resemble chutney.

Mix the *rujak* with peeled and sliced fruit such as apple, pineapple, mango, Japanese pear or jicama as well as cucumber. It is also delicious with grated carrot and grilled meat. It is important to achieve a balance of sweet, sour, salty and spicy flavours in this dish.

Note: Fish sauce can be added instead of roasted shrimp paste. If mixing *rujak* with green mango, do not add the tamarind.

Makes 5 tablespoons of dressing.

Kangkung Pelecing
Spinach with sambal

The Balinese have a great fondness for *kangkung*, or water spinach. Part of the secret of this dish is to mix the cooked spinach and tomato-chilli sauce robustly by hand adding kaffir lime leaves, fried shallots and sweet soy for the final layer of flavouring.

Kangkung is the favourite green vegetable of all our children. Nowadays, Dewi likes to make this dish. She has been helping in the kitchen since she was eight and has already mastered the art of grinding spices. The kitchen staff usually help her by advising on quantities and frying techniques, while Laksmi watches in admiration. In between cooking, Dewi jots down her favourite recipes in a book given to her by her Australian grandma.

250 g (8oz) or one bunch water spinach or kangkung
1–2 teaspoons sea salt for boiling leaves
2–3 tablespoons fried shallots
1–2 teaspoons kecap manis
2–3 kaffir lime leaves, shredded

TOMATO SAMBAL
3 large red chillies
1 red shallot, peeled
2–3 small chillies (only if you like hotter flavour)
8 cloves garlic, peeled
3 medium-sized tomatoes

1 teaspoon shrimp paste
3 candlenuts
sea salt, to taste
4—6 tablespoons oil

Slice the stem of the *kangkung* in half by running a knife lengthwise and cutting it in half. Slice into smaller pieces.

Bring a large pot of water to the boil and add the *kangkung* with the sea salt. Boil, covered, for 2 to 3 minutes until the stem of the spinach is al dente. Drain and set aside, covered.

To make the tomato sambal, remove the seeds of the large chillies and discard, by slitting with a sharp knife and then washing them away under a cold tap. Chop into three or four pieces each.

Grind all the sambal ingredients, except the oil, in a mortar and pestle until a coarse red paste is formed or place all the ingredients in the bowl of a food processor and blend until fairly fine, like a homemade tomato sauce.

Heat the oil in a wok over a medium flame. Fry the sambal until it reduces nearly by half and the oil rises to the surface. If the mixture looks too dry, add more oil. This will take at least 3 minutes. It should be a beautiful bright red colour with a clear tomato fragrance.

Remove from the heat and cool. You can pour off some of the oil if you like and keep it in the refrigerator to add to salad dressings and grilled dishes.

In a large bowl, thoroughly mix the sauce with the drained spinach, tomato sambal, most of the fried shallots, *kecap manis* and shredded lime leaves. It should be a juicy combination of sweet, sour, salt and spice. Check seasonings and adjust if necessary.

Top with remaining fried shallots and serve with steamed rice. Serves 4–8.

Babi Kecap
Pork in sweet chilli sauce
Always eaten for the festivals of *Nyepi* and *Galungan*, *babi kecap* is one of those dishes in which the flavours intensify after a day

or two. Like all Balinese, it's one of my children's favourite dishes. The sweet soy blends affectionately with the aromatic gingers and chilli, resulting in a comforting stew that would also taste delicious with a pile of potatoes.

My young brother-in-law, Wayan, is famous for his *babi kecap* and is always called upon to make it for family gatherings. He usually adds extra chunks of pork fat for deeper flavour and richness, and I must say it does make it taste more delicious.

500 g (1 lb) lean pork, chopped into chunks
1 tomato, optional
2 salam leaves
2 tablespoons oil
1 stalk lemongrass, bruised and tied in a knot
6 cups water
3 tablespoons kecap manis
1/4 teaspoon salt
2 tablespoons fried shallots, for garnish

SPICE PASTE
8 cloves garlic, peeled
3–4 small red shallots, peeled
1 tablespoon chopped ginger
3 large mild red chillies, trimmed and de-seeded
4 small chillies, trimmed
1 stalk lemongrass
2 teaspoons palm sugar
1/2 teaspoon shrimp paste
1/4 teaspoon white pepper

Grind the spice paste ingredients in a mortar and pestle or place the ingredients in the bowl of a food processor and blend to a paste.

Slice the tomato into large chunks.

In a large glass or china bowl, mix the spice paste, lemongrass, tomato and leaves together with the pork.

Heat the oil in a wok over a medium flame. Fry the meat for 2 minutes until just coloured and sealed on all sides.

Add the water and bring to the boil. Simmer, uncovere[d] about 1½ hours or until the meat is tender and the wate[r] evaporated. Add the *kecap manis* and sea salt.

Garnish with fried shallots and serve with steamed rice.

Serves 4–6.

Acar
Fresh carrot and cucumber salad

Laksmi adores this bright salad. She'll eat mouthful after mouthful and then drink the pool of sweet and sour liquid left at the bottom of the bowl, relishing every drop. It is a perennial favourite for all children's parties at our house, and is also popular served with *nasi goreng*.

It can be stored in the refrigerator for up to a week and is, in fact, more delicious when chilled.

1 carrot

2 cucumbers

2 tablespoons white sugar

1 teaspoon sea salt

1 red shallot, peeled and finely sliced (optional)

½ cup Chinese rice vinegar or white vinegar

1 cup water

Peel the carrot and cucumbers. Slice into julienne sticks or any other shape you prefer.

Mix the sugar and salt into the vegetables, crushing and bruising to release the flavours. Add the red shallots, if using. Add the vinegar and water.

Check seasonings, making sure there is a balance of sweet and sour.

Store in the refrigerator.

Serves 4–6.

Ayam Goreng
Fried chicken

Served throughout Indonesia, *ayam goreng* is one of those classic dishes that varies from island to island. In this version, the chicken pieces are first sealed in hot oil then tossed with a tomato-based sauce for further cooking.

My late brother-in-law taught me this dish in his restaurant, Ubud Restaurant, near the Monkey Forest many years ago. I'd spend hours in his simple kitchen, which overlooked a tropical garden of fuschia-coloured bougainvillea and hot-pink hibiscus, nestled between stripy leaves and ferns. It was an overgrown burst of colour. He had more roosters than children and treated these proud smooth-feathered heroes with great affection. If he slept too long in the mornings, his wife would come and beat him with a stick — or at least that's what he told us. In the quiet steamy afternoons I would watch him cook up bright spicy dishes with easy confidence. He would grab the cleaver with his large hands and energetically chop and grind piles of spices. On his fingers he wore enormous antique-looking rings set with crudely shaped murky stones. They seemed to pulsate with energy as he cooked and chatted about his favourite food.

The meal that followed was always irresistible. We'd enjoy every mouthful, with a glass of icy rice wine, while soaking up the view of endless rice fields stretching towards the Monkey Forest.

If you add a touch of rosemary and oregano, the chicken takes on a sunny Mediterranean flavour.

Simple to make, this dish can be frozen, or made a day before serving and reheated in a covered casserole.

2–4 chicken thighs
pinch of sea salt
3 red shallots or ¹/₂ medium brown onion, peeled
6 cloves garlic, peeled
2 baby leeks or ¹/₂ a large leek, trimmed and washed
2 large red chillies, trimmed and de-seeded
2 small chillies (for hotter flavour)
2 medium tomatoes
one bunch choi sum or spinach
3 tablespoons oil
1 cup water or chicken stock
2 teaspoons fish sauce
3 teaspoons palm sugar or kecap manis

2 teaspoons tomato paste (optional)
¹/₂ teaspoon sea salt
¹/₄ teaspoon black pepper
2 tablespoons fried shallot to garnish

Chop each thigh into 4 or 5 pieces, roughly the length of the middle joint of your finger. Mix with a pinch of salt. Chicken breasts may be used for this dish, if you prefer.

Slice the shallots, garlic, leek, chilli and tomato finely, in uniform size. Slice the choi sum into 6 cm (2½ in) lengths.

Heat the oil in a medium-sized wok over a medium flame.

Fry the chicken for 5 minutes or until half-cooked. Set aside on a paper towel. If there is too much liquid in the wok, you may need to wash it and start again with fresh oil.

In the same wok, fry the onion, garlic, leek and chilli, stirring constantly, for 1 minute or until the ingredients are soft.

Add the sliced tomato and fry for 30 seconds, keeping everything moving. Add the chicken stock or water, fish sauce, *kecap manis*, tomato paste, salt and pepper to the wok and bring to a boil.

Smash the chicken with a cleaver to flatten out the meat.

Add the chicken to the wok, simmering for at least a minute until the chicken is fully cooked.

Throw in the choi sum. Simmer together for another minute or until the greens are just cooked.

Garnish with fried shallots and serve with white rice.

Serves 2–4.

Jukut Kacang Panjjang Goreng
Stir-fried beans

This is a simple and effective way of retaining the flavour and colour of beans. Snake beans or French beans work equally well for this dish. This is one of the first dishes I learnt from my sister-in-law when I lived at her house. She varied the dish every time she made it, sometimes adding lime leaves or extra sliced tomato, or fish sauce instead of shrimp paste. You can even take it a step further by adding adzuki or kidney beans.

250 g (8oz) snake beans
3 small red shallots, peeled
5 cloves garlic, peeled and sliced diagonally
1 large red chilli, trimmed and de-seeded
½ tomato sliced
1 small knob ginger
2 tablespoons oil
½ teaspoon shrimp paste
3 salam leaves
½ cup water
1 teaspoon kecap manis or brown sugar
½ teaspoon sea salt
1 tablespoon fried shallots

Trim the beans and slice diagonally into lengths of approximately 3 cm (1 in).

Finely slice the shallots, garlic, chilli and tomato. Bruise the ginger by smashing with the back of a knife.

Heat the oil in a wok over a medium flame. Fry the shallots for about 30 seconds, followed by the shrimp paste, garlic, ginger, and chilli, stirring constantly. Squash the shrimp paste on the base of the wok as you stir. If the garlic burns, lower the heat. Add the salam leaves and fry for a few more seconds.

Add the water to the wok and bring to the boil. Throw in the sliced beans.

Add the tomato and *kecap manis* or brown sugar and sea salt. Cook another minute or until the beans are al dente. Check seasonings.

Garnish with fried shallots and serve with steamed rice.
Serves 4.

Bakso Ikan

Glass noodle and fish ball soup

The *bakso*-seller is one of Indonesia's most famous sights. In the late afternoon, he takes to the streets with his *kaki lima*, small food cart, and walks from house to house, selling this famous clear soup brimming with chicken balls, glass noodles, rice cake, fresh chilli and herbs. You can hear him before he arrives, as he hits one of the glasses in his case with a fork to create a sharp tinkling sound — the distinctive call of the *bakso*-man. It has the same effect as the jangling bell of the ice-cream van in the sixties, when everyone would run to the gate to buy swirls of freshly whipped ice-cream in a cone.

Children love *bakso*, especially my children. Nowadays, we make our own, in an effort to perfect the flavours, and we use fish instead of chicken. At least once a week, we sit together and slurp on the transparent noodles floating with seasoned fish balls in clear chicken broth infused with lemongrass. It's a gentle nourishing meal that we all enjoy. Don't be deterred by the long list of ingredients, as it's very easy to make.

300 g (10 oz) chicken thighs
2 tablespoons water
4 salam leaves
3 lemongrass stalks, bruised and tied into a knot
1/2 leek, bruised
5 kaffir lime leaves
1/2 medium onion, chopped in half
2 L (3 1/2 pints) water
3 teaspoons oyster sauce
100 g (3 1/2 oz) glass noodles
fried shallots, to garnish
Chinese celery or spring onion, to garnish
fresh large red chilli, sliced, to serve
lime wedges, to serve

FISH BALLS
500 g (1 lb) fish such as mackerel, skinned, boned and sliced into cubes
1/2 teaspoon white pepper
1 teaspoon sea salt
3 teaspoons sesame oil
2 teaspoons soy sauce
3 teaspoons fish sauce
6 garlic cloves, peeled and chopped
3 tablespoons cornflour

Preheat oven to 180°C (350°F). Place the chicken in a baking dish with water and bake for 20 minutes or until golden brown.

Put the cooked chicken, salam leaves, lemongrass, leek, lime leaves and onion in a large saucepan. Add the water. Bring to the boil over a medium flame and then lower the heat and simmer for at least 20 minutes.

To make the fish balls, combine the white pepper, sea salt, sesame oil, soy sauce, fish sauce, garlic and cornflour in a small bowl, making sure the cornflour has dissolved thoroughly and there are no lumps. Place the cubed fish in the bowl of a food processor and blend the fish adding the cornflour mixture, a little at a time, until all the fish has been processed. It should be a smooth, sticky paste.

With two wet teaspoons, take a small amount of fish and shape into balls the size of ping-pong balls. Drop into the simmering broth. Repeat the process until all the fish is finished. Makes 40–45 balls.

Place the glass noodles in a large bowl and soak in boiling water to cover for 5 minutes. Drain in a colander and set aside.

Divide the glass noodles between 8 to 12 serving bowls. Ladle the hot soup and fish balls over the noodles and cover heavily with fried shallots and spring onion. Serve with sliced, fresh chilli and wedges of lime.

Serves 8–12.

Mie Goreng
Fried noodles

Usually iridescent pink in colour, noodles in Bali are served for breakfast, lunch or dinner.

For successful noodles, you must first arm yourself with a good wok and cooker, preferably gas. Then prepare all your ingredients and set up your workspace. Once you're ready, the cooking process doesn't take long and is always worth the effort.

We always serve *mie goreng* at our children's birthday parties. These have become an institution at our house, with as many as eighty small friends, family and neighbours attending and playing games such as how to eat *krupuk* from a string, pass the parcel and musical chairs. Recently, I have been to parties of employees' children in remote villages and played the same games. They've even served decorated birthday cake with candles, sung 'Happy Birthday' in English, cut the cake with wishes for better grades, and given out bags full of lollies to take home. It seems the Western birthday party is the one custom I have passed on to the Balinese. I used to think I was starting an unnecessary tradition, as Balinese children don't usually celebrate these occasions, but the pleasure they get from it is lovely to see.

250 g (8 oz) egg noodles
100 g (3½ oz) chicken or any meat
3 small red shallots, peeled
1 small leek, trimmed and washed
3 cloves garlic, peeled
1–2 large red chillies, trimmed and de-seeded
½ a medium carrot, peeled and sliced julienne style
125 g (4 oz) cabbage
125 g (4 oz) choi sum
2–4 tablespoons oil
¼ cup water or chicken stock
2 teaspoons fish sauce
3 teaspoons soy sauce
1 tablespoon kecap manis
2 teaspoons tomato sauce (optional)
salt and pepper, to taste

GARNISH
fried shallots
sliced cucumber
sliced tomato

Boil the noodles as instructed on the packet. Drain in a colander. They should be al dente.

Slice the chicken into narrow strips and then into tiny pieces. Slice shallots, leek, garlic, chilli, carrot and cabbage very finely. Slice the choi sum into thumb lengths.

Heat the oil in a wok. Over a medium heat, fry the meat for about 2 minutes, stirring constantly until it is cooked. Push the meat to the side of the wok or remove from the wok and rest on absorbent paper. If the chicken exudes too much water, tip out the liquid, wipe the wok and start again with 3–4 tablespoons of fresh oil.

Fry the shallots and garlic for 20 seconds or until translucent, stirring and swirling around quickly. Then add the chilli and leek, keeping up the same action. Stir in the cooked meat, then water or chicken stock and bring to the boil. Add the carrot, cabbage and choi sum. You can cover the vegetables for a minute so they'll cook quicker.

Add the noodles with the sauces. At this point you may need to turn off the heat. Use tongs to mix them all together.

Turn the heat on and toss for another minute or two until the noodles are heated through.

Check seasonings. Garnish with fried shallots and serve with a slice of cucumber and tomato on the side or *acar* (see recipe, page 65).

Serves 4.

Satay Manis
Beef satay

There's something very satisfying about eating food on a stick. One of my jolly Balinese cousins from Denpasar gave me this recipe. She makes this satay for any special occasion and is very proud of it. When I first made this for the children, they were so excited. Arjuna wouldn't leave my side and sat on the kitchen bench so he could see every part of the process. He watched me grind and roast the spices and thread every chunk of meat. The others helped, and together we ate every morsel.

15 satay sticks
500 g (1 lb) lean beef
1 tablespoon kecap manis
1 tablespoon oil

SPICE PASTE
3 teaspoons roasted coriander seeds
1/3 teaspoon roasted ground cumin
1 teaspoon black pepper

4 garlic cloves
3 large red chillies, trimmed and de-seeded
$^1/_4$ teaspoon sea salt
2 teaspoons lemon juice
2 teaspoons palm sugar

Soak the satay sticks in water to cover for 30 minutes to prevent charring during cooking.

Chop the beef into satay-sized chunks approximately 2 cm ($^3/_4$ in) square. Grind the spice paste ingredients in a mortar and pestle or place in the bowl of a food processor and grind to a paste.

Mix the chopped beef with the spice paste, *kecap manis* and oil. Marinate for 15 minutes.

Thread 4 or 5 pieces onto each satay stick. Grill or barbecue until golden brown. Serve with peanut sauce (see recipe, page 134) or *sambal kecap* and steamed rice.

Garnish with fried shallots.

Note: You can also use pork in this recipe.

Serves 4–6.

SAMBAL KECAP
6 small bird's-eye chillies
1 shallot, peeled
1 tablespoon kecap manis
$^1/_2$ teaspoon calamondin lime juice, optional

Slice the chilli and shallot finely and evenly. Mix with the *kecap manis* and optional lime juice.

Timun Mesantan
Cucumber in coconut milk

Golden fragrant spices are mixed with coconut milk, thin slices of cucumber and then scented with lime leaves, resulting in a dish of delicately fresh and perfectly balanced flavours. I remember we served this dish at Arjuna's ground-touching ceremony. My sisters-in-law took turns to cuddle our precious new baby making cooing noises and funny faces. He was passed from one loving aunt to another as they chatted endlessly about his features, especially admiring his Western-style pointed nose. Arjuna laughed and gurgled at all the attention.

2 cucumbers
1 teaspoon salt
2 teaspoons sambal goreng (see recipe, page 200)
2 tablespoons oil for frying spice paste
1 cup roasted coconut milk (see instructions, page 183)
4 kaffir lime leaves
sea salt to taste
1/4 teaspoon white pepper
2 tablespoons fried shallots
1 tablespoon suna–cekoh (see recipe, page 180)

Peel the cucumber. Slice the cucumber in halves lengthways, then slice each half again lengthways. Slice the quarters into thin slices. Mix with a teaspoon of salt to soften and set aside.

Heat the oil in a medium-sized wok. Fry the *sambal goreng* over a low–medium flame, stirring constantly, scraping the wok at the same time. This is a wet, sticky mixture and can be difficult to cook without burning. Add a little water if necessary. Cook for 3 to 5 minutes or until the oil has risen to the surface and it appears separated. Set aside to cool

Strain the salt-water off the cucumber.

Mix the cucumber, *suna-cekoh* and *sambal goreng* together thoroughly.

Add the coconut milk, lime leaves, salt, white pepper and fried shallots.

Check seasonings. Garnish with extra fried shallots and serve with steamed rice.

Serves 4.

Kare Ayam

Chicken curry

Probably the most wonderful thing about making a curry is the heavenly fragrance that drifts through the house when it's being prepared. My sister-in-law often throws a handful of small potatoes into this dish, making it even more appealing for children. The potatoes add a lovely soft texture and soak up the flavour of the spices so beautifully. Make sure you use fresh galangal and turmeric for this dish as the flavour, aroma and texture will be far superior to the powdered varieties.

You can replace the chicken with any other meat, fish or vegetable, or even tofu or tempe. For maximum flavour, I always use chicken thigh or leg for a curry.

750 g (1½ lb) chicken pieces
5 tablespoons oil for frying
4 kaffir lime leaves
1 stalk lemongrass
2 salam leaves
2 cups water
1 cup coconut milk
sea salt, to taste

SPICE MIX
2–3 red shallots
5 cloves garlic
4 large red chillies
2–3 bird's-eye chillies
1 tablespoon chopped ginger or one thumb
2 tablespoons chopped galangal or 1½ thumbs
1 tablespoon chopped fresh turmeric or ¾ thumb
2 teaspoons chopped kencur (optional)
2 teaspoons tamarind pulp
½ teaspoon shrimp paste
5 candlenuts
¼ teaspoon black pepper
2 teaspoons coriander seeds
½ teaspoon cumin (optional)
¼ teaspoon grated nutmeg
2 teaspoons palm sugar
2 tablespoons oil

Chop the chicken into small chunks or curry-sized pieces.

Grind all the spice mix ingredients in a mortar and pestle or process them in the bowl of a food processor on high speed with a little oil until paste-like. (If using a food processor, remove the seeds from the tamarind pulp.)

Heat the oil in a large wok and fry the spices over a medium flame, stirring constantly, for 2 or 3 minutes or until the spices are glossy and fragrant. Throw in the lime leaves, lemongrass and salam leaves, moving them around the base of the wok for 30 seconds until coated with the spices. Add the chicken and fry for at least 3 minutes or until the meat has changed colour and is sealed in the hot oil.

Add the water and simmer uncovered, to develop full flavour, until the meat is tender. You can decide at this point how soupy or dry you would like your curry.

When the water has reduced by half or more and the meat is cooked, stir in the final layer of coconut milk and bring to the boil. Simmer for a few minutes and then turn off.

Check seasonings and garnish with fried shallots. Serve with steamed rice.

Note: Potatoes, beans or carrots may be added. Tempe/tofu may be used instead of meat.

Serves 3–4.

Body and soul

THE ESSENCE OF THE INDIVIDUAL

. . . in the web of existence, two forces ebb and flow —
Good and evil, both are encountered, both are ever-present . . .

PARTHAYANA, THE JOURNEYING OF PARTHA

The Balinese religion, officially known as Hindu Dharma, is a subtle blend of Animism, Hinduism and Buddhism. Since early times, Java has exerted considerable influence over Bali. The greatest Hindu-Javanese empire, known as the Majapahit Empire, which prospered during the fourteenth and fifteenth centuries, is perhaps most responsible for the cultural and religious elements in Balinese life today. With the incoming flood of Islam in the sixteenth century, many princes, scholars, priests and artisans fled to Bali and established an 'exclusive' kingdom on the island. A unique 'Hinduised' culture developed there, whose age-old customs still apply today.

Balinese cosmology is based on the principle that the universe is divided into three spaces: the underworld, place of Brahma, lies to the south, in the direction of the sea; the middle space, place of Siwa, is where mankind lives; and the heavens, place of Wisnu, lies to the north, the direction of the mountains and lakes. The same cosmic laws that apply to the universe, the macrocosmos, also apply to humans, the microcosmos. In Sanskrit, the macrocosmos and microcosmos are described by the same word: *bhuana*.

The spectacular volcanoes that dominate the landscape give this magically charged island an ethereal quality. You can understand why these gentle folk incorporated the worship of mountains, lakes, rivers and trees to form the basis of their religion. Gunung Agung is Bali's highest mountain and the home of Besakih, the mother temple. Climbing the many stairs of this ancient temple to pray in the main courtyard, you feel as if you are already halfway to heaven. In all the years I've prayed here, I have only seen Gunung Agung once, as a thick layer of grey misty clouds usually covers it. I had actually forgotten that the temple is nestled into the mountainside, until one day it appeared before my eyes. Sitting in the courtyard, surrounded by chanting priests dressed in white, black and white checked umbrellas, banners of red, yellow and black, smouldering incense and people praying, I saw the curtain of clouds slowly part. The sight was breathtaking. The mountain loomed in the distance like a gentle giant and reached into the sky as far as the eye could see. Mount Gunung Agung is the most sacred part of Bali.

The cosmological laws apply to all levels of life, the seen and the unseen: how the Balinese see their place in the universe, how they live their everyday lives, how they set up their homes and even how they prepare and eat their food. It is for this reason too that orientation is crucial to the Balinese sense of well-being; not knowing which direction is north and which south is the one thing that can send a Balinese into a state of absolute panic — what they call *pusing*. I don't know any other culture that identifies these opposite poles in all situations. Whether it's parking a car, moving a table or looking for a street in a remote village, it's all determined by north and south. Even moving a cup on a table will be directed by north and south instead of just saying 'move it to the other end'.

The soul, or *atman*, is the venerated essence of the individual, the unseen and untouchable everlasting spirit. The Balinese believe that a life of purity and virtue will lead them to their fundamental origin: God himself, or Brahma, the Supreme Being, but there are many steps of higher learning required for entry to this holy paradise. The body is the vehicle of the soul and represents the flesh and blood that can lead the *atman* astray. The penalty for straying is empowered by the Law of Karma: the fruits of our deeds that may be manifested either in this world or the next.

On the physical plane, the head is believed to be the spiritual centre, the body is the home of man and earthly desires, and the feet are connected to the land of evil, illness and negative forces.

The head is the seat of wisdom, knowledge and power; it is the temple of Brahma, the soul of our being. At the temple, it is the head that receives the holy grain that helps unite our spiritual power after prayer. The *udang*, the cloth that men tie around their heads to wear to the temple, is like an antenna that opens a direct link to God, a means of focusing on the soul and receiving blessings. Tied at the front, the knot of the *udang* points to heaven, the land of the deified ancestors and God. The sarong tied around the waist points to the netherworld. Between these worlds, we must maintain balance and harmony by observing the laws of dharma, the way of virtues. The head is sacred and you should never touch the head of anyone older than you or of greater importance. When Nyoman places flowers in my hair to wear to the temple, she always says '*permisi*' first, 'excuse me'.

When Ketut first saw an Australian clothes line with its assortment of worn clothes and underwear flapping in the breeze, he was shocked. In Bali, the only items placed high up are offerings, shrines and holy matter. Washed clothes are thrown on the grass or over a shrub to dry; in other words, as close to the ground as possible. It was at this point that I realised how little I knew about Ketut's culture. I hadn't noticed that the only things to occupy the top shelf of his cupboard in Bali were his temple sarongs.

When Ketut and I went to Europe with my mother, all three of us often slept in the same room to save our meagre rupiah, which wasn't worth much when changed into other currency. In Munich, we stayed in a quaint little room that had the luxury of its own small washbasin, which proved very convenient as it meant we didn't have to walk miles down the cold corridor to brush our teeth. My mother had a habit of hanging her silky undies to dry on the small rail above the basin. I hadn't noticed them flapping against my face when I brushed my teeth, but eventually I realised that Ketut never used this handy washbasin, preferring instead to rug himself up and walk down the corridor to the bathroom. He hadn't said a word about it, but once I'd noticed I mentioned it to Mum, and after some laughter at the sight of the pink bloomers, she stopped hanging them there — or at least waited until after Ketut had brushed his teeth.

Similarly, whenever Mum neatly folded her cotton nightie and popped it under her pillow, Ketut would remove it when she wasn't looking and place it at the end of her bed. I think Mum thought the housekeeping staff were responsible — she kept commenting on how her sleepwear always ended up at the bottom of her bed — but Ketut kept moving it. 'The place where the head lies is sacred,' he told me, 'not a resting place for cotton nighties or flannelette pyjamas.'

Although the body is the location of earthly desires, it is also revered as a symbol of worldly splendour. It seems that in striving to attain eternal liberation, or moksha, it helps if you are beautiful and well groomed, for the Balinese are surely one of the world's most graceful people and attention to personal hygiene and cleanliness is paramount. After washing, the aromatherapy ritual begins with the application of fragrant creams and oils to their soft skin and hair. In the early days, when I was travelling between Australia and Bali, I would buy duty-free French perfumes for Ketut as he loved the scent of flowers and roses. Friends would comment, 'I love that fragrance you're wearing' and I'd reply, 'Actually, Ketut's wearing it!' He refused to wear the musky colognes designed for men.

As in the West, the Balinese ideal of female beauty is a slim hourglass figure with tiny waist, slender arms and glossy black hair (not brown like mine). An overweight body is a sign of imbalance and lack of harmony, proof that worldly passions obviously prevail. The body is treated with great respect and this is evident in the poise and grace of each person. Movement of the body is gentle and slow and handshakes are a featherweight, a polite gesture of contact rather than a show of strength. In prayer, there is a certain way to hold your hands and even cross your feet when kneeling. The Balinese innate self-assuredness comes from knowing exactly who they are, where they are going and what happens when they get there. It is only people without that faith in their place in the universe who need to 'find themselves'.

In Bali, the hands create and receive magic and mystery and are sacred symbols of strength, creativity and skill. The right hand represents Brahma, the creator, and the left hand represents Wisnu, the protector. The right hand receives all that is good and the left hand receives impure, suspicious things. When we unite our hands to pray, the union of the hands, called *desa indria*, represents the ten tools of the body.

It has taken me many years of observation to be able to verbalise the subtleties of how the Balinese use their hands. I've watched as they've gently ground spices, prayed with fragrant flowers in the temple, drunk scented holy water after praying, mixed and bruised vegetables, massaged the weary limbs of my children and made beautiful offerings from young coconut leaves. For the Balinese, the hands provide a link with God and the ancestors through prayer and the receiving of holy water, and a link with friends, family and others through love and affection. The powerful mantras and hand gestures of the chanting priest at a temple festival is a hypnotic act of beauty and mysticism. The expressive gestures of a Balinese dancer or the graceful blessings of offerings on the night of the dark moon echo a thousand memories of ancestors and ancient times. When my children say the *Trisandhya* or *Gayatri* at the temple, the sacred hymn from the *Rig veda*, they unite their hands in a manner that echoes the shape of a lotus flower, the symbol of everlasting life. And from an early age, they were taught to receive gifts by cupping the right hand over the left, and to give in return with the same right hand. The magic of all these movements is an expression of love, respect and harmony with nature.

I have watched many Balinese preparing food and have come to the conclusion that the hands are the element that brings life and vitality to the ingredients, be it through mixing, grinding or chopping. The deliberate circular motion of mixing the ingredients is an echo of an ancient Hindu mantra that protects all those within the circle, just as Laksmana drew the circle to protect Rama's wife, Sita, in the *Ramayana*. The hands can assist in the delicate art of balancing textures and flavours through feeling, and of course are the means by which the results are carried to the nose for the final appraisal. When Nyoman makes Balinese satay, her hands work overtime, while her eyes direct the assembly. She bruises the ingredients robustly, throws in extra fried shallots and lime leaves with great determination, and smells her hand moistened with golden spices with the astuteness of a proud mother breathing in the scent of her freshly bathed and powdered baby.

Balinese feet are firmly planted on the earth with their toes spread wide like the roots of a banyan tree. Their feet support the men as they squat to chat by the side of the road and hold the women upright as they kneel to pray. Feet help to support the weight of offerings, rocks, tables laden with snacks and growing babies. It is considered rude to use your feet as pointers; they walk in the realms of evil spirits and are considered unclean. When seated on a chair, the Balinese rarely cross their legs, preferring to keep the soles of their feet tucked away underneath the chair.

The cosmology of the universe is also applied to the Balinese village and the home. Seen as a living unit, the family compound is roughly mapped out in the shape of the human body, with three main parts: the family shrine, which faces north, represents the head; the courtyard, living and sleeping areas represent the body; and the kitchen, bathroom and compost heap, located towards the south, represent the legs.

If you wander into a Balinese compound, you will see that it is set out in a certain pattern. In the entranceway beyond the gates, there is usually a small pond to absorb evil spirits and a path that leads you right or left. This is a subtle trick to confuse evil spirits, who, luckily, cannot turn corners. Beyond the gates and temple, the compound unfolds into a network of small cottages, with wide verandahs and small windows, surrounding the central pavilion or *bale dauh*.

In the early hours of the morning, food and rice for the daily meal is transformed by fire and water. For this, the Balinese give thanks by making offerings. Small squares of banana leaf, called *saiban,* are graced with a few grains of rice and a tiny amount of cooked food. The blessings are then put in magically charged places around the compound. Only after rice and food for the offerings has been set aside may the people eat. The Balinese believe that if you don't share your food with the spirits, harm and bad fortune will certainly come your way. Therefore, good and evil spirits are treated equally.

Several families usually live together in the compound, including parents, aunties, uncles, children and the married sons. It is communal living, where everyone has certain duties and commitments to family. The sons stay with their parents and the daughters follow their husbands and set up house in his family compound. I often wonder how we will accommodate our own daughters and whether they will live with their parents-in-law or choose to have a place of their own, as Ketut and I did. Ketut was from such a large family that they pooled their resources and bought land for each brother and sister to set up their own compounds.

Balance and harmony is essential to all aspects of Balinese life. The poise and serenity so important to the ritual of praying at the temple also apply to eating and the Balinese have complex customs related to the meaning and function of traditional food. There are rules and regulations concerning what may or may not be eaten according to space (*desa*), time (*kala*) and situation (*patra*).

In preparation for your first meal of the day, you should wash yourself and tidy the kitchen. Most of the time, the Balinese sit close to the ground at mealtimes, preferring contact with the earth, rather than the comfort of tables and chairs. In an atmosphere almost equivalent to the morning prayers, there is little talk as spiritual nourishment is received from the soul of the rice. The food on our plates is like an offering that we are given to share, a gift of God's bounty, and deserves great respect. It took me years before I understood my staff's insistence that my children wash before eating, but then I realised that, like praying, you have to prepare yourself for the food that provides fuel for the body. I always felt that small children should wash afterwards, as they make such a mess. Nevertheless, I abided by the rule — I was outnumbered anyway.

A person must never be disturbed when he or she is engaged in a meal as eating time is considered a private time. To be given the privilege to finish a meal was always such a treat for me as a young mother. Phone calls and even crying babies had to wait until I had eaten my food. The Balinese prefer to eat in quiet places. I am for ever stumbling over one or another of my staff sitting on the floor in some hidden corner of the kitchen, eating their meal. One of the first songs all children learn at kindergarten reinforces that there must be no talking at mealtimes. You have to eat all the food on your plate quietly and the spell is broken when the meal is finished.

I remember eating with Ketut in our early days together. In accordance with my culture, I saw mealtimes as an opportunity to catch up on the day's events, a time to socialise. And that's exactly what I did: I'd burst forth with all I had done during the day while Ketut would keep on eating quietly, his head lowered over his plate, not saying a word. You can imagine my frustration. Ketut, on the other hand, was wondering why it is that when you give a Westerner a plate of food, they immediately break into conversation and won't stop. Eventually, out of desperation, he told me to be quiet when eating, to stop disturbing him and allow him to appreciate his meal. Initially, I sulked, but eventually we understood our cultural differences. Nowadays we meet in the middle by chatting when we feel like it.

At mealtimes, food and rice is artfully scooped between the fingers of the right hand and popped into the mouth with very little mess being made. This delicate action requires skill and care, and makes for slower eating which results in more thorough digestion. In this part of the world, it is said that good digestion is the core of good health. Lack of chatter aids this process by allowing the body to steadily assimilate the food. The Balinese will tell you passionately that their food tastes more delicious when eaten with the fingers and that cutlery creates an unpleasant steely coolness on the tongue that interferes with all spicy flavours. Whereas Westerners think that eating with the hand is unhygienic, some Balinese feel the same way about cutlery. A meal that has been so diligently prepared by hand should be eaten by hand. And ceremonial food is always eaten with the hand, in reverence to God.

Offerings and Woven Leaves

The fragrance of burning incense inspired pangs of love as it diffused its delightful fragrance without cease.

PARTHAYANA, THE JOURNEYING OF PARTHA

Offerings are a way of life in Bali. Every day, small coconut-leaf trays containing petals, leaves and rice are placed at busy crossroads, outside shop fronts, in shrines and homes. A walk into town becomes like a spiritual journey, each step marked by a precious feast of Mother Nature's bounty and saturated with the perfume of incense, the holy scent that follows you from house to house. The dashboards of cars and motorbikes also enjoy these sacred blessings as a protection from the evil spirits that linger on the roads. On auspicious days, more elaborate offerings are made. In the afternoon of the full moon, you'll see smouldering coconut husks at the entrance of each compound, gently burning amidst bright flowers and decorative coconut leaves, their fragrance trailing quietly to heaven. The phases of the moon and sun determine the schedule and size of these offerings and all Balinese Hindus follow these time-honoured rituals.

The five elements of air, fire, water, earth and ether are the catalysts to activate the spirit of the offering. The Balinese believe that the world is a place occupied by many beings, good and evil, seen and unseen. Great care must be taken to ensure that balance and harmony is maintained between all members of this metaphysical world. I heard a friend telling Ketut how she sometimes sleeps on the beach at night. He was very disturbed by this and replied that the world does not exist only for humans. The sea is not always a playground for people and it does not belong to us during the hours of darkness. Negative energies awaken after midnight and occupy areas such as the oceans, and they should be respected as they can create havoc with our health, mind and our energy, known as *bayu*. If illness or trauma disturbs the gentle force of our consciousness, then offerings must be made to revive the spirit and restore the troubled soul to normality.

The making of offerings is a way of quietly practising the worship of God to cleanse your mind and control worldly passions. It is an act of love and respect that enriches a pure heart and helps us receive the wisdom and guidance of God. The essence of offerings is contained in Krishna's advice to Arjuna in the *Bhagavad-Gita*. In this legendary passage, Krishna explains that the perfect gift to God should contain leaves, flowers, fruit and water in order to receive his blessings. Incense and flowers symbolise prayers and water symbolises spiritual purification. Whether great or small, this is the recipe for all offerings.

As a gesture of thanks, the first meal of each day is presented to God, the deified ancestors, and good and evil spirits. After returning from the market, the daily meal is prepared and the necessary offerings are made. When our cook Kadek makes the food in the morning, she places the various bowls of steaming hot curries, coconut vegetables, banana-leaf packages and seductive sambals under an open-weave plastic cover. While they rest, she tidies the kitchen and prepares the offerings. A ritual cleansing follows, which requires washing, tying back the hair and dressing in a *kebaya*, sarong and a brightly coloured sash. The holy communion with God and the universe now begins. After the offerings have been placed around the compound, it is time to eat.

More than eighty offerings are placed around our compound each day in cosmic hot spots determined by the priest. These generally consist of small coconut-leaf squares laden with red, yellow, pink and blue petals, a slice of areca nut and betel leaves smeared with lime paste, fragrant shredded pandan leaves and some cooked food with a sprinkling of rice and fried shallots. This garden paradise of tropical palms, sun-drenched flowers and fruits offers all the ingredients necessary to balance life's opposing forces. The combination of the areca nut (otherwise known as betel nut) with betel leaves and lime is a symbol of the Hindu trinity of Brahma, Wisnu and Siwa and is known as *porosan*. And the red, green, yellow, blue and white petals are the essential colours that represent the deities. Nowadays, we buy the coconut-leaf containers from the grandmother of one of our workers. It provides her with extra pocket money and saves us a little time in between attending to ceremonies and daily duties. God doesn't mind who makes the offerings, just as long as they're done.

Before we built our house, we were instructed to make offerings to the spirits of the land, in order to maintain the harmony of nature and safeguard our family. A *daksina* for building, an offering comprising a shaved coconut, Chinese coins, leaves and rice, along with several bricks wrapped in cloth, was buried in the foundations on a day chosen by the priest. Some people say the *daksina* ignites the spirit of the land; others say the coconut inside represents us, members of the human world. These offerings are nestled under every building on our property. On completion of the construction, a more elaborate ceremony called *melaspas* was required. This is a purification ritual that breathes life into the building; once the rites had been performed, our house was considered a living being. The next day we moved into our new abode, now fully occupied with happy unseen tenants. When we have ceremonies in our family temple, we all get dressed in our precious festive clothing and the house gets dressed up too. Just as the Balinese wear a sarong and *udang*, the stone columns are wrapped in shiny gold-painted fabrics and a band of decorative fabric is pinned to the eaves. Whenever we travel away from Bali, we ask the stone guardian of the land that protects our compound for permission to leave and to grant us blessings for a safe journey.

At both our restaurants, we make larger offerings to appease the spirits that live in the swirling waters of the rivers below us. Their three-course buffet includes a piece of cake with a tiny cup of coffee and sometimes a clove cigarette. These invisibles can appear as beautiful nymphs, old grandmas or ferocious beasts and have been known to beckon innocent victims to the depths of the netherworld.

Coconut leaves are essential for offerings and celebrations; the young smooth lemongrass-coloured fronds are woven into thousands of intricate containers and decorations. Coconut leaves at the entrance of a compound are a sign to announce a young couple's wedding. When we pray at the temple, we hold a *kwangen* up to the sun — a small cone made of banana leaves containing a delicate lacy coconut-leaf fan and fragrant flowers with a Chinese coin tucked inside, said to represent the moon and the Hindu trinity. It is one of the most beautiful of the small offerings and I love holding these glorious works of art between my hands, raised to God for blessings. The individual decorative style of the *kwangen* varies from village to village. Sometimes the tiny fan is as fine as that held by a Spanish maiden; sometimes it has only a minimalist touch of detail. The older deep green coconut leaves are used for sturdier offerings and can be stored for later use, as opposed to the young coconut leaves which turn brown after a day or two. These stronger leaves are also used to make the sacred *daksina*, the essential offering. Sturdy *lontar* leaves are also used for special occasions and they don't wilt or fade.

Ketupat is rice cooked in a beautiful diamond-shaped small container woven from young coconut leaves. The making of these is like Balinese origami or basket-weaving, with long strips of the coconut leaves wound around and around and in and out to form the container. When you boil the filled containers, the rice expands and becomes a solid block, similar in texture to potato. *Ketupat* is used for auspicious days such as *kajeng-kliwon*.

For the festival of *Galungan*, a *penjor* — a piece of trimmed bamboo artfully decorated with tufts of colourful leaves that represents the tail of the dragon and symbolises prosperity — bunches of Balinese rice and a crown of young coconut leaves is placed outside the front gates of every household to ensure prosperity and longevity for all. My children always love to watch the process involved in making these glorious celebratory *penjors*. During this festive season, a drive through the villages beneath the shade of these huge triumphant bamboo poles is a bit like the tradition of driving through a Western town to admire the Christmas trees.

Larger offerings for ceremonies and grand festivities are spectacular displays of creativity and beauty. I will never tire of seeing Balinese women carrying offerings on their heads to the temple. Towering pyramids of pink and green cakes, exotic fruits and sometimes grilled chicken are a thanksgiving to God by proffering the best of the season. The precious bounty is carefully attached to banana tree trunks with a network of skewers to create a design of rainbow shape and colour. The offerings are blessed with holy water at the temple and then brought home to be enjoyed by the family. My children always get very excited about eating the blessed fruit and cakes, and relish the sacred energy of each bite.

Together we share in your happiness; together we share in your sadness

CEREMONIES: A WAY OF LIFE

There he performed the most excellent, paramount ritual gestures,
Praying to the Lord of One Thousand Rays, the Sun
Together with the recitation of esoteric formulas, his meditation
Penetrated to the highest Inconceivable truth . . .

PARTHAYANA, THE JOURNEYING OF PARTHA

An expression in Indonesian, *suka-duka*, translates as 'together we share in your happiness; together we share in your sadness'. The emotional bonding that occurs when working and eating together with friends and family is constantly strengthened in a culture that relies on the participation of all its members. Ceremonies, family gatherings and village activities are all a part of life's obligations.

The Balinese year seems to revolve around *Galungan*, the festival that occurs every six months, the dates being determined by the phases of the moon and the Balinese calendar. Leading up to *Galungan* we celebrate festivities for human folk, such as weddings, tooth-filings and cremations. *Galungan* itself marks the start of the elaborate temple festivals, during which the bearing of offerings to receive divine blessings is one of the most spectacular sights in Bali. After *Galungan* we observe the baby ceremonies that celebrate different stages in a child's life, and all sorts of other festivities.

The men of the house and the *banjar* are the culinary experts for ceremonies. Together they are responsible for the preparation of elaborate foods that will become offerings for the ceremony and the symbolic meal that is shared by friends, neighbours and all those who have helped with the hard work. For a large ceremony, the family will slaughter several small pigs around two in the morning, and fresh chunks of the meat are set aside to become the basis for a multitude of spicy dishes and offerings. The preparation of ceremonial food is traditionally carried out at night, as it has to be ready in the morning when the celebrations begin.

Some of the dishes are prepared as religious symbols or offerings, their meaning signified by shape and colour. Others are for sharing with co-workers and members of the *banjar*. Packages of rice, blood-seasoned vegetables and satay, wrapped carefully in banana leaves, are also delivered to the homes of extended family and friends. These are a gesture of thanks for those who have helped, as well as providing a way of keeping up with village ceremonies.

For any ceremony, the kitchen and surrounding area of the home is transformed into a lively workplace. In the early hours of the morning, the men start preparing the sacred menu of *lawar*, satay, soups and so forth. The women make the offerings and refreshments for the guests and helpers, while the men chop meat, coconut, spices and vegetables with carved Balinese knives. The pretty young daughters always hand around the tea, coffee and Balinese cakes and the flirting and teasing that follows adds to the jolly spirit.

The delicate task of mixing *lawar* is a performance in itself. Fresh congealed pig's blood, fried chilli, grilled shrimp paste, cooked chopped entrails, stomach lining and meat are mixed with roasted coconut, vegetables and seasoned coconut milk. The initial mixing, performed by one central figure, is followed by the taste-testing, and this is when the action really starts. More salt, more chilli, more fish paste is called for and the debate continues. When men from different villages prepare together, the process can be even more time-consuming. I once saw the ingredients for making *lawar* taken out of the huge mixing bowl to start again. The person mixing them was from a nearby village and had been invited to help prepare the food for our daughter Dewi's ground-touching ceremony. All the local Ubud men were horrified, as the order in which he was about to mix the vegetables and coconut was not the way it's done in our *banjar*. Amidst the spirited chatter, the visitor shyly started the mixing process again, this time putting the spices into the coconut and then adding the cooked vegetables. The others watched closely to make sure he didn't have any other unacceptable methods up his sleeve. When he had finished we all tasted the ceremonial fare. The men claimed it was delicious and well worth the effort. But they would say that anyway!

Ceremonies such as weddings, cremations and tooth-filings can turn into a gastronomic feast in Bali, as food has to be prepared for days on end to feed the multitude of helpers from the village. Eating at festivals is a communal event, whereas daily meals are more solitary and silent.

I was amazed by and deeply grateful to the army of people who worked happily day and night to make all sorts of offerings for my wedding. I couldn't believe they would do this for me, as I didn't even know most of them. Fragrant curries, steamed banana-leaf parcels, tofu, tempe, green leaves with coconut and other favourites were part of the ongoing feast that was cooked by both the men and women. Snacks of black rice pudding, sago pudding, mung-bean porridge and poached fruits were served between meals. For the wedding banquet that followed the ceremony, pinkish-red noodles, snake beans in coconut milk, assorted satay, chicken curry, deep-fried fish with a sweet chilli sauce, spicy potato fritters, luscious pork stew and jackfruit curry were part of the huge spread.

Once married, you become a member of the local *banjar* and this means taking part in and helping with all village festivities. On auspicious days, you might be required to visit up to six compounds to celebrate weddings, tooth-filings or maybe even a cremation, as these activities often happen on the same day. For temple festivals, you are expected to help prepare offerings for a week or two in advance; you might spend days on end working together with your community. I am always amazed that businesses manage to keep going amidst all the religious commitments.

Temple Ceremonies

Odalans, or temple ceremonies, are the most spectacular events in Bali. Celebrating the anniversary of the temple, *odalan* is a time when the deities drift down to earth and take up residence in the decorated shrines of the holy sanctuary to enjoy the festivities. A grand procession of all the village members heralds the start of this special occasion. It includes small children dressed like dancers in glorious Balinese costume, boys carrying painted banners, beautiful young girls carrying offerings of fruit and sacred effigies, a *barong* — a mythical animal similar to a lion and the protector of the village — a gold shrine for the spirit and a *gamelan* orchestra. Other village members grasp the long white cloth that trails for many metres, a symbol of the road to God.

Probably the most exciting temple festivals in Ubud happen at the Pura Dalem, the temple associated with Siwa and death. This is where you'll see wonderful dance, shadow-puppet and drama performances. It is here that you'll also see the most stylish Balinese men and women on the island, dressed in *pakaian adat*, or ceremonial costume, made from glorious silks and handcrafted gold jewellery.

Odalans vary greatly in size. Some might last for only three days, but the more spectacular ceremonies can last for weeks. They generally occur around the same time each year, often commencing on a full moon. The preparations for the ceremony can take more than a month. I have helped many times for these occasions and have become adept at some of the more simple coconut-leaf offerings. I can also shape warm rice into miniature mountains and tiny round cushions. The weeks of working together create a wonderful feeling of well-being and happiness, giving you a sense of purpose, a focus to occupy your thoughts and strengthen the bond between all members of the village. The rest of the world might be caught up in danger, but in the village, life revolves around a magnificent ceremony. If a family that prays together stays together, then the same must hold true for a whole community.

For the last major ceremony in Ubud, the mothers in our *banjar* had to learn a dance called the *rejeng*, in which many women dance slowly in long lines, bearing offerings to the gods. I had three short lessons with the women and was amazed at their grace and flexibility. Some of the grandmas were so beautiful in the way they swayed and moved their hands, fingers arched like a bow, the languid movements of youth still flowing through their veins. I felt rigid and clumsy by comparison, but everyone was so encouraging and told me I was a natural. When Dewi watched, she told me I was doing everything wrong! When we finally danced at the temple, I hid at the back where I thought no one could see me. But everybody can see a tourist. My Australian friend, Olive, observed my performance and thought I did a fine job. She even wrote a poem about my achievement.

When the ceremony begins, the excitement in town is immense. For a large festival, the streets will be adorned with handcrafted *penjors* and the experience of driving through town under the shade of hanging bamboo adorned with lacy coconut fronds and tufts of golden rice is exhilarating.

Within the inner sanctum of the temple, peace, splendour and opulence prevail. Lofty shrines line the walls, surrounded by colourful umbrellas, graceful banners and flags painted with deities. Streams of fabric, sometimes black and white checked and other times bright satin, pour forth from the small niches at the top of these shrines and spill onto the ground below. Seated in pavilions embellished with white and gold cloth are several *barongs* that stare at you from within their well-lit dreamland. They are surrounded by a mound of hair, usually strung with frangipani, beneath a patterned gold leather headdress. Seen as the protector of the village, these mythical animals are reminiscent of a Chinese lion and are always present at temple ceremonies.

A huge statue symbolising the Balinese universe usually stands near the central shrine. Made of small fried rice cakes in pinks, yellows, oranges and greens, it represents mankind perched on a turtle, surrounded by the skies and heaven. On the other side is usually a massive statue similar to a pagoda, made from fried pork and glistening pork fat. Offerings of pink and orange rice set in gold pyramids, piles of folded fabric on pedestals, coconut-leaf rice goddesses, mangosteen, snakefruit, mangoes and apples sit in the main pavilions. Long tables full of more offerings brought by each family, receive blessings of holy water and sweet incense from priests and women dressed in pure white. Terracotta burners on the ground charge the air with the captivating fragrance of smouldering sandalwood. The temple is like a perfumed fairyland full of worldly treasures, decorated animals and exotic people. The soft tinkle of the *gamelan* sends gentle petals of sound to the clouds. A chorus of chanting women sings ancient songs of worship, deep mantras that penetrate the soul. The atmosphere can be overwhelming. It's like visual meditation, where all other thoughts disappear and the focus turns to God and greater things, to a realm beyond our own lives, where ancestors and deities reside.

There is almost as much activity outside the temple as inside. Food stalls abound with all sorts of snacks, drinks and meals. A crowd of young men play games of chance on the ground. Performances of dance, drama and shadow-puppetry are held in the surrounding pavilions or under the stars. The atmosphere is like a carnival. And by the time the ceremony is over, plans for the next one are often beginning.

Baby Ceremonies

Starting from birth, baby ceremonies of varying detail are performed every month. The ground-touching ceremony at three months, and the *otonan* at one and a half years, are probably the most elaborate a small child will experience. Suckling pig is the traditional food for these occasions. Small ceremonies called *oton* are performed every month for the baby until he or she loses the first tooth. For these occasions, rice, fried chicken, cakes and fruit are prepared. The baby is given a small amount of the blessed food to eat as part of the ceremony and the remainder is shared later with the family.

When the umbilical cord fell off each of our children, we collected the dried skin and wrapped it in white cloth. This breaks the final tangible bond to the four brothers that accompanied the baby through birth and the first days of his or her existence. They now depart and become an intangible spiritual link, like a guardian angel or mystical brother. Special offerings were made to mark this event and a ceremony was performed. This was also the time when I was allowed to return to the kitchen. My sister-in-law was called in to help organise proceedings. She placed some cotton wool on a stick and burnt it over the gas burner in our kitchen. The ashes that fell in a silky black mass were collected in a banana leaf and rubbed onto my forehead.

The offerings for the baby were blessed and we placed the umbilical cord in the *kumara* — a small ornate throne often painted in bright red and gold — until the baby's three-month ceremony, when it would be tucked inside his or her gold amulet to be worn that day. Some children wear this sacred talisman for years. The *kumara* usually sits beside the parents' bed where the baby sleeps. Sanghyang Panca Kumara is the son of Siwa, and legend has it that Kumara called on Siwa for help when fighting with his brother, Ganesha. Siwa saved Kumara from death, but in exchange for his protection ordered Kumara to be the guardian of all small children until the time they lose their first milk teeth.

The umbilical cord is said to have magical healing powers. I remember hearing the story of a Western man staying near us who was violently ill. There seemed to be no medicine that could cure him. For days he lay in his bed with a high fever and the doctors were baffled by his condition. Finally, the Balinese family he was staying with took the dried umbilical cord of their youngest child from where it was stored in the *kumara*. They mixed it with holy water, strained it and then gave the liquid to the ailing man. The next day he made a miraculous recovery and was back on his feet in no time.

* * *

Forty-two days marks the first important ceremony for babies, when any impurities that have lingered since birth will be cleansed. It also celebrates a child's introduction to the world around them, a time when babies really start to open their eyes and recognise shapes, sounds and smells. The ceremony acknowledges the awakening of all the senses and from now on the baby's personality unfolds. At this time, the baby is also given a Balinese name — a tradition I unknowingly broke with every child. Seven names of flowers, including a name the parents like, are written on individual *lontar* palm leaves and each is attached to a homemade candle amidst a pile of offerings. The name that is the last to burn becomes the baby's name. In the early days, people must have added vegetables and kitchen utensils to the choices, as I know people whose names in Indonesian mean 'tomato', 'plate', 'table' and even 'kitchen'.

I remember celebrating this occasion with little Dewi. Motherhood was still new for me and I was particularly protective of our beautiful child. The priest began his chant in the temple pavilion while I sat below him on the step, surrounded by my sisters-in-law and cuddling Dewi, who was asleep. Forty-two days also marks the end of temple abstinence for the mother and I was now allowed to participate in ceremonies again. A pile of coconut-leaf offerings, cakes and fruit faced the priest, waiting to be blessed. While we listened to the prayers, I noticed a small chicken nearby. I suddenly became nervous about the proceedings and hoped the bird wouldn't be sacrificed in our presence.

The blessings began and we were showered with scented holy water. The priest placed some grains of rice on Dewi's forehead and his wife grabbed the chicken, holding its small body in her hand. She held it to Dewi's brow and encouraged it to peck the white seeds off her tiny face as a symbol of purification. I held Dewi anxiously as she slept blissfully in the comfort of my arms. A haze of sweat trickled down my neck as I waited for blood to appear, but she was left unscathed and continued to doze. After incense had been wafted towards us, we were blessed with more holy water and grains of rice. The ceremony was finished.

The chicken came home with us to commence its new role as a guardian to protect the baby from negative energies and evils. I watched it roam happily on our land. It quickly grew into a feathery bird, but then suddenly died. I hoped this wasn't a bad omen. I'd thought it would live for years in the compound, but nobody seemed worried so I decided not to take its death too seriously.

At three Balinese months the ground-touching ceremony is performed, the first time a baby will touch the ground. This is my favourite infant ceremony to protect the baby from danger and disease. I remember the last time we performed this ceremony, for Arjuna. As usual, the men arrived in the morning to start the preparations for the feast. By seven o'clock, the back courtyard of our house was full of the sound of the chopping of spices. The sweet smell of clove cigarettes, roasted coconut, galangal, ginger and lemongrass mingled with the aroma of thick black Bali coffee, jasmine tea and human sweat. My brother-in-law, Wayan, a marvellous cook, was chosen to make his speciality, a spicy pork stew, our cousin was in charge of the jackfruit curry and an uncle was appointed as the chief mixer of spices for the *lawar*. Sticky rice cakes layered with chocolate and coconut milk and freshly cooked fried golden bananas were served with the drinks. Loud chatter and laughter carried through the house and into the front yard. When you throw a dozen Balinese men together, for any occasion, the noise can be deafening. The young children sat with their fathers and shyly answered questions about whether they'd already had a wash, eaten breakfast or started school. These are essential questions for every Balinese child to master. In the meantime, the women organised the offerings outdoors in the central pavilion, while others chased away roosters, cats and dogs.

By ten o'clock it was time to enjoy the wonderful feast, made all the more exciting by the presence of so many friends and family. The men were pleased with their efforts and, one by one, went home after eating to wash away the smell of fresh meat and spices. Women from our *banjar*, wearing colourful sarongs and simple shirts, came in a constant procession bearing offerings of sugar, rice, coffee and bananas neatly balanced in a bowl on their heads. Each bowl was topped with a brightly wrapped present for the baby and a beaded lid. My job was to help collect the gifts and converse with the guests. Coffee, tea and cakes kept pouring forth from the kitchen for all the visitors. After a polite chat, the gifts were emptied into the appropriate sacks and the bowl was refilled with satay, rice and *lawar*. The custom in Bali is to bring a gift and return home with an assortment of ceremonial food. It's that old routine where you give and receive at the same time.

The priest arrived after midday and my favourite ceremony began. We had also employed the services of Ubud's chief offering-maker, a plump middle-aged woman with a round cheery face, to help make the more elaborate offerings. She always wears bright *kebayas* that add a rosy warmth to her complexion and complement her jolly nature. Together with the priest's wife, she coordinated the ceremony, making sure that all was in the right place, including me.

The first part of the ceremony took place under the shade of a leafy green tree strewn with yellow trumpet-shaped alamanda. The priest stood facing us and began the gentle chant of purification. The smoke from the sandalwood incense held to his chest made a peaceful path through the garden. My sister-in-law and I stood in front of the priest, facing north-east towards the main family pavilion that lies in the middle of our compound and in the direction of Mount Gunung Agung. At our feet sat colourful offerings of young coconut leaves filled with flowers, a small golden coconut and burning rice husks set in a terracotta pot. These surrounded a large terracotta bowl which had been wrapped in white cloth and filled with fragrant flowers, a few pebbles and water.

A mortar and pestle is the focal point of this part of the ceremony. I stood on the south side of the stone mortar, holding a large soft-pink banana flower wrapped in a rich purple Indian silk sarong tied with a yellow satin sash. Gold jewellery that we had bought especially for the baby had been carefully tucked into the folds of the fabric. The jewellery included a gold amulet set with a tiny opaque sapphire, a small gold cap the size of a twenty-cent coin to place on the fontanelle, a tiny ring carved with the letter 'A' and tiny gold bracelets and anklets with little baubles. The decorated flower looked like a strange doll with a mouse-like head. My sister-in-law stood to my left, holding Arjuna. The lull of the priest's chanting had rocked him to sleep for a brief moment.

As I listened to the priest's prayers, I heard him utter the names of Siwa, Brahma, Wisnu, Sang Hyang Widi, God and Surya, the sun. All the forces were called on to protect our baby. After a further few minutes of chanting, the priest announced that Arjuna was now a member of the human world and no longer a divine angel. The women assisting the priest instructed me to swap the flower, the symbol of life, for my healthy rosy-cheeked baby. 'Welcome,' I whispered in baby Arjuna's ear as I took him in my arms, and for a minute was a little sad that this would be my last celebration of this ceremony of life and love with my own children.

We dressed Arjuna in the silk sarong and bright sash that had adorned the banana flower and the priest placed some rice on his forehead. Two small chirping chickens and a beautiful sandy-coloured duck with a single Chinese coin tied around its neck were held at Arjuna's head to peck away the pearly grains. As I watched them deftly picking up tiny grains of rice, I was again anxious they might break the skin, but not a speck of blood appeared. The pecking of the rice represents the cleansing of the head after childbirth, a symbolic gesture of removing any impurities or negative spirits that may harm the child.

With Arjuna in my arms, I walked around the offerings on the ground three times, just as I had in our wedding ceremony. The circle represents the journey of birth, life and death, the eternal trinity. Arjuna's jewellery was then dropped into the pot of blessed water. I watched the glittery gold sink to the bottom and settle between the pebbles. My job was to fish it out again with my baby, so holding Arjuna's tiny hand in mine, we plunged into the cool water and collected all the treasures. The water and jewellery are symbols of life and prosperity. Our duty as parents is to provide as best we can for our children so that their journey through life will be blessed with material success and golden opportunities. Water is the symbol of knowledge and learning, the sacred element that heals and purifies. In its contact with the blessed water, the jewellery gains a cosmic energy so it may serve as a sacred talisman for the small child. Ketut owns many rings that he wears for mystical protection, and always chooses his rings to match the occasion rather than his outfit. When he goes to the Pura Dalem, the temple associated with Siwa, death and destruction, he wears a large decorative gold and moonstone ring surrounded by a dozen small rubies. It's his favourite, and most expensive, security guard.

Arjuna was adorned with his new jewellery and the rest of the ceremony was held in the *bale*, which had been decorated with elaborate offerings of fruit and cakes. The wooden pillars supporting the roof were wrapped with purple and gold *perada* fabric painted with gold Balinese patterns and the ceiling was hung with white cloth. The overall feeling was one of lightness and abundance. From where I sat, I could see a small suckling pig, ordered especially for the occasion, perched on a large tray and wrapped up like a birthday present in young coconut leaves. The crisp skin was golden brown and glistening and the distinctive aroma of sweet roast pork infused the air. A mother is not allowed to eat certain foods, such as suckling pig, after the birth of her baby and this celebration marks the end of these taboos. When the ceremony was over, we all feasted on the blessed food.

Tooth-filing Ceremony

One of the most important rites of passage in Bali is the tooth-filing ceremony. Known as *potong gigi* or *mesangih*, it is one of the five rituals of mankind, or *manusia yadnya*, that every Balinese must complete before he or she dies, and symbolises maturity and becoming civilised. It is an elaborate ceremony that costs families thousands of dollars. Consequently, as many young folk as possible are gathered together for this grand occasion, as it doesn't amount to much more to file a dozen people as it does a few. The Balinese say that the essence of the six vices, or *sad ripu*, of *matsaria* (jealousy), *kroda* (anger), *kama* (desire), *lobha* (greed), *moha* (confusion) and *mada* (drunkenness) enter through the top six teeth. It is believed that the filing of these teeth is a way of balancing these evils within us that can create havoc and lead us to despair — and inner harmony guarantees inner peace. In the early days, tooth-filing was a more serious smoothing of these teeth; nowadays, it is not so severe and depends on the wishes of the individual. The idea is to soften the appearance of the canines, so as not to look like a demon, and thus be admitted to heaven, meet your ancestors and maybe even God.

I knew from the time of my marriage that I would one day have to undergo this ceremony; I've also known that my children could not jump the queue and take part in this ceremony before me. The filing of the teeth gives you the necessary papers to enter heaven. Without it, you're left in the immigration office for ever. If it's anything like the immigration office in Denpasar, I shudder to think of a lifetime sitting on hard crimson vinyl sofas watching stern officials in ever-so-tight uniforms stamping papers all day. And I certainly wouldn't want to be responsible for my children not being allowed to pass through the gates of heaven because their mother was too busy to get her teeth filed.

So the priest selected an auspicious day and it was decided that I would join sixteen younger nieces and nephews in the tooth-filing ceremony. You are usually not allowed to have this sort of ceremony in your husband's temple, but an exemption had been made for me, the non-Balinese member. Two months of preparation followed.

In my spare time, in the afternoons, evenings or on the weekend, I went to Ketut's uncle's home, where the ceremony would be held. This is also the place of my husband's larger family temple and where his father was born. For certain ceremonies we pray here and also at our clan temple in Denpasar. The temple had been renovated especially for the occasion and the shrines glowed with a new layer of gold leaf. The preparations included making a zillion offerings and all sorts of structures necessary for the big celebration. I always love these occasions when everyone gets together and has loads of fun. It's family bonding at its best, with joking, laughing and good spirits all around. This time I decided to hang out in the kitchen to help prepare the daily meals necessary to feed all the workers, and I learnt even more about the local food. For the first time, I saw the roasting of spices in preparation for a spice paste (I had been told that this was never done) and many different ways of preparing vegetables. I also found out that one of my sisters-in-law knows how to make some of my favourite Javanese dishes. So the weeks of preparation became a learning ground for all of my passions.

The week before the tooth-filing ceremony I had my first *oton* — one of those ceremonies that commences at six weeks of age and a necessary preliminary for the tooth-filing. In this instance, because of my age, it was a summary of several ceremonies covering the period from six weeks to one and a half years. I was so excited to finally have one of these ceremonies. As I sat behind the priest, listening to his soft chanting, all sorts of strange emotions drifted through me. I thought of the many times I had shared this ceremony with my own children, and then looked up to see their curious faces affectionately watching me. As you can imagine, the proceedings were also rather hilarious as my sister-in-law had to wrap her arms around me and pretend I was a baby. I was exchanged for a banana flower and had to fish my new jewellery out of the stone pond, just as I'd helped my children to do. I was also given a Balinese name. The priest inscribed the names of two flowers onto two small *lontar* leaves and then attached each one to its own long white candle set amidst a pile of offerings of coconut leaves and flower petals. It reminded me of a birthday cake, or the candles we used to light for Christmas at home in Melbourne. The offering was placed in the kitchen and the candles were lit. They slowly burnt in a dreamy haze, the ashes falling on the petals like fine grey gold dust. The first to burn to the base revealed my new name, Nyoman Jepun, which means frangipani.

The following week, I had to pack my overnight bag and go to the house where the tooth-filing was being held. In nervous anticipation, all seventeen of us gathered under the stars around a pile of offerings on the ground and received blessings from the priest. He brushed our hands with leaves and eggs and tied cotton around our wrists. We had to dip our fingers three times into a coconut bowl, walk in a circle, and were sprinkled with holy water. During the tooth-filing ceremony, those taking part are temporarily killed, which releases the same dangerous frenetic energy as a cremation, so great care is taken to appease all and to keep those evil spirits at bay.

Just before midnight, we gathered to have our hair cut. For women, the tradition is to cut the pieces of hair around the face to chin length, so one of the experts was called in and the cutting commenced. First she smeared our hair with a thick black candlenut paste that resembled tar. It was combed through until stiff and thick — it reminded me of a Geisha's hairstyle. Our hair was then shaped out in a wide curve around our ears and the blackened pieces were left to dry into a dull black mass. Once dry, it was cut to jaw length. I'm probably the world's most unadventurous person when it comes to haircuts, so this was a major event for me. We had to leave the black glue in overnight; I was anxious to sleep, so I tossed the cut pieces to one side and slept for four hours. Some of the young ones stayed up all night, and Ketut and the fathers sat in a nearby pavilion playing cards.

We were woken at four in the morning to start getting ready. The first step was the shaving. This was more terrifying for me than the tooth-filing itself. I watched out of the corner of my eye as my young sister-in-law slowly edged a shiny silver razor blade across my face to shave off all my facial hair. I shivered, imagining lots of tiny stinging cuts appearing on my cheeks and forehead. But she was very careful and I was left with a shiny, smooth face that rendered me pure. It is said that the head is contaminated through childbirth, so every measure is taken to correct this.

A smart young Balinese make-up man arrived an hour later. He applied a layer of thick matt foundation over my smooth skin to hide all flaws then added copper lids, dark eyebrows, eyeliner, thick mascara and red lips. The rest of my hair was tied back and an artificial hairpiece strung with fragrant flowers was attached to create a long ponytail. Then came the crown: hundreds of gold flowers were pushed into my hair to form an almighty headdress. You can imagine the pressure on my skull, weighed down by hundreds of metal skewers. The things we have to do to be beautiful, I thought. The face and hair ornamentation completed, I was then wrapped into a gold sarong and bustier with a long yellow and gold sash tightly binding my torso. This was a similar outfit to one a dancer would wear. Finally the jewellery was secured in place and I was ready, only three hours later.

We were all instructed to wait in my niece's small bedroom until the ceremony began. The small airless room became more stifling as we sat squashed together. I managed to find a spot on the corner of the bed near a small fan. There was a lot of nervous laughter and chatter at this point. In fact, some of my nieces were petrified. I wasn't so worried as I figured that a tooth-filing couldn't be any worse than a tooth-filling.

The actual ceremony was to be held in the main pavilion in the family courtyard, which had been beautifully decorated with colourful textiles stamped with gold and offerings. A new mattress had been bought for the occasion and covered in a bright cotton-polyester sheet with matching pillowcases. This was where we were to lie for the tooth-filing.

The ceremony began at around 10.00 a.m. Being the eldest, I was the first in line, with two others joining me. The carved wooden doors were pushed open and we appeared to a chorus of 'oohs' and 'ahhs'. We made our way down the steps to the open ground, where two family members emerged from the crowd and tucked their arms into mine to support me. As I moved across the courtyard, through a sea of familiar faces, I felt like a delicate princess, shimmering in gold: the immense crown of gold flowers forming a halo around my head, the ornate gold earrings studded with Indian rubies on my ears, the matching pendant around my neck and the bangles that sparkled on my wrists. With the aid of my consorts I moved trance-like towards the family pavilion as the soft tinkle of the *gender wayang*, the music that normally accompanies a shadow-puppet performance, drifted through the air.

I was guided to the pavilion and helped onto the mattress with the two others. Together, we kneeled in front of the priest, ready for blessings and holy water. I was thrilled to see that my favourite high priest from Padang Tegal was performing the ceremony. Dignified and charismatic, he has a lovely softness in his eyes and an air of wisdom acquired from a lifetime of dedication to God and the greater powers. He began chanting in a voice at first transparent, yet as deep as the ocean; gentle, yet as powerful as a bolt of lightning. I was calmed by his presence and almost hypnotised by the *mudras* his hands performed. The tight clothing, the pressure of the immense headdress and the fragrant incense, bells and chanting combined to create an interesting effect on my state of mind. I felt almost intoxicated and was enveloped in an intense stillness, while my thoughts drifted in a misty cloud around my heavy body. I was instructed to open my mouth and the priest gently tapped on my top six teeth with a large ring and inscribed them lightly with the Hindu symbols for male and female using a tool dipped in honey. Delicious, I thought. And so, the greedy evils within me were awoken, then symbolically killed with a mantra and inscription. I was also killed by the sacred words and waited in limbo for purification and restored life. That was the first filing.

We returned to the tiny stuffy bedroom where we had to wait while the others went through the same procedure. 'What was it like?' they asked nervously. For the second stage, we were guided out again and this time instructed to lie down on the mattress, on top of a small line drawing of Semara Ratih, the god of beauty. In Bali, beauty and aesthetics always prevail, and I was pleased to see it was just as important to be beautified through this process as spiritually blessed. We rested our heavy heads on the new pillows and were given a small yellow and gold cloth to cover our chest. My parents were called to stand beside me on the high pavilion and held my arms to protect me from evil spirits. The real filing began.

With my mouth prised open with moist sugar cane, I saw the file appear before my eyes. It was small, the kind you would buy from the local hardware store. The priest rolled it across my top six teeth five times or more in an attempt to make them even. I didn't feel a thing; the noise was worse than the actual process and I saw people near me wincing at the grating sound. I'm so glad my teeth are straight, I thought. With the expertise of a stone-carver, the priest then rubbed a flat stone along my teeth to smooth them out.

I sat up and was given a small mirror to view the results. I gazed at my mouth and focused on the top six teeth: there was very little difference. A golden *jamu*, or tonic, of pure turmeric juice mixed with lime and honey was handed to each of us. I took a small mouthful, swished it around my mouth and spat it into a golden coconut. I was allowed to drink the remainder and concluded it was one of the most delicious tonics I have ever tasted. The priest completed the ceremony with a mantra that brought life back to my teeth and I was then instructed to bite into betel leaves and finished by having tobacco brushed across my teeth. I hadn't realised this whole experience was going to be such a wonderful taste sensation. I had tasted the six flavours, one after another, and it had created a warm awakening throughout my body. My mother and father helped me step onto an offering of flowers and coconut leaves before touching the ground. The filing was over, although I still had to return to the small hot bedroom to wait for the others.

After the ceremony was finished, we changed part of our clothing and sat near the pavilion, on display. My children looked at me shyly. Arjuna was intrigued and stared at me constantly, hoping I wouldn't notice. My daughters were ecstatic at the layers of heavy make-up I was wearing and thought I looked beautiful, a Western goddess in Balinese clothing. Dewi thought I should wear it all the time! Visitors arrived with gifts of rice, coffee, bananas and small presents. I sat between my nieces and heard the word 'tourist' mentioned constantly. I had hoped they wouldn't notice.

By the afternoon, we were allowed to mingle with the guests. Another ceremony with all the children followed and then we could relax. By nine o'clock, all was quiet. I pulled out the hundreds of gold flowers that were entwined into my hair and unbound, untied and unzipped the layers of tight clothing. My body heaved a sigh of relief. A *joged* performance had been arranged for that evening in the pavilion across the road and together with my children, I watched one of the finest dance performances I have ever seen. After a long day, I returned home with my overnight bag and placed a handful of *cempaka* flowers beside my bed. I filled the bath with warm water and fragrant oils and washed away the hours of perspiration and make-up. The black tar remained until the next day. I sank into bed and was already dreaming by the time my head hit the pillow.

The next day, Dewi proudly informed me that because my teeth are filed, I will never experience anger, greed or jealousy again. She proclaimed that I am now a truly balanced person, possessing harmonious spiritual virtues to last a lifetime.

'That's all very well in theory, Dewi,' I said, 'but you can't tell me that a girl who's had her teeth filed isn't jealous of the beautiful girl that steals her boyfriend.'

Dewi was deeply upset by my cynical response and decided I could never be Balinese. 'It's not like that. You never believe anything I say,' she uttered in frustration and walked off in a huff. I decided I'd better keep certain thoughts to myself and have tried to be as balanced and positive as possible ever since.

Nyepi, the Balinese New Year

Nyepi, Balinese New Year, is one of my favourite events and occurs at the end of the ninth month on the Balinese calendar. *Nyepi* is the celebration of Surya, the sun, who gives life to all beings, and Chandra, the moon, who influences the oceans and the human spirit. At the time of *Nyepi*, generally in March, the sun begins turning to the north, the direction regarded as the positive path towards purity. This is the dawning of springtime in Bali.

A few days before *Nyepi*, a massive ceremony is held at the crossroads of every town, during which all sorts of animals are sacrificed. This is followed by a procession of the village members to the sea. We pray together on the warm, black sand of Sukawati beach in the late afternoon, the ferocious ocean lapping at our toes as the tide charges in. The offerings are left on the sand to be consumed by the sea. The following day sees the procession of ogres, and more special offerings that are made for the home.

About a month before the big day, the young boys start building huge monsters of all shapes, sizes and colours to be paraded through town on New Year's Eve. The skill and innovation that goes into these constructions is amazing. Every year we drive around the neighbouring villages before the big day to admire all the different creations and we've seen some spectacular monsters. I recently saw a huge red one, about four metres high, wrapped around with a massive serpent and balancing his whole ferocious body on one hand. Sometimes, famous local leaders are recreated as ogres, as well as television characters. (This year, a massive model of Amrozi, one of the accused Bali bombers, holding two bombs in the hands of a huge demon, led the Kuta parade.)

Last year, Krishna and his pint-sized mates spent many days working together on a small purple dragon with huge fangs and claws. It stood over a metre high and was attached to a bamboo frame for transportation. Of course, a few of the older boys assisted in the project too. The basic frame was made out of thin strips of bamboo artfully woven to create the skeleton of a human body and a layer of thin foam was then stretched and nailed over it. The final touch of paint brought the dragon to life.

The boys in our street, Jalan Bisma, made a terrifying demon with a huge snake wrapped around him. It must have been more than three metres high. The snake was made from layers of thinly cut foam to create the perfect snakeskin, then painted in shades of green and brown. The monster was painted red, black and white. Music blasted from its mouth (there was a transistor radio connected inside) and its eyes flashed. At night, they covered its face so it couldn't roam the streets and spoil children's dreams. My two boys watched its progress every day and were in constant awe of its creators.

These demons are called *ogoh-ogoh*, which sounds a little like 'ogre'. The tradition of building these ogres started only about fifteen years ago and provided the Balinese with yet another creative opportunity to rid the island of *kala*, or evil spirits, in order to begin the New Year in peace and harmony. The act of parading through the streets and spinning around at the crossroads of each village chases the *kala* away, and there's nothing better than a demon to do the job. Of course, it doesn't take much to fuel Balinese artistry, especially when it has a religious purpose, so they embraced this new tradition with whole-hearted vitality.

This annual parade has a carnival-type atmosphere as the frenzied din of the *gamelan*, crowds of people, loudspeakers and colourful demons take over the town. There is laughter and squeals of excitement as the young boys and men shake and bounce the ominous giants on their bamboo frames. This year Krishna helped his friends carry a frightening red monster with blue hair through town, and Arjuna wished he could join in. Krishna looked so handsome in his black T-shirt, black and white checked sarong and white headband. The demons can be frightening too. Somehow an eerie Lord of the Flies element creeps into things when fervent young boys are running the show. Small children often cry with fear, or hide behind their mother's sarong. I've seen these giants tumble over many times and the crowd runs in all directions as the huge demon's head lunges to the ground.

I love watching Krishna and Arjuna in the build-up to *Nyepi*; it holds the same excitement as Christmas, but without the presents. They spend hours watching the development of the local ogres, and when not looking at these amazing creations, they spend their spare time drawing them on large sheets of paper. Piles of drawings of demons with claws, fangs, wings, horns and muscles are scattered across our terrace. You can hardly see the floor and the ogres grow more ferocious every day.

After the parade, the demons are returned to their respective *banjars* to wait for the next year, or sometimes they are burnt in a halo of flames at the cemetery. The excitement dies down and we all relax and wait for next year's show, but for months afterwards, my sons watch videos of these parades. A thousand viewings later, they still hold the same fascination.

The day after *Nyepi* is one of silence, when the whole island shuts down. Everything is closed, including the airport, and cars are forbidden on the roads. All people, including tourists, are confined to their hotels or family compounds. And within the walls of the compound, silence must prevail. Fires are not supposed to be lit, so all food is prepared the night before, and lights should not be switched on. In our household, we always make a huge pot of jackfruit curry, pork stew and bundles of steamed spiced pork packages the night before. Ideally, one should fast and meditate on this day, but, not surprisingly, in our household it's become a day of feasting and entertaining, while the children laze around watching television. The belief is that all the noise made the night before will scare away the *bhutas* and *kalas*. The day of silence following is designed to confuse the spirits into thinking that Bali is deserted and therefore not worth occupying. In this way, the year starts off peacefully with no disturbances.

Death and Cremation

I have come to the conclusion that there is definitely a season not only for weddings, tooth-filings, temple festivals and cremations in Bali, but also for dying. Death in Bali is much like death anywhere: the loss of a loved one is a sad occasion that can lead you to despair. But in Bali, with that despair comes an enormous sense of duty that governs all thoughts and actions. Sorrow and grief is balanced by an obligation to those they have lost, and when there's a ceremony to be performed in Bali, there's no time to think of anything else. The body must be cremated and offerings made so that the soul may be released and eventually returned to God. This is a time when my admiration for these gentle people is supreme.

When my aunty lost her son, like any mother she was in a deep depression for many, many months, but the single element that brought her light was the attention to the rituals of death that guaranteed her son a safe journey to heaven. It was as if there was some kind of communication between them that kept her going, and a belief that he had left this world for certain reasons. Now his spirit rests in her family temple, and she speaks to him every day through the offerings she places in the seat of the shrine dedicated to deified ancestors.

Death of my Father-in-law

My father-in-law — one of Bali's veterans who fought in the hills for independence and a man who had, until recently, bicycled all over town — passed away after he had been ill for a couple of months. Once the word spread through town, women began to appear in a constant stream at the family house, wearing sarongs and black *kebayas* and bearing on their heads the traditional gift of sugar, coffee and rice. The local men wore sarongs, *udangs* and casual shirts. They sat cross-legged together and revived their memories of the man they had all loved. Many people had a peek at his body where he was resting in peace in the eastern pavilion, behind traditional gold-patterned curtains, to pay their last respects.

By the afternoon, the house was a hive of activity as the family went into action to prepare the necessary offerings for this most important rite of passage. Sweet tea, coffee and cakes poured forth from the kitchen and were served to all the guests. The priest arrived and the gentle sound of chanting and the tinkle of holy bells commenced. The body was moved from the *bale* to a bamboo stretcher and placed on a bed of banana leaves in the middle of the courtyard. A piece of white cloth was stretched above as shelter from the sun. The members of the family crowded around this small resting place and the cleansing of the body began. I watched Krishna, who was eight at the time, share in the duties of pouring holy water over his grandfather and, together with his father, wrapping him in white cloth. I was so proud of him. I watched his brave, young face as he threw flowers over his grandfather's withered old frame and saw how emotion mingled with an overwhelming sense of duty and respect as he stood beside the quiet strength of his father.

I always marvel at the reverence and care the Balinese spend on their loved ones, not only in life but also in death. Someone once told me that a measure of a culture is in the way they treat their children and their old, and how they educate their people. The Balinese revere all of these and my children are learning this from an early age. Ketut says that people in the West spend their time on things that don't matter, but fail to take care of the issues in life that are so important.

Once washed and wrapped, my father-in-law's body was carried outside and placed in a small bamboo house-like structure, decorated with Balinese motifs made from bright red paper. Banana-leaf streamers hung like curtains from the roof. The men in our *banjar* had quickly put together this final resting place before burial.

The procession to the nearby cemetery began. Years ago, I was told that you mustn't cry when someone dies as tears interrupt the path to heaven. So we all laughed and chatted as happily as we could. At the cemetery, several men had already dug a large hole and his body was gently lowered into the grave. We peered in and watched as the men lay temple silks on top of the white cloth. The priest commenced his prayers and instructed the men to open the cloth on my father-in-law's small wrinkled face. He sprinkled him with holy water and flowers while chanting and holding incense. The cloth was wrapped over his face again, for the last time. More flowers were tossed on top and we were instructed to throw a handful of dirt three times on top of the wrapped corpse. The grave was filled over and we prayed together, before slowly going back to the house for a three-night vigil.

The body still lies in the cemetery and will stay there until an auspicious day is chosen for a cremation. This is the way old Grandfather wanted it to be. We have visited the cemetery many times since then. Each time we take an offering of all the things he liked to eat, such as rice with vegetables and chicken (the only meat he would eat), a freshly baked cinnamon roll, a small glass of papaya juice and a tiny cup of coffee. We place the offering on the grave and say, 'Wake up, Grandpa, it's time to eat. We're all here to see you, even your grandchildren. Come and eat with your other friends in the cemetery' — gesturing to the others who have passed away — 'Come and eat to make your grandchildren strong.' It's a fine feast that I know he enjoys.

Every time we drive past a cemetery, the children insist that I toot the horn. Dewi says it's to ask the spirits for permission to drive on their road and to prevent them following us home.

Ubud's Mass Cremation

A cremation can be a very costly ceremony. Your obligation in life is to cremate your loved ones with all the fanfare they deserve, so no expense is spared for this final send-off. Families sometimes have to sell precious rice fields to pay for these grand events, as there is a belief that an unhappy departed soul can wreak havoc. If Grandma was troublesome in this world, it is possible she might be just as troublesome in the next. Consequently, mass cremations have become commonplace as families can save millions of rupiah by sharing the costs.

In Ubud a couple of years ago, the departed souls of seventy-five people were cremated in a mass ceremony. The lengthy preparations for the cremation started about six weeks before the scheduled day. From morning until night, Ubud's married folk were required to attend the local *banjar* to help make the ornate bull sarcophagi, a multitude of offerings and other decorative paraphernalia for the big day. I tried to help as often as I could by going to the North Ubud *banjar*, of which I am a member. I must say, sitting on a cement floor for seven hours or more with only a bamboo mat between you and a hard cold surface is not very easy; nevertheless, despite the aches and pains, the Balinese women still laugh and joke. My job was to make banana- or coconut-leaf containers and other simple fare. One day we filled hundreds of small banana-leaf cones with a sprig of holy basil, a tiny fragment of coconut flower, a single pennywort leaf, some dried betel leaf and a Chinese coin. I found myself wondering what would happen if we left one out. Was God really keeping track of all these details?

For me, probably the most exciting part about the *banjar* activities was the meal and snacks that were always provided. A wonderful banquet appeared every day, featuring all sorts of delicious spicy curries, salads and sambals. I suggested the mothers could make a little money on the side by selling the food to the inquisitive passers-by — they thought this was hilarious. But probably the best meal I had over those weeks was the one served at the house of Ubud's special offering-maker. One Sunday morning we gathered on the shady verandahs of her compound to make tall bamboo cylinders and other bits and pieces. Glorious orchids were bursting out between the branches of flowering frangipani trees, beside pots of pink and white lilies. We were full of admiration. It seems the modern Balinese wife must be a master of many things, including the nurturing of these delicate orchids, somewhat like a Western woman's passion for growing roses. By midday we were given the polite gesture to eat and I piled my plate with all my favourite food: cucumber-coconut salad, Asian spinach with loads of chilli and tomato, chicken curry, gentle pork stew, crunchy fish with coconut and sambal — what a feast! Of course, I had to suffer the consequences. Eating a big meal when you're strapped into a corset and sarong is not advisable.

The Balinese grandmas always steal the show on ceremonial occasions, as they are the undisputed experts in all things holy. I watched them making iridescent rice flour offerings in all shapes and sizes and marvelled at their dexterity. I also wondered why they are so insistent on dyeing their hair black when half their teeth are missing! One of the Ubud grandmas always likes to tease me whenever she sees me. She's one of these small robust women with a deep voice and a dry sense of humour. Married to a local priest, she's always present for ceremonies and assists with all sacred duties. When I'm at the temple and she has to bless me with holy water, she'll make some sort of comment: 'Here's that tourist again. Can she speak Balinese yet? She ought to by now, she's been here long enough.' She spotted me at the *banjar* as I sat devouring my lunch and I waited for her response. 'I didn't know we had a "hello" in our *banjar*!' she roared with her powerful voice. 'Can she eat this sort of spicy food? Good Lord, she's even eating with her hand!' Everyone laughed and I smiled shyly between mouthfuls of rice.

After days of praying and preparing at the cemetery, the cremation finally took place. Many of the bodies had been exhumed three days beforehand, and others had been brought there from home. My brother-in-law — who had died several months earlier — had already been cremated. After his cremation, the remains of his body were carefully wrapped in white cloth, strewn with brilliant bougainvillea, marigolds and frangipani flowers, then carried on a small bamboo stretcher to the sacred Tjampuhan River. As his remains were thrown down the river, the family cheered and waved goodbye to their brother and friend. What a lovely way to leave this world, I remember thinking.

A large animal-shaped sarcophagus made of wood is used to carry the body to the cemetery. The animal must have four feet, symbolising the four brothers, *kanda empat*, and the bull is the preferred animal as it is the vehicle of Siwa, the aspect of God that symbolises death, destruction and the recycling of the spirit. The beautifully decorated red and black bulls and lions had been lined up for a week near the crossroads waiting for takeoff, and now the procession began. Its progress down Ubud's main road was spectacular as the festive red, black and white animal coffins travelled to the cemetery amidst the noise of the *gamelan*. The young boys carried the bull of our nephew, with his soccer number plastered over the tail, down the road, singing 'Joni, Joni, Joni!' and jostling the bull around as if he was galloping to heaven. Two months of hard work then went up in triumphant flames that licked the leaves of the overhanging trees. After the cremation we prayed together, and gathered later that night to throw the ashes into the sea at Sanur. We returned home at four in the morning.

The next part of the ceremony began a week or two later. We spent several hours praying together late into the night. A tooth-filing was held the next day for about fifty young people; dressed in gold and white, they sparkled in the hot sun. The following day, at five in the morning, we set off to Goa Lawah and Besakih to mark the final release of the departed souls. By the time we climbed the final steps to the inner courtyard at Besakih, it was five in the afternoon. I was so proud of Dewi and Krishna, who, throughout this long and exhausting day, never once complained. We said the final prayers together as the sun was starting its descent, and I watched the clouds drift across the sky around the souls of the seventy-five people on their way to heaven. Their journey was over and our job was done. Back in Ubud, the

TOP: Jogjakarta Airport, 1974: Dad, Mum and my brother Tim, the surfer, at the back; my sister Susan and me in front, with our Javanese tour guide. My mother, father and sister continued to visit Bali after this first holiday, but my brother only returned for the first time sixteen years later, when Ketut and I got married.

BOTTOM: Twenty-six years later: my father, Ketut, Dewi, Laksmi and Krishna on my parents' farm in Bonnie Doon.

TOP: Ketut and I had three weddings. The first one was in Melbourne on a cold winter's day.
BOTTOM: (l-r) Nyoman Suwitera; Ketut; Ketut's cousin, Made Sugiartha; and Ketut's brother, Koming.

Our Balinese weddings were filled with music, dancing and feasting, and Ketut and I were dressed up like a prince and princess. The people of our *banjar* made elaborate offerings for the ceremony.

TOP: Ketut building Casa Luna in the main road of Ubud, 1991.
BOTTOM: The Honeymoon Guesthouse: a paradise amidst the rice fields.

TOP: The happy couple! Ketut and me in the grounds of our home, the Honeymoon Guesthouse, 2001.
LEFT: Laksmi, Dewi and me at a recent ceremony at our house, 2003.
BOTTOM: Krishna, Arjuna, Dewi and Laksmi, 2003.

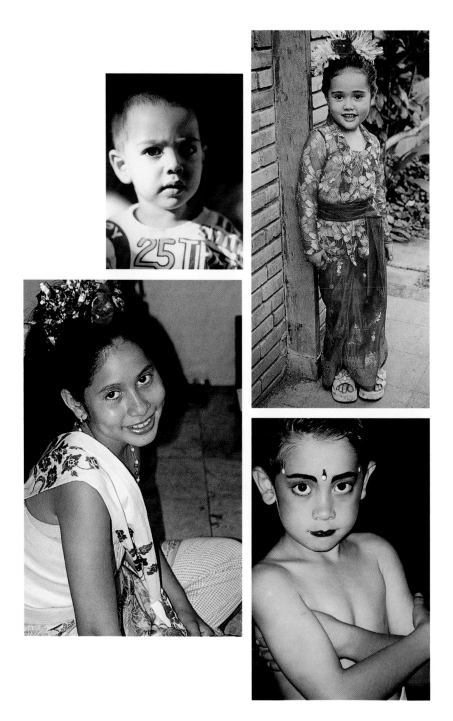

Our beautiful children: (clockwise from
top left) Arjuna, Laksmi, Krishna (made
up for a school performance), Dewi.

Temple festivals are determined by the Balinese calendar. They can be elaborate occasions lasting up to ten days, or more simple events over one or two days.

TOP: Laksmi, touching the ground for the very first time. This ceremony is performed at the age of three months, to protect the baby from danger and disease.

MIDDLE: Arjuna's ground-touching ceremony. Gold jewellery is tucked into the folds of the silk sarong wrapped around the banana flower.

BOTTOM: Laksmi's forty-two-day ceremony; the priest is pouring grains of rice into a piece of bamboo. Later, a duck and a small chicken pecked grains of rice from Laksmi's forehead.

The tooth-filing ceremony is an important rite of passage in Bali; it symbolises maturity and becoming a civilised being. I joined sixteen nieces and nephews for this elaborate ceremony in our family temple. My parents and my children came along too.

TOP: Laksmi's fifth birthday party. We seem to have introduced the Western concept of birthday parties and birthday cake to Ubud. MIDDLE: Some friends from a nearby village performing a Balinese dance at the party. BOTTOM: Krishna (at the back) and his friends with the terrifying demon they made for the Balinese New Year's Eve parade.

TOP RIGHT: The Balinese kitchen is a simple room with a stove and a chopping bench.

TOP LEFT: Cooking satay at a nearby beach. There are many *warungs* set up around the coast, selling Balinese fish satay and other seafood dishes.

MIDDLE: Ketut's cousin preparing a chicken dish for all the helpers at the tooth-filing ceremony.

BOTTOM: Shredded coconut is a key ingredient in ceremonial food.

TOP: The waitresses at Indus making a marigold flower decoration called *canang rebong*. These are made for special occasions.

BOTTOM: Any visitor to Bali will have seen the offerings placed on the street outside shops and houses, comprising small coconut leaf trays containing petals, leaves and rice.

TOP: In Bali we buy our food fresh every day and
bargaining at the market is a pleasurable ritual.
BOTTOM LEFT: In 1992 I opened the Casa Luna Cooking
School, which is now known all around the world.
BOTTOM RIGHT: *Kangkung pelecing*, a favourite dish in my
cooking classes.

TOP: The *dalumen* lady pours a glass of her slimy green herbal tonic and I try to persuade my market tour group of its health-giving properties.

BOTTOM: There is an abundance of vegetables, herbs and spices available at the Ubud market.

TOP: The long leaves are young coconut leaves, which are essential for making offerings.
BOTTOM LEFT: Chicken curry, served at Casa Luna.
BOTTOM RIGHT: *Pepes ikan* — fish in banana leaves — with coconut bean salad and yellow rice, served at Indus.

Two dishes that are always a favourite with visitors to Casa Luna and Indus: (top) Balinese chicken satay; (bottom) black rice pudding.

effigies of the dead were placed in the respective family temples, where they remained until next *Galungan*.

I will never see death in the same light again. The Balinese sense of duty and dedication to their loved ones is to be greatly admired. When it comes to the celebration of life and death, nothing else matters. All business comes to a halt. Isn't that the way it should be?

Ayam Gerang Asem
Sour chicken stew

Ketut always said his dad made the best *ayam gerang asem*. Somehow, he always created the perfect balance of gingers and aromatics, that piquant combination of flavours evolved from years of culinary wisdom. He preferred to use an athletic free-range Balinese chicken and claimed this is how chicken is supposed to taste. An invaluable part of the preparation of anything he made was the compulsory joking and flirting that went with it. In the kitchen, a team of young girls always surrounded him and the laughter amongst them could be heard for miles. I used to hear the Balinese women say my father-in-law was so youthful and sprightly and you could taste this in his food.

Sometimes a friend or neighbour gives us a gift of a defeated rooster from the local cock fight. *Ayam gerang asem* is the traditional way to cook it; the long slow simmering tenderises the meat and heightens the flavour of the fresh spices.

500 g (1 lb) chicken
3 tablespoons oil for frying spices
1 lemongrass stalk, bruised and tied into a knot
3 salam leaves
3 kaffir lime leaves
5 cups water
sea salt, to taste

SPICES
1/4 teaspoon white pepper
1/2 teaspoon black pepper
3 candlenuts

¹/₂ teaspoon shrimp paste

1 teaspoon coriander seeds

2 teaspoons tamarind pulp

1 lemongrass stalk

¹/₂ teaspoon sesame seeds

¹/₄ teaspoon nutmeg

2 small red chillies

3 large red chillies

2—3 red shallots, chopped finely

2 teaspoons palm sugar

5 cloves garlic, chopped finely

1 tomato

2 teaspoons chopped turmeric

2 teaspoons chopped ginger

1 tablespoon chopped galangal

1 teaspoon chopped kencur

Chop the chicken into curry-size chunks approximately 5 cm x 4 cm (2 in x 1¹/₂ in).

Place the spices in the bowl of a food processor and blend to a coarse paste. Add oil if the mixture is too dry. In this case, the spices do not need to be smooth. Otherwise, chop with a cleaver.

In a large saucepan, heat the oil over a medium flame. Fry the spices until fragrant, for about 30 seconds. Add the lemongrass, salam leaves and lime leaves.

Add the chicken and toss around in the oil until sealed.

Cover the chicken with the water and bring to the boil.

Simmer for at least an hour, until the liquid has reduced and the meat is tender.

Check seasonings and serve with steamed rice.

Serves 4.

Lawar Kacang Panjang

Snake bean lawar

Lawar is a ceremonial food and part of a sacred task known as *mebat*, which signals the start of the celebrations. *Mebat* refers to the chopping of all the ingredients to be used in the ceremony, carried out by the local men. They say the name comes from the blunt chopping sound the knife makes on the thick wooden board. Our recipe is a simplified version!

500 g (1 lb) snake beans
2 kaffir lime leaves, shredded
3 tablespoons fried shallots
1¹/₂ cups coconut, grilled and grated (see instructions, page 121)
sea salt, to taste

MADAM (CHICKEN AND COCONUT MILK DRESSING)
2 tablespoons oil
3 tablespoons basa genep (see recipe, page 179)
2 kaffir lime leaves
2 salam leaves
1 stalk lemongrass, bruised and knotted
100 g (3¹/₂ oz) chicken mince
1 cup water
¹/₂ cup light coconut milk
sea salt, to taste

To make the *madam*, heat the oil in a small saucepan over a medium flame and fry the *basa genep* spices with the lime leaves, salam leaves and bruised lemongrass for 1 minute, or until fragrant. Add the chicken mince to the spices and fry for a further 3 minutes, stirring well or until the meat is nearly cooked.

Add the water and simmer until the chicken is cooked and half the liquid has evaporated.

Add the final layer of coconut milk, and sea salt to taste. Bring to the boil for 1 minute and then turn off. Check seasonings.

Trim the beans and then steam or boil until al dente. Drain and then chop finely.

In a large bowl, first mix the shredded lime leaves, fried shallots and *madam* thoroughly with the grilled, grated coconut. Add the cooked, chopped beans.

Add salt, extra fried shallots and shredded lime leaves if necessary. Serve with steamed rice.

Note: Madam can also be made with just water or just coconut milk.

Serves 6–8.

Urab Buncis

Bean and coconut salad

I first developed a passion for *urab buncis* at my late brother-in-law's restaurant. It was one of the accompaniments to *nasi campur*, so whenever I ordered it from the menu I'd race into the kitchen to watch the cooks making it. In those days, nothing was made in advance: the spices were freshly ground and fried, the coconut roasted and grated and the vegetables boiled. I could watch the whole process from start to finish and then eat the results minutes later at one of the bamboo tables out the front. Years later, I finally perfected the dish. The flavour of juicy tender beans with golden spices and *sambal goreng* marries perfectly with the sweet chewy shredded coconut. We now serve this at Casa Luna with *nasi campur* and it never fails to please.

There are a number of steps involved in creating this dish, but do persist because it is well worth the effort. Use any other green or legume, such as kidney beans, as a substitute for the beans. You can also use shredded packaged coconut in place of fresh roasted coconut. It tastes great with chicken satay or just about any Balinese dish.

1 cup coconut milk

1 lemongrass stalk, bruised and tied in a knot

2 salam leaves

2 kaffir lime leaves

300 g (10 oz) green beans

1¹/₂ cups coconut, grilled and shredded (see method below)

2 teaspoons sambal goreng (see recipe, page 200)

3 tablespoons fried shallots

2 kaffir lime leaves, extra, shredded

salt, to taste

SUNA-CEKOH

5 cloves garlic

4 candlenuts

3 teaspoons chopped kencur

1 tablespoon chopped turmeric

5 tablespoons oil

Prepare the sambal first by following the recipe on page 200.

Grind the spices for *suna-cekoh* to a paste. Heat the oil over a medium flame. Fry the *suna-cekoh* spices in hot oil making sure they don't stick to the base of the wok. Add a splash of water if necessary. Fry for at least a minute or until the earthy flavour of the turmeric has dissipated. Now add coconut milk, with the lemongrass, salam leaves and lime leaves and slowly stir until the milk thickens like a light custard. Set aside.

Boil the green beans in salted water for 3 minutes or until al dente. Set aside to cool a little and then chop finely in 5 mm (¼ in) widths. Roast the fresh coconut over a flame until charred. Clean the skin by scraping with a knife as you would burnt toast, then shred the coconut flesh. Otherwise, dry-roast packaged shredded coconut that is available in supermarkets and health food stores. Once all the separate ingredients and seasonings are prepared, you can assemble the salad. Mix the chopped beans with the *suna-cekoh*, roasted coconut, *sambal goreng*, fried shallots, shredded lime leaves and sea salt. Check for a balance of sweet, sour, salty and spicy.

Substitutes: Use galangal if *kencur* is not available. Use ground almonds in place of candlenuts.

Serves 6–8.

Sate Lembat Ayam

Chicken satay with grated coconut

This is a delicious and aromatic combination of ground meat, spices and coconut. It is always prepared for religious ceremonies, with the number of sticks varying for each occasion. The fragrant raw meat mixture is artfully spiralled around bamboo sticks and grilled over glowing coconut husks.

The task of making *sate lembat* is always performed by men. It is one of those phallic symbols that appears all over Bali and is said to also represent war weapons, coming back to that old theme of good versus evil.

wooden chopsticks, soaked or fresh lemongrass stalks
½–¾ cup grated coconut

4–5 tablespoons basa genep (see recipe, page 179)
2 teaspoons palm sugar
3 tablespoons fried shallots
¹/₂ teaspoon sea salt
5 kaffir lime leaves, shredded
300 g (10 oz) chicken mince

Soak the chopsticks in water to cover for at least 30 minutes.

In a large bowl, mix the grated coconut with the *basa genep*, palm sugar, fried shallots, sea salt, and lime leaves. In Bali, the mixing is done by hand so that the spices blend thoroughly.

Add the minced chicken and knead the flavours together to develop a doughy texture. The mixture should be fragrant, deep yellow in colour and slightly sticky.

Take a dessertspoon of this mixture and shape into a small pear, about the size of a golf ball. Place the meat on the end of the chopstick and spiral it firmly around until it reaches halfway, resembling a drumstick.

Grill or barbecue until golden brown, turning the sticks constantly to prevent burning.

Serve with steamed rice as a main course with *lawar kacang panjang* (see recipe, page 118). *Satay lembat* is also ideal served as part of a buffet or with cocktails.

Makes approximately 15.

Hari Saraswati

Hari Saraswati is one of my favourite days and luckily it occurs every six months in Bali. It is the day that celebrates Dewi Saraswati, the gracious goddess of literature and fine arts, who glides through the heavens on a swan, strumming a guitar. She is the essence of intelligence and accomplishment. The Balinese pay homage to her on this particular day by placing offerings on all books, including those in the universities, schools and at home. Even my magazines and cookbooks are blessed with a pile of fragrant flowers and incense. On this day, it is said that you should not read, as all literature is being sanctified, and Dewi always polices this holy law with great efficiency. She finds me no matter where I am, usually secretly browsing the pages of a magazine or reading a novel.

On *Hari Saraswati*, the children go to school in ceremonial costume and pray for clarity of mind, extra wisdom and, of course, better grades. Later that night, we pray in the temple under the stars.

The following day, known as *Banyu Pinaruh* — the first day of the new lunar year — is the most exciting part of the ceremony. A lengthy early morning wash, preferably in the cool waters of the nearest river, is followed by a marvellous feast. Dewi and her young aunty, Dek Lis, always drive to the sacred temple at Tampaksiring to bathe in the clear spring water that pours forth from small jets in the side of the hill. This ancient shrine overlooks an equally ancient thick jungle, which surely must have been the home of travelling sages and other mystic folk in the old days. After a lengthy wash, they pray in the temple then return home looking refreshed and almost chilled to the bone. Water is the symbol of purity and knowledge and great powers are received through its cleansing properties.

The feast that follows includes the famous Balinese smoked duck, yellow rice and a selection of ingredients, such as raw eggplant, mung beans, cucumber, salted fish and fried egg, to represent all the earth provides. The duck is chosen for this feast because it is the sister of the swan that carries the goddess and is an important member of the complex eco-system that lives in the rice fields, protecting the growing rice from pests and insects. And of course they also provide people with rich golden eggs.

Betutu Bebek
Smoked duck

Years ago I remember watching a man who lives near the Pantheon gallery prepare smoked duck. They were having a temple ceremony and this was part of the feast. I was so excited to have the opportunity to see one of the old folk cooking and he was equally excited by my enthusiasm. I watched his careful selection of spices and the delicate balancing of ingredients that would result in a perfect marriage of flavours. While he ground the spices, I listened to his animated speech alongside the rhythm of the huge volcanic stone mortar and pestle. The old man communicated to me with simple gestures that a great Balinese chef can taste with the tips of his fingers and the palm of his hand. As I watched, I saw that he never tasted what he was preparing; instead he carefully mixed the ingredients with his large broad hands and, from time to time, would smell the tips of his fingers intently, as if the elixir of life were upon them. We sat together for about an hour, laughing and enjoying each other's company. I'll never forget that day and sometimes I see the old man riding his bicycle along the main road near the gallery. He always smiles warmly as if we're old friends, and I guess we are.

The sweet perfume and flavour of freshly made coconut oil is the key to a delicious smoked duck. Cooked over a period of eight hours, the tender gently seasoned flesh melts in the mouth. It is delicious with yellow rice, but also with salad greens. The duck can be baked in the oven or even barbecued instead of smoked.

1 x 1 kg (2 lb) duck
1 tablespoon sea salt
2 teaspoons shrimp paste
2 teaspoons tamarind
$^{1}/_{3}$ cup coconut oil
3 teaspoons kecap manis
5 salam leaves
coconut tree bark or oven bag, string
2 staghorn sprigs, to speed up the cooking process (see Note)
$2^{1}/_{2}$ cups water

SPICE PASTE
8 red shallots, peeled
12 garlic cloves, peeled
4 large red chillies, trimmed and de-seeded
5 medium chillies
5 bird's-eye chillies
6 candlenuts
2 tablespoons chopped ginger
$1^{1}/_{2}$ tablespoons chopped turmeric

2 tablespoons chopped galangal
2 tablespoons chopped kencur
1 base wangen (see recipe, page 180)
3 teaspoons tamarind pulp, soaked in water
1 tablespoon palm sugar

Place the duck in a large bowl. Rub with half the salt, shrimp paste, tamarind and 2 tablespoons of the oil to break the bones and soften the meat, for approximately 3 minutes. Set aside.

Place the spices in the bowl of a food processor and blend to a smooth paste. Put the ground spices in the bowl. Mix on the side with half of the remaining oil, the remaining salt and the *kecap manis*. When it is thoroughly mixed, add all the oil.

Push a tablespoon of the spices down the duck's throat. Add the salam leaves to the remaining spices in the bowl and push into the duck's cavity. Rub the skin with a thin layer of spices.

At this point, the duck is wrapped in coconut tree bark. You can use local tree bark, an oven bag or a terracotta pot. Wipe the tree bark with a clean cloth and place a sprig of staghorn on top. Place the duck on top of this. Place another sprig of staghorn on top of the seasoned duck. Tie up one end of the tree bark securely with string. Pour the water into the package and tie up the other end. Alternatively, place the duck and half the water in an oven bag or in a terracotta pot. It is not necessary to add the staghorn.

The smoked duck is now cooked under a terracotta lid, surrounded by rice husks and burning coconut fibre. It takes at least 8 hours to cook and the slow cooking process yields wonderfully aromatic, delicious tender meat. Alternatively, place in a pre-heated oven set at 180°C (350°F) and cook for 1½ hours or set the oven to 120°C (250°F) and cook for 4 hours. The duck can also be cooked in a pressure cooker.

Note: The staghorn is an unusual ingredient. It is included to speed up the cooking process.

Serves 4.

The vibrant heart of village life

THE MARKET

Mpu Dibia taught Kusuma Sari
the science of the market:
how many eggs for how much salt;
so many bushels of sweet corn for a bolt of cloth.

THE PAINTED ALPHABET

The Ubud market lies at the crossroads opposite the palace and is the vibrant, bustling heart of village life. It is typical of markets found in Bali's larger towns, and is the place where the local women socialise with friends and neighbours early every morning, while gathering fresh provisions for the daily meals, offerings and ceremonies.

Entering from Monkey Forest Road takes you past rows of noisy old ladies dressed in faded sarongs and long-sleeved lace or printed polyester *kebayas*, selling fluorescent cakes dyed with pink and green food colouring, fluffy blue hydrangeas, coconut leaves, green bananas and vegetables bursting out of small bamboo baskets.

Around the corner lies my favourite section, where a network of low tables is set up for the morning's take-away trade. Shaded from the hot morning sun, you can buy sweet or savoury rice porridges or *bubur* and *nasi campur* from four of Ubud's grandmas, who have been selling take-away rice for as long as I can remember. The *bubur* is my favourite and consists of soft boiled rice topped with steamed greens and soy sprouts mixed with shredded coconut, shrimp-paste chilli seasoning and golden coconut sauce. The grandma who sells the *bubur* has a soft round face that somehow matches the gentle quality of her food. Next to her is the sticky rice and *nasi campur* seller. The meals are all carefully wrapped in waxy green banana leaves, to be eaten for breakfast or an early lunch.

For an unusual refreshment, *dalumen*, the slimy forest green drink smelling of wheat grass, can be purchased nearby from a woman whose personality is as intriguing as the tonic she sells. In fact, I adore this woman and her *dalumen* is the finest in town. She's an unusual mix of elegance, comedy and melancholy and always has the women laughing. Her stall, set with its supporting cast of mysterious green *dalumen*, creamy roasted coconut milk, palm sugar syrup and pink squiggly rice flour bits, is her stage where she combines all the ingredients, stirs each glass and delivers her lines with the drama of a Shakespearean actor. Once her potion is finished for the day, she quietens down and looks a little forlorn. I've never seen her with any family members and there's somehow a hint of sadness about her. If I see her at the temple, she always hugs me and tells me I'm *cantik* (pretty). When all her pots are empty — usually by ten o'clock in the morning — the table and all its contents are carried home on the top of a coiled towel on her head.

In the dazzling sun, huge overflowing tubs of small red and green chillies, smooth brown snakefruit, bright red hairy rambutans, small yellow bananas, glossy betel leaves, red shallots and mangoes, hold pride of place amidst a million deep-brown spotty coconut spoons, rustic baskets from Lombok, large black rubber sandals and decorated photo albums. The Javanese tonic-seller, her basket brimming full of golden-yellow drinks or *jamu*, sells cure-all potions that give extra strength and stamina for early morning shoppers.

But the real action takes place in the far-eastern corner of the market complex. Deep inside are rows of shiny white eggplant, frilly winged beans, pale green bitter melon and all sorts of lush green Chinese leaves. Piled alongside are mounds of dazzling red chillies, tiny earth-coloured potatoes, white sprouted mung beans, small brown peanuts, tiny fragrant limes and aromatic gingers still covered with a fresh layer of moist soil. From time to time, I'll spot tiny succulent fresh seaweed that bursts with flavour in your mouth. Mixed with galangal and roasted coconut, it makes a delicious salad. At other times, I'll see the wide leaves of the resurrection lily rhizome, tied in small bundles with bamboo twigs. This is delicious when blanched and mixed with spices.

Every third day is the larger market day and a time when the village trading place becomes chaotic. An abundance of more exotic fruits and vegetables in all colours, shapes and sizes are proudly displayed inside and outside the main market area, with vendors from all around Bali setting up shop. Unusual fragrances, pungent aromas, iridescent colours, gangly roots and musky unfamiliar spices assault the senses. The small crowded passageways become a frantic migratory path as baskets of squealing pink-nosed pigs are carried home or to the next ceremony. Bulging sacks of red and green chillies, bundles of fat green bananas and old brown coconuts in hessian bags meet in near collision with startled tourists and loads of vegetables. 'Hello, hello, hello!' yells the bearer of a huge sack of white rice, straining under its weight as he seeks an exit from the shopping pandemonium. Shouting and laughing, the stallholders greet discerning local customers while defending their usually inflated prices.

Next to the spice-seller, small bright-eyed fish lie alongside chunks of fresh red tuna dotted with fat flies, tiny grey shrimp and silvery pilchards. Smoked sardines called *pindang* are tightly packed and artfully layered in tall square tins. The air is thick with the odour of seafood and fermented shrimp paste. Slithery brown rice-field eels make a last attempt at slipping out of the huge black buckets in which they're always kept. Sold by the plastic bag, two hundred grams is all you need to make a wonderful sambal. When deep-fried, these tiny eels taste like a mixture of bacon and whitebait.

In the livestock section you can purchase small pigs and take them home alive in large bags or woven bamboo baskets. Ducks always seem to be sold in multiples of two. Tied together at the feet, they're thrown across the handlebars of the family motorbike and transported home, quacking at the passing traffic. Chickens are thrown into cloth bags and can often be seen pushing their beaks out of the opening to view the world as it whizzes by.

The well-worn crumbling cement stairs take you down into the depths of the market. This level offers a selection of firm creamy-white tofu or thick tempe, wrapped in plastic or banana leaves. When you hold it in your hands, you can feel the warmth from the fermentation process. The intense yeasty aroma that lingers around these food stalls is like the smell of freshly brewed beer. Tempe is a fermented cake of soya beans bound together by a mould culture, and is an important source of protein and fibre. It is one of Indonesia's greatest inventions but is now available in health food stores around the world.

Behind one of the main stalls are more rows of lumpy tempe in the making, brimming with pale yellow soy beans, to be sold the next day. A band of young smiley Javanese men puffing on sweet clove cigarettes are happy to show you their product. A breakfast of wok-fried creamy tofu tossed in a spicy chilli sauce can be ordered here and taken home in a plastic bag, with a few crunchy tofu skins thrown in for good measure.

Throughout the market, mounds of delicate, waxy-green ylang-ylang blossoms, powerful white *cempaka* or Himalayan magnolia, creamy yellow-tinged frangipani and bright orange marigolds are displayed on painted Chinese pink and green tin trays or bursting out of woven bamboo baskets. A fresh *cempaka* strung into the hair is one of the world's most alluring fragrances and the ideal ornament for the temple. Ylang-ylang, redolent of sandalwood, is said to be a powerful aphrodisiac and usually grows near the family temple shrines. Infused with leaves, bark and petals, it creates the delicious sacred water that we drink when we're blessed at the temple. Bamboo baskets brimming with shredded green pandan leaves and petals in shades of pinks, reds and purples line the wide cement stairs. For those too busy to make their own offerings, coconut-leaf offerings scattered with red, blue and white flowers can be bought in bundles of ten. Sweet incense, oils, young coconut leaves and offering containers wrapped in gold-patterned cloth provide a colourful backdrop to this perfumed paradise.

One of my favourite stallholders is the old woman who sells fresh honeycomb. Her round face and kind smiling eyes are framed by dark grey hair that is always smeared with coconut oil and tied in a loose bun. I imagine she's the beloved grandma in her family compound. She would surely be the one who offers you all sorts of treats when Mum isn't looking. Opposite her is an elderly betel-chewing woman who sells local green oranges and pale blue duck eggs. Her head adorned with the obligatory coiled towel for carrying heavy loads, she always wears a faded brown sarong, held firm with a long thick band of forest-green cotton around the waist and an old army-style shirt. These battlefield colours give her an authoritarian air. The long overstretched holes in her ears, from years of wearing heavy Balinese earrings, are always full of rupiah, curled up tightly to fit the space. This was something that intrigued me on my first visit. Who would have thought you could use your ear lobes to hold money? This old grandma has become a self-appointed leader for my cooking school market tour groups. When I hold up leaves to show the group, she tells them they're *daun pandan, sereh* or *daun sirih*. She nods her head knowingly when I, in turn, tell her in English the names of the respective ingredients.

Amidst soft grey tofu, pink temple cakes, blue and gold shiny sarongs, frilly nylon hairclips, tweetie-bird shoes and green coconut fruits, the ground floor also offers a range of delectable snacks, including juicy Balinese fish satay brought in by a lady from nearby Lebih beach, freshly cooked chicken satay grilled to order by the sprightly man from Madura, grilled golden spatchcocks from the woman from Lombok, or *gado-gado* from the lady under the plastic roof. The aroma of barbecued meat mingles with the smell of body sweat and ground peanuts. You can sit and enjoy suckling pig, roast chicken, *nasi campur*, or sip

Balinese coffee on the long bench that overlooks the inner courtyard and ravaged fighting dogs, while discussing life and politics with the local artists.

For something sweet, there's a lady offering colourful Balinese cakes topped with thick palm sugar syrup, near the comical jackfruit-seller and his huge chunks of this golden-yellow bubblegum-like fruit. In this damp dark corner the smell of fermented fruits and rotting leaves surrounds you like a blanket. Small golden steamed cakes that taste like chewy pancakes are cooked to order, and if you're lucky, the pudding-seller from a nearby village will be perched on the side of the cement stairs, selling the most delicious array of desserts I have ever tasted. For next to nothing you can buy black rice pudding, creamy sticky rice and simmered banana in palm sugar topped with roasted coconut milk and pearly pink sago. I have even dreamt about her glorious treats.

Kitchen necessities such as spiky coconut graters, plastic containers and scoops sit alongside caramel-coloured coconut-shaped palm sugar, pink prawn crackers, salted dried fish and small bags of palm oil. Bamboo rice baskets and conical bamboo containers for steaming rice look like farmer's hats. I've seen grandmas sell these to tourists, who promptly pop them onto their sweaty heads and walk out into the tropical sunshine.

The knife-seller is nearby, with his handcrafted wares neatly stacked in a bright blue plastic basket. A butcher who joined us for the market tour remarked on the quality of the knives, saying that carbonated steel is the finest metal to use for cutting meat as it's very strong and easy to sharpen. This steel is no longer permitted in the Australian meat industry because it rusts, and the butcher looked rather wistful as he recalled using it.

In this dimly lit haven, fermented shrimp paste, rotting leaves, animals and fragrant tropical flowers combine to produce an overwhelming odour, punctuated by the busy sounds and vibrant colours that add up to a rich sensory experience. Bargaining for a kilo of coffee might leave you wondering whether you've paid too much, but the interaction with the seller is just as important as the sale itself.

Nestled between the old and new section of the market on the main road is the market temple. Dedicated to Dewi Melanting, the goddess of seeds, markets and gardens, it is a hive of activity as stallholders wearing sashes and bright sarongs diligently place the sweetest offerings and incense in front of the shrine that will guarantee abundant takings. Twice a year this temple celebrates its anniversary and this can be a huge festival that lasts for up to three days. On these occasions, all of Ubud must bring an offering. I certainly would not want to offend the goddess of good fortune by taking a meagre gift. So for this feast day we always prepare a bountiful gift of purple mangosteens, bulbous snakefruit, fat yellow bananas and a sponge sprinkled with chocolate to sit on the top.

In the north-eastern corner of every stall, perched above the head of each stallholder, there also sits a small shrine. This is the throne that holds the *daksina*, usually a silver conical container about the size of a small ice-cream carton, wrapped in gold-patterned fabric and decorated with a halo of frangipanis, red, yellow or white hibiscus and sometimes ylang-ylang. Inside lies a palm-leaf pot containing a shaved coconut, Chinese coins, leaves, a sprinkling of rice and an egg. This is the essential offering that holds the soul of each stand, each stallholder. It is like the beating heart that symbolises life and humanity. Take this away and you take the spirit with you.

Outside the market can be as exciting as shopping inside. Tofu tossed in sweet peanut sauce, clear pork-ball soup and green mung-bean porridge are sold in plastic bags from pushcart-sellers who gather in the car park. Mothers in shiny floral dresses with huge white collars pass by, gracefully carrying home their towering loads on their heads. Motorbikes laden with one or two cheerful children, bright plastic baskets bursting with edible leaves and frantic feathery chickens, tear down the road past *bemos*, the small local transport buses, which are usually leaning under the weight of sacks of rice, onions, coconuts and livestock. For the faint-hearted, this is the time to avoid any public transport, as you are likely to be squashed between sticky children slurping on sugary pink drinks, sweaty grandmas with bright red lips from chewing betel nut, clove-cigarette-smoking sweaty men, quacking ducks, boxes of noodles and tons of garlic. Take a deep breath and savour the memory. It all adds up to an exciting, cultural experience.

Krupuk
Crackers

These crunchy rice crackers come in all shapes and sizes. At the market, they are sold everywhere, sealed in plastic bags. Children especially love to munch on them and I've also seen adults mix them with chicken broth for afternoon tea.

krupuk, shrimp or other flavour
vegetable oil

It is best to dry the *krupuk* in a slow oven for half an hour before cooking. Then, half fill a wok with the oil and heat over a medium flame. Fry the *krupuk*, just a few at a time until puffed up. This will only take a few seconds. Remove with tongs, drain on absorbent paper and then serve. They will keep for a few days if stored in an airtight container.

Sate Ayam
Chicken satay

In Bali, you'll see the vendors in the markets busily fanning and twirling satay over glowing coconut husks. Every now and then they splash them with a marinade that makes the flames jump and crackle, adding a delicious smoky finish to these succulent treats. Tossed with a fiery sweet peanut sauce and wrapped in banana leaves or brown paper, they become a hearty take-away snack or meal.

My children love the chicken satay from the man from Madura at the market. Tiny chunks of meat are basted over hot smoky coconut coals; a small plastic fan perched on a table nearby keeps the flames fired. A light peanut sauce is drizzled over the warm meat before it's wrapped in brown paper to take home and eat with rice. It's a special market treat.

12 satay sticks
300 g (10 oz) chicken fillets
3 cloves garlic
3 tablespoons oil
2 tablespoons fried shallots
1 teaspoon soy sauce
3 teaspoons kecap manis or brown sugar
2 teaspoons cracked black pepper
3 kaffir lime leaves, shredded finely
fried shallots, to garnish

Soak the satay sticks in water for half an hour to prevent charring during cooking. Chop the garlic.

Remove the skin and fat from the chicken. Slice into small cubes approximately 2 cm x 2 cm ($^3/4$ in x $^3/4$ in). Mix all the ingredients in a bowl with the chopped chicken, making sure the meat is well coated with the marinade. Leave for at least 10 minutes. If leaving longer, cover with plastic film and put it in the refrigerator. Thread 3 or 4 chunks of chicken onto each of the sticks. Barbecue or grill until golden brown for about 4 minutes on each side, basting with the marinade from time to time to prevent them drying out.

Serve with peanut sauce (see recipe below) and rice. Garnish with the fried shallots.

Makes 12 sticks.

Peanut Sauce
Bumbu kacang

Peanut sauce is one of Indonesia's most popular condiments. Varying in degrees of spiciness and sweetness, it is exceedingly simple to make and can be served with snacks or a main course.

In order to make a delicious peanut sauce, first you must begin with delicious peanuts and these are abundant in Bali. Sweet organic garlic also adds a wonderful bite. For a successful sauce, the trick is to not reheat it, as it is inclined to curdle. I always buy my raw peanuts at Asian food stores but you can buy freshly ground peanuts from any health food store. My children love to eat peanut sauce with compressed rice cake and tofu, but you can add whatever you like.

1 cup oil for frying peanuts
150 g (5 oz) raw, unsalted peanuts
1 teaspoon sea salt
½ teaspoon shrimp paste
1 large red chilli, trimmed and de-seeded
2 bird's-eye chillies
4 cloves garlic
¼ medium tomato
1 tablespoon palm sugar
2 teaspoons kecap manis
2 kaffir lime leaves, finely shredded
2 tablespoons fried shallots
½ cup water

Heat a wok with the oil over a medium flame. Fry the peanuts a handful at a time, until just golden brown. Remember that they keep cooking after they've been taken from the wok. Do not discard the skin. Remove with a slotted spoon, place on absorbent paper and sprinkle with ½ teaspoon sea salt. This will keep the peanuts dry and crisp. Remove most of the oil from the wok, leaving about two teaspoons. Heat over a low flame and fry the shrimp paste for 30 seconds. Place all the ingredients, except for the peanuts, in the bowl of a food processor and blend to a paste. Add half the fried peanuts and blend until fairly smooth; then add the remaining half. Add more water if necessary. If you'd like a sweeter, darker sauce, add more *kecap manis*. Check seasonings, balancing sweet, sour, salty and spicy.

Serve with satay or *gado-gado*, garnished with fried shallots.

Makes 1 small bowl.

Note: For a quicker, easier option, use cooked beer nuts instead of raw, unsalted peanuts.

Gado-Gado

Vegetables in peanut sauce

This is another Indonesian dish that varies from island to island. In Bali, *gado-gado* — or *jukut mesantok* as it is known here — consists of spinach, bean sprouts, snake beans, tofu and compressed rice cake. It is served in small *warungs* or sold by street vendors, who mix the sauce with the other trimmings to order using a large mortar and pestle. It is then wrapped up in the ubiquitous banana leaf to eat on the spot or take home. My favourite *gado-gado* is sold downstairs at the Ubud market. The peanut sauce is made to order and then tossed with freshly steamed vegetables and compressed rice cake. Then you can sit on a wooden bench, eat *gado-gado* and watch the world go by.

In Java, *gado-gado* is served with a wider variety of vegetables, often including potato and cabbage. In Bali, *kangkung*, bean sprouts and snake beans are used.

250 g (8 oz) snake beans or French beans
150 g (5 oz) bean sprouts
500 g (1 lb) kangkung or English spinach
400 g (14 oz) firm tofu
oil for deep-frying
4–6 tablespoons peanut sauce
sea salt, to taste

Chop the beans into bite-sized pieces. Boil in lightly salted water until tender but not soft. Refresh under cold water. Blanch the bean sprouts in the boiling water for 25 seconds then refresh under cold running water. Split the stems of the *kangkung* in two by running a sharp knife through the centre. Break into shorter pieces. If using English spinach, wash the leaves in several changes of water to remove the grit.

Boil the *kangkung* or spinach in boiling, salted water for 25 seconds. Remove with a slotted spoon.

Chop the tofu into even-sized cubes and deep-fry in hot oil until brown and crispy.

In a large bowl, mix the *kangkung*, bean sprouts and beans with the peanut sauce. Check seasonings and garnish with fried shallots or shrimp crackers. Serve warm or chilled like a salad.

Serves 2–4.

Bregedel Tahu
Tofu fritters

Sometimes I drive to a nearby village to buy organic tofu to make such things as tofu fritters. These thick fragrant blocks of soy bean curd are prepared by a couple of smiley old Balinese grandmas, who have been making tofu all their lives. Their rustic workroom is full of ancient-looking pots and boilers that have, like these tiny women, withstood years of turbulent times and natural disasters. The warm strained soy milk is packed onto beautifully tarnished homemade bamboo trays that glow with a golden sheen. Entering this tiny compound is like walking over the threshold of bygone days and their tofu is the loving symbol of their honest endeavours.

Tofu is a cheap nutritious food popular throughout Indonesia, and there are countless ways of cooking it. My children love these fritters. They're a wonderful snack in the afternoons and are also delicious eaten with *nasi campur*. The mild flavour of the tofu is infused with fresh spices to create a delicately seasoned and deliciously fragrant snack. Even if you don't like tofu, I'm sure you'll love these soft fritters.

250 g (8 oz) firm tofu
2 tablespoons flour
2 eggs
1 tablespoon fried shallots
2 kaffir lime leaves, finely shredded
1/2 teaspoon sea salt
1/4 cup oil for frying

SPICE PASTE
2 cloves garlic
3 teaspoons chopped galangal
2 teaspoons fresh chopped turmeric
1/4 teaspoon shrimp paste
1/2 large red chilli
1 teaspoon palm sugar

Wipe the tofu with a paper towel.

Grind the spices in a mortar and pestle or place in the bowl of a food processor and blend to a paste. Add the tofu to the spices and whiz around for a minute until the tofu is smooth.

Put the tofu and spices in a bowl and stir in the flour, egg, fried shallots, lime leaves and salt. The consistency will be like thick pancakes.

Heat the oil in a wok over a medium flame.

Take a dessertspoon of the fritter mixture and drop it into the hot oil. Fry the fritters, a tablespoon at a time, until golden brown. Remove and set aside on absorbent paper. Serve hot with steamed rice or as a snack.

Makes approximately 15.

Sager Gerang
Spicy dried fish and coconut sambal

We were preparing for a cremation at the head offering-maker's house in Ubud. The compound was busy with the activity of women working together to make holy paraphernalia for the big day. The kitchen was humming with the sound of oil sizzling in the wok, grinding spices, chatter and laughter. Fresh coconut oil, fragrant gingers, salted fish and sweet shallots teased our senses as we waited for lunch to be served. Eventually the table was set with a dozen glossy dishes and one of them was *sager gerang*. I took a mouthful and was blown away by the sweet mellow flavour of roasted coconut with lime leaves, nutty mung beans and roasted dried fish. I invited the woman who cooked it to our house several weeks later and we duplicated the feast. The only element missing was the crowd of women working and the sea of colourful offerings.

Salted dry anchovies are available in Asian food stores, usually under the name of *ikan bilis*.

100 g (3¹/₂ oz) salted, dry anchovies
2 teaspoons sambal goreng (see recipe, page 200)
1 cup roasted grated coconut (see page 121)
1 cup warm water
2 tablespoons mung beans (optional), soaked for 8 hours

2 teaspoons fried shallots
2 kaffir lime leaves, shredded
1 calamondin lime, halved
1 teaspoon palm sugar
salt to taste
2 teaspoons torch ginger bud

Break the heads off the fish and discard (makes great cat food!).

Wash the fish in the water, drain and set aside. Grill, broil or dry-fry the fish a handful at a time, until crunchy. Set aside.

Chop the anchovies very finely. It should almost look like grey sand. Mix 2 teaspoons of *sambal goreng* with the roasted coconut. Add the remaining seasonings, including the mung beans. Squeeze the juice of the calamondin lime in and then thrown the halves in as well. Lastly, add the ground anchovies. Taste seasonings. If you'd like it spicier, add more sambal.

Serves 4.

Kering Tempe

Sweet crunchy tempe

This is a popular way of serving tempe and is a regular on the *nasi campur* circuit. The success of this dish will depend on the quality of your tempe and peanuts. My children love it because it is so sweet and tasty.

300 gm (10 oz) plain tempe (fermented soy bean cake)
1 cup oil
100 g (3¹/₂ oz) peanuts, skins (not shells) left on
1 teaspoon sea salt
5 large red chillies, trimmed and de-seeded
2 teaspoons tamarind pulp
¹/₄ cup water
1 stalk lemongrass
1 salam leaf
2 kaffir lime leaves
2 teaspoons palm sugar
1 tablespoon kecap manis
3 tablespoons fried shallots

SPICE PASTE
  4 cloves garlic
  2 tablespoons chopped galangal
  4 red shallots
  2 small red chillies

Slice the tempe into matchsticks. Heat the oil in a wok over a medium flame.

Deep-fry the tempe, a handful at a time, in the oil until golden brown. Remember it will keep cooking after you take it out of the wok. Remove with a slotted spoon, strain and set aside on absorbent paper. It should become crunchy as it cools.

Deep-fry the peanuts in the same way, leaving the skins on, stirring constantly in the hot oil. Remove with a slotted spoon, strain and set aside on absorbent paper. Sprinkle with a pinch of salt.

Slice the large chilli finely and neatly.

Soak the tamarind in ¼ cup water, mix together and strain, reserving the water.

Place the spices in the bowl of a food processor and blend to a paste. Add a tablespoon of oil if the mixture is too dry to move the blade. If the galangal is too hard to blend, add two thick, bruised slices instead.

Pour out most of the oil from the wok, leaving two tablespoons remaining.

Heat the oil over a medium heat. Fry the mild chilli for a minute until slightly wilted. Strain and set aside with the tempe.

Fry the remaining spices with the lemongrass, salam leaves and lime leaves in the oil for 30 seconds or until fragrant.

Add the tamarind water, palm sugar, *kecap manis* and sea salt. Simmer over a low flame for about 1 minute, until thick.

Add all the fried tempe, fried peanuts, fried shallots and fried chilli. Mix thoroughly, making sure the sauce coats the tempe and peanuts.

Check seasonings and serve with extra fried shallots on top.

Note: You can use potato instead of tempe.

Serves 4.

Pepesan Ikan
Grilled fish in banana leaves

What would the Balinese have done without banana leaves? Pliable and porous, they are perfect for grilling and steaming as they retain natural flavours while imparting their own subtle aroma. In this dish, fragrant gingers, chilli and fresh fish are wrapped together and grilled over hot coconut coals. The result is a deliciously golden and healthy meal.

Try parchment paper if banana leaves are not available. Barbecue, grill or roast the parcels in the oven. Steaming the parcels will create a tender juicy package.

300 g (10 oz) fish
3 kaffir lime leaves
1/2 teaspoon sea salt
1/4 cup oil
banana leaves
salam leaves

SPICE PASTE
3 cloves garlic
2 teaspoons palm sugar
2 tomatoes
2 tablespoons oil
3 candlenuts
1 stalk lemongrass
1/4 teaspoon shrimp paste
4 large red chillies, trimmed and de-seeded
2–4 small chillies
1 1/2 tablespoons chopped galangal
3 red shallots
1 tablespoon chopped ginger
2 teaspoons chopped turmeric
1 teaspoon tamarind pulp
1 teaspoon ground coriander seeds
1/4 teaspoon ground black pepper

Cut the fish into large chunks.

Shred the lime leaves, by rolling the leaves into a tight cigarette shape and slicing finely. Mix with the fish and set aside while preparing the spices.

Grind the spices in a mortar and pestle or place in the bowl of a food processor and blend to a smooth paste.

Mix the blended spice paste, sea salt and the oil thoroughly with the fish. Taste a little for flavour.

Cut banana leaves into pieces about 8 cm x 8 cm (3¼ in x 3¼ in). Steam the leaves to soften if necessary.

On each piece of banana leaf, place a salam leaf first and two or three chunks of fish.

Wrap the fish in the banana leaf by rolling it over like a Christmas bon-bon and secure each end with a wooden tooth-pick or short bamboo skewer.

Alternatively, wrap with string. Baking or parchment paper can also be used instead of banana leaves.

Steam over gently boiling water for 5–7 minutes or until cooked.

You will need to open one up to see if it's cooked inside.

The parcels can also be grilled, baked or barbecued.

Serve the fish in their neat little packages and allow guests to open their parcels on their own plates.

Serve with steamed rice and *kangkung pelecing* (see recipe, page 62).

Makes 6 small parcels.

A haven of good and evil spirits

THE BALINESE KITCHEN

Abundant were their gifts of delicacies:
there were fruits and roots and sweet young coconuts.
PARTHAYANA, THE JOURNEYING OF PARTHA

Charming in its simplicity, the Balinese kitchen, *paon*, is steeped in ancient folklore and magic. Literally meaning 'ashes', the *paon* is a haven of good and evil spirits and always lies in the south-western corner of the compound, or in the direction of the sea. The north, where the great mountain Gunung Agung is situated, is the home of the gods, and all holy places must face this direction.

In the villages, the kitchens are dark and smoky from years of burning bamboo and local firewood to steam the precious rice, make rich aromatic coconut oil and cook sweet and savoury foods. The ceilings are layered with black soot that was once believed to have healing properties. In these corners where sunlight rarely penetrates, memories and magic seem to linger.

The kitchen is a powerful space where evil spirits can be neutralised. Brahma, the creator, and Wisnu, the protector and symbol of male fertility, are said to dwell in the kitchen. A large terracotta pot of water, *gebeh*, always sits beside the oven, *cangkem paon.* Revered for its purifying powers, water is believed to be the manifestation of Wisnu and is an essential part of all Balinese ceremonies. The Balinese oven represents Brahma, whose manifestation is fire. Ashes are also believed to have sacred properties and are placed at the entrance of the house when a person dies, to appease evil spirits.

Most village kitchens are still built of mud-brick with a simple tiled or grass roof. There is a small window on either side of the main entrance, usually covered with wire to keep out chickens and other unwanted visitors. A mud-brick oven is used for cooking. For wealthier folk, a low tiled bench usually runs the length of the back wall, with a gas burner perched in the middle and perhaps even a sink nearby. The bench provides a working area for the meticulous job of peeling onions and garlic and the chopping and grinding of spices. It's also somewhere to sit so you can chat while working, but generally the Balinese kitchen is not the kind of welcoming place where you would sit and have a cup of tea; its sole purpose is to prepare food. Pots, pans, and hand-made knives are usually stored underneath the workbench. From this active workplace, exotic flavours and aromas drift like incense to the heavens, awakening all the senses. Dishes are always washed outside and stacked in a separate area to dry in the sun.

The traditional Balinese oven has three holes in the top and an opening underneath to burn the firewood. The rice is always cooked over the most powerful middle hole, with other dishes cooked on either side. A Balinese folk story about the celestial twins Komara and Kumari explains why there are three holes in a Balinese oven. Bhatara Kala, the evil demon-king, was looking for humans born the same day as his birthday to feast on. As Komara and Kumari were born on this day, they jumped into the kitchen stove in an effort to hide from the wicked king. Bhatara Kala spotted them and covered two of the holes with his huge hands, but the sprightly twins jumped out of the central hole and escaped. To this day, it is believed that bad fortune will fall upon those who build a stove with only two holes.

* * *

For me, the kitchen has always been the heart of the house. So when we drew up plans for our new home, I decided to create a Western-style indoor kitchen, instead of one in a separate building. I longed for a kitchen where I could make coffee any time of day, bake cakes or even write letters while the kettle boiled. I looked forward to entertaining friends and sipping cups of tea with visitors from all over the world. I love the charm of a rustic Balinese kitchen, but I wanted a bright tiled space with powerpoints for my kitchen tools and a soot-free, spider-free environment. I wanted to see big bowls of fruit on the bench, tomatoes on the windowsill and my favourite teapots on shelves on the wall.

On completion of our house, many friends visited, eager to see the finished product. 'You're so lucky,' exclaimed my Western friends who live in Bali. 'You have a kitchen inside your house.' They looked enviously at the smooth pink granite benchtops and jade-green teak cupboards full of sparkling cups and plates. They oohed and aahed when they saw my smart cutlery drawer. I was so proud. Teak shutters overlooked the back courtyard and the new stainless-steel oven sat smiling in the corner. I also had a shiny white fridge with the cutest pantry nearby. At the same time, a Balinese friend dropped over. He stood in the doorway and gazed over the entire space for a few minutes with a look of disdain on his face. 'Great house,' he said, 'but why did you put the kitchen inside?'

One of my favourite kitchens belongs to the high priest in Ubud, Ida Bagus Pedanda Manuaba. Whenever we need blessings or holy water for special ceremonies, we make the journey to the other side of town and arrive at the *pedanda's* compound laden with fragrant offerings and usually one or two children. Morning is the appropriate time to be blessed, and the sweet smell of fried shallots always greets us while breakfast is being prepared. Huge blackened pots of steaming rice sing on the traditional wood-fired stove, sending the comforting smell of warm grains and fragrant leaves drifting through the compound.

Nearby in the temple grounds, the priest carries out his purification ceremony in a small pavilion high above the ground, surrounded by shimmering fabrics, vessels of holy water and offerings. From his lofty setting, he chants Hindu mantras and performs the sacred hand gestures. Sweet incense floats on the notes of delicate brass bells that he rings at his altar while tossing fragrant flowers into the courtyard. We always watch the ritual from the nearby pavilion under the shade of the *cempaka* tree. Others who need blessings or holy advice sit alongside us. I've even see tourists line up for purification ceremonies.

To the gentle rhythm of the prayers, the priest's wife prepares the first meal of the day, as well as attending to her other duties as a priest's wife. Kind and cheery, she always makes you feel at home with her constant chatter and simple questions. The bundles of fresh dark green leaves, bright smooth chillies, spices, tempe and eggs somehow look joyful, as if they're honoured to be part of this special meal. Hens with fluffy chicks scatter across the yard. The Indian mynah bird sings '*selamat pagi*' repeatedly from a huge cage nearby, surrounded by flowering purple orchids. A small pond at the temple entrance is teeming with bright goldfish. A small sleek cat wanders lazily between the offerings, looking for a mouthful of food. The whole compound seems to be brimming with contentment.

There are two parts to this ancient kitchen, joined by a small semi-open area. On one side is a small dark smoky room where most of the cooking takes place. The aroma of fried spices, shrimp paste and toasted coconut lingers in the gaps between the old faded red bricks, frangipani flowers and brilliant red hibiscus. On the other side is another small room where sacks of rice and other daily necessities are stored. It has a well-worn charm that has evolved from years of feasts and festivities.

Recently we went to the priest's house for Arjuna's purification ceremony, a rite that occurs every six months. This is similar to baptism, where you are drenched with delicious fragrant holy water laden with petals. We arrived on an auspicious day for the priest and his family, and after receiving our blessings were given a small selection of the ceremonial foods from the priest's wife, piled neatly on a banana leaf to take home. I was thrilled by their generosity and carefully placed our precious gift in our silver temple bowl, covered it with the small ornate carved lid and carried it home with due reverence. Ketut called a few friends over to share in the divine assortment; we were all deeply honoured to receive ceremonial food from one of the most holy places in town. Together we ate our meal eagerly but silently, and we all went back for seconds. The subtlety of the flavours and contrasting textures were beyond compare. It was one of the most delicious *lawars* we had ever eaten.

Basic Equipment
Mortar and pestle: mother and child

The mortar and pestle is one of the most important utensils in a Balinese kitchen and is affectionately referred to as the 'mother and child'. A woman at one of my cooking classes commented that it was appropriate for the child to be the pestle, considering that it eventually wears away the mother part! Essential for the preparation of Balinese food, this rustic food processor can wield magic in seconds as it grinds and bruises a multitude of exotic spices to make the senses sing. The fragrances released are redolent of essential oils, with lemongrass intermingling with gingers, pepper, chilli and aromatic leaves. These ingredients are said to be anti-depressants because of their uplifting and heart-warming qualities. It's certainly true that the grinding of brilliant earthy spices seems to comfort the soul.

The Balinese-style mortar and pestle is either round and fairly shallow or very deep like the Thai-style pounder. The former is used for spice pastes and vegetables, while the latter is mainly reserved for meat. Made out of volcanic stone, it is porous and tends to gather flavour with each use. After many years of hard work and a thousand layers of spices, the thick stone will eventually wear away and split in half. Nowadays, most mortars and pestles are made from a blend of volcanic rock and stone. They don't grind as smoothly as pure volcanic rock but are still effective in getting the job done.

If you are able to get hold of a volcanic stone mortar, the first step for sealing it is to grind fresh turmeric into it and then plunge it into hot water, soaking it until the water becomes cool. If it is a particularly gritty stone, you'll need to soak it for several more days and it may also be necessary to grind coconut or peanuts into it, to add natural oils. After that, you may have to soak it in water again until it is ready for use.

I always enjoy watching the women at our house cooking and like to observe their different grinding styles. Jero, our family cook, has a delightfully gentle manner which almost seems to allow the ingredients to communicate with her. She has an innate knowledge of spices and their harmonious combinations, which is apparent in everything she makes. She never measures anything. When she grinds her spices, she uses short sweet strokes, often with one hand held behind her back, surveying her ingredients as carefully as a mother with young children. She gently rolls large red chillies between her hands to coax the seeds away from the tenacious hold of the membrane. I watch her as she slowly and respectfully removes the outer layer of purple shallots or tenderly peels her gingers. She cooks as if she is preparing an offering for the temple and I always feel great pleasure and happiness after eating her food. Since her marriage and the birth of her little girl, Jero has acquired an added maturity and glow that makes her food even more satisfying.

Nyoman, our other cook, is more aggressive in her approach and cooks with great gusto, seeming to immerse her whole being into the food. When she grinds spices, she grips the pestle firmly with both hands and charges into the mortar with a deliberate definite rhythm. There is an inherent power in each dish and eating her food gives me great strength and confidence.

The basic principle of grinding is to roll the pestle back and forth in the same spot with a rhythmic action similar to kneading bread. It is a very satisfying therapeutic activity and great for releasing the day's stress. The slow action of grinding is like alchemy and the transformation of exotic spices into fragrant vibrant pastes a secret art.

If you are unable to find a volcanic stone mortar and pestle, try experimenting with a marble or wooden one. Otherwise the food processor will do the job, although you will miss out on a whole sensory experience and the wonderful texture.

The rice steamer, goddess of the kitchen

In Bali, the comforting fragrance of steaming rice always greets us in the morning. Reflecting the hourglass shape of Dewi Sri, the rice goddess, the rice steamer is the focal point of the kitchen. The base, *dandang*, is made of thin grey aluminium or sheet metal and holds the precious water for steaming the rice. A conical-shaped bamboo basket, *kukusan,* holds the grains and sits comfortably inside the base. The lid, *kekeban,* is made of terracotta and prevents any moist air escaping.

Modern families sometimes use rice cookers — a great option for the serious rice eater — and nowadays Magic Jars are also very popular. These look similar to a rice cooker but only keep the rice warm, they don't cook it. In our household, we cook the rice in the traditional way and then pop it into one of these containers.

Knives for all occasions

In every Balinese household, as in any kitchen where serious food preparation takes place, you will find sets of extremely sharp knives. Handcrafted and beautiful in their simplicity, these knives are excellent for chopping and slicing. Made of carbonated steel, they can be quickly sharpened on the mortar and pestle. In our kitchen we mainly use small paring knives and ceremonial knives for the chopping of spices and other ingredients.

I am always fascinated by the knife-sellers at the market, with their bamboo baskets overflowing with knives of many sizes. They sell the full range of small paring knives, general-use knives and dangerous-looking Balinese-style cleavers. These are usually combined with a few other kitchen necessities, such as different types of coconut graters and ladles, made out of oil-tin scraps.

Ketut has his own selection of knives stored away in special leather sheaths. These are reserved for the early-morning task of chopping piles of meat and spices for ceremonial food. Their handles are lightly carved, while the blade is also etched with Hindu symbols. When new, the handles are a lovely clean brown colour, but after a few weeks of use they soon turn a well-worn deeper brown.

Graters for great events

The Balinese grater is very rudimentary: a plank of wood with rows of small extremely sharp nails banged into it. This model is a follow-on from the even more old-fashioned version made of spiky *rottan*, held together and trimmed with bamboo. One of the cake-sellers in the market still uses this type of grater because she feels it lends a more natural flavour to her food. They are also suitable for grating gingers, such as turmeric, and other spices.

There are two types of coconut graters used in Bali: one is for fine grating, required for making coconut milk, desserts and certain vegetable dishes; and the other is for shredding — the texture required for ceremonial food. Both are hand-held utensils as opposed to the Western-style standing version. The grater used for shredding is made out of tin punched with elongated holes and framed with wood. It is a strong, quick and effective tool for shredding the large quantities of coconuts needed for ceremonial foods. Up to a dozen coconuts may be used for these occasions and shredding them is the work of several men. Sitting cross-legged on the ground, this rustic utensil held firmly in the left hand, they leisurely shred piles of freshly roasted white coconut meat to be incorporated into a whole host of sacred dishes.

The usual style of Western domestic cheese grater is often not strong enough or sharp enough for dealing with hard coconut. A food processor is probably a better option.

Woks and pots

Most Balinese food is cooked in a wok. Its broad rounded shape and thin metal base distributes heat most effectively and is perfectly tailored for fast Asian-style cooking. It is generally used for stir-frying, deep-frying and boiling.

I have two woks. My favourite is a large one made from shiny stainless steel with a sturdy wooden handle. When seasoned meats, vegetables and fragrant spice pastes are tossed around the base, they glisten with enthusiasm and cook to perfection. Even thick coconut curries never fail in this particular wok. My other wok is made of aluminium and is the type you see in most Balinese homes. This one works well, although food is inclined to burn if not properly supervised. When choosing an aluminium wok, make sure the metal is not too thin.

Chinese-style dishes, such as *nasi goreng* (fried rice), *mie goreng* (fried noodles) and *cap cay* (stir-fried vegetables), are always cooked in a wok, generally over a high flame. After using our woks, we wash them lightly and wipe them dry. They never have a chance to rust as we use them so often.

For the boiling of certain curries and stews, aluminium pots of varying sizes are used. These are the most popular cooking vessel nowadays because they're so cheap. The theory that aluminium may be linked with senility certainly hasn't been heard in Bali, and there are very few senile seniors in the community. Jackfruit curry, sour chicken curry and certain ceremonial dishes are simmered in large aluminium pots for many hours, and usually kept overnight to be enjoyed the following day.

Spoons

The hand is the main measuring device in a Balinese kitchen. However, rice spoons are usually made from the smoothed halves of pale-coloured coconut wood or even plastic. For salt, the most popular container is still a coconut.

The heart of every Balinese meal

RICE

'Have you ever noticed, Kerti,' said Siladri,
'that our children are like the rice cycle?'
The Painted Alphabet

Since ancient times, rice has been central to complex customs and religious beliefs in Bali; it was held that to worship rice would guarantee an abundant harvest. Life here still revolves around this highly respected grain and the cultivation of rice is a ritual process that requires prayers, ceremonies and offerings. A drive through the villages will take you into a lush emerald world of floating rice terraces lined with shady coconut trees and slender shrines — and seeing this graceful beauty it is easy to understand why rice is so revered here.

White, black and red rice is grown in Bali, representing three of the four sacred colours. Yellow is the fourth sacred colour and a Balinese mythical story tells how yellow rice came into being. Sanghyang Kesuhun Kidul, a divine god and incarnation of Siwa, sent four birds, one carrying red rice seeds, one black, one yellow and one white, as a gift to King Pretu, the incarnation of Wisnu and one of Bali's early rulers. On their journey, a giantess attacked the bird carrying the yellow rice seeds. In its efforts to protect itself, the bird dropped the tiny seeds and they fell to earth. The angry god cursed the seeds, deeming they would remain as a plant, not grow into food. The seeds grew into a rhizome that has become a favourite ingredient in Balinese food and herbal medicines ever since: turmeric. It is revered for its healing properties and, when mixed with rice, produces the holy golden colour necessary for certain offerings.

Dewi Sri is the legendary goddess of rice and fertility in Bali. Dewi Pertiwi, Mother Earth, first bore the seeds of rice through her celestial union with Wisnu, male god of fertility and water. In his book, *The Island of Bali*, Miguel Covarrubias states that 'as the principal source of life and wealth and as a gift from the gods, rice was born from the cosmic union of the divine male and female creative forces represented in earth and water'.

Dewi Sri is represented by the *cili*, considered to be the symbol of Bali. This is a bundle of rice stalks tied together tightly in the middle to form a tiny waist with a triangular-shaped face and a full skirt. You will see *cili* in the rice fields during certain stages of the grain's life cycle, often attached to the growing rice, as well as represented in ceramic or terracotta on the tables of many popular restaurants, holding bunches of frangipani, salt, pepper and even toothpicks. Small *cili* woven from lontar leaves are sold in the marketplace or gift shops and the image of the *cili* also appears in countless bright paintings sold in every gallery on the island. Even the traditional rice steamer echoes the hourglass shape of the rice goddess. Offerings are made to this deity of beauty to protect and nurture the rice fields that provide the people with the food of life.

Nearby at Mount Batur, the complex irrigation system of Bali begins. It is here that the cool waters from the mountain lake make their way down the fertile slopes through a network of rice fields that eventually lead to the sea. This complex watering system dates from early times. The *subak*, a collective organisation of local farmers, controls Bali's rice fields. Members of every village donate money to the *subak* and we all share in the ritual of making offerings and praying in the rice field temples. For without rice, there would be no life.

The cycle of rice is similar to the cycle of life: from a tiny seed nurtured by water the grain eventually matures into a ripened plant. At the final stage before harvest, the rice is said to be pregnant, and this last phase is the most crucial. Even on *Nyepi*, Balinese New Year, which is a day of absolute silence and confinement to the family compound, I've heard farmers in the rice fields banging tin cans and yelling energetically to protect the precious grains from hungry birds and insects.

The Balinese calendar determines which days are suitable for planting rice, and offerings are made to the growing grain every fifteen days as it fattens in the fields. The cycle begins with the hoeing of the fields, known as *ngendag*. When the hoeing is finished, the field is flooded with up to ten centimetres of water and then ploughed. In the rice fields surrounding our house, the farmer uses a small tractor to assist with this labour-intensive task. Tiny rice seeds are planted in a small seed bed in the corner of the flooded fields and dark green woven coconut mats are placed around the area to protect it from the wind, sun and animals.

The rice seedling is called a *bulih*. After about three weeks, when the seedlings have grown into long blades of grass, they are quickly planted into the prepared muddy fields with precision neatness. The tops of the plants are trimmed to encourage even growth and to protect the delicate shoots from the sun. Once the plants are established, the fields are usually drained once or twice for weeding and subsequently reflooded.

After two months, the rice is considered to be *beling*, pregnant, and extra care is taken to protect the fattening grain. A network of plastic bags is usually strung up in the fields and left to flap in the wind to scare away the birds. In the bright sunlight, the billowing bags appear as fine as silk and add to the beauty of these verdant fields. The fields are drained and allowed to dry prior to harvesting.

When the rice is golden and ready to be harvested, an offering is made to Dewi Sri. This is called *biukukung* and consists of a small bundle of cut rice from the field. During the harvest, the rice stalks are cut and tied in bundles, then the rice is threshed in the fields. The grain is collected in sacks and taken to the local rice mill. The mountains of rice straw left behind in the fields are burnt, to add calcium and other important nutrients to the soil. Our house sits enveloped in a gentle smoke for days when the farmers burn the straw in the fields along our street.

The rice fields have influenced Balinese eating in other ways. They are a paradise for ducks, which wander there freely and feed on whatever organic matter they can find. Consequently, one of the most popular dishes in Bali — with locals and tourists alike — is *bebek betutu*, roast duck. Salted duck eggs are a favourite too. Small dark brown elvers also thrive in these muddy insect-infested fields and roasted eel, finely chopped and mixed with purple shallots, loads of chillies and coconut oil, is one of the most popular sambals on the island.

Used in all offerings for all ceremonies, rice is moulded into different shapes for various occasions. Rice flour is the main ingredient in most of the pink and green cakes that adorn the towering offerings, and the daily offerings, known as *saiban*, consist of a few freshly steamed grains of rice and a tiny amount of food placed on top of fragrant pandan leaves and pink, red and blue flower petals in small pale yellow coconut-leaf baskets. The offering is a gesture of respect and gratitude to a god that provides such abundance. After praying in the temple, we are blessed with a few moist grains of rice called *bija* placed on the forehead, temples and throat. Three grains are then swallowed and the remainder tossed over the head. Fermented sticky rice, *tape*, is the obligatory gift that newly-weds give to the members of the *banjar* at *Galungan* in return for offerings. And rice wine, *brem*, is a cloudy sweet alcohol coaxed from the soft fermented grains.

Cooked rice is considered to be the heart of every Balinese meal. The word *nasi* (steamed rice) is synonymous with food, and the Balinese for 'to eat' and 'to eat rice' is the same word: *ngajengang*. As far as the Balinese are concerned, you have not eaten until you've had rice. Ancient Balinese wisdom claims that rice, as for all food, holds a vital spirit called *amerta*, which is brought to life by the cooking process. *Amerta* — a Sanskrit word — translates as 'that which is essential for life'. With each mouthful of cooked rice, the sacred power or essence of life can be ingested, thereby providing us with spiritual and physical nourishment. Chatter disturbs the *amerta*, so one of the first songs children learn at kindergarten emphasises eating without talking. Mealtimes should be silent, in homage to the life-giving force of this holy grain.

Because rice is the essential element in every meal, the selection of highly seasoned foods served with it are viewed as mere accompaniments to this main course. The rice is always taken first, with the other dishes following. Boiled, steamed or fried rice has a soft soothing quality that makes it as pleasurable to cook as it is to eat. The gentle aroma of steaming rice calms the soul, and when fragrant leaves are added it has the scent of a perfumed garden. Creamy sticky rice topped with a curry sauce is sustaining and comforting. The powerful flavours of spicy fish, sambal and steamed rice are a nutritious Balinese favourite. Fragrant yellow rice is the perfect partner to tender smoked duck, and compressed rice cake tossed with peanut sauce is a popular afternoon snack. The local cuisine has been shaped by rice and most dishes are finely chopped, pounded or stewed to complement its texture and absorbing qualities.

The traditional style of eating, *megibung*, involves all the participants sitting in a large circle and eating together. Bowls of water are passed around to wash the fingers first, followed by steamed rice and various other dishes. The meal ends with fresh tropical fruit. Palm wine, *arak,* might accompany the meal, or perhaps sweet tea or water. The tourist equivalent to *megibung* is Rijstaffel, which is a Dutch-colonial expression meaning 'rice table'. You will find a version of this in many restaurants throughout Indonesia.

Besides the many varieties of white rice grown throughout Bali, there is also white sticky rice, *ketan*; black sticky rice, *injin*; and red rice, *beras barak*. White sticky rice is used for certain desserts and velvety porridges, while black sticky rice is the basis for Bali's famous black rice pudding. Red rice is nutty and wholesome like brown rice, but is seldom eaten by the Balinese as it is harder to chew. Prized for its nutrients, red rice porridge is one of a baby's first foods.

The original short-grained Balinese rice, known as *beras Bali*, which was the most commonly grown variety until the mid 1970s, is claimed to be the most delicious. Similar in appearance to Italian *arborio* rice, it is a larger, more expensive grain — due to its six-month life cycle — with more flavour and goodness. It is now mainly grown in North Bali. For older folk, eating *beras Bali* brings back memories of days when life was simpler and the food was more delicious. Today, most people eat the newer strains of white rice, or dwarf rice which is a long-grain rice and takes only four months to mature. The newer rices are identified by a code determining the type and quality; C4 is the most popular in Bali. Buying by numbers like this always reminds me of ordering a meal in a Chinese restaurant in an Australian suburb.

Recently, an Australian rice-grower in my cooking class examined my C4 white rice and declared that it would never reach the shelves of a Western supermarket. But he was actually being complimentary. He said there is too much bran in C4 to be considered 'white' and that the bran content would shorten the six-month shelf-life required by supermarkets. In other words, our C4 rice is more wholesome!

In my early days in Bali, if I was anticipating a busy day I wouldn't eat rice for lunch. Rice takes more energy to digest than noodles, for example, and so slows you down. However, I soon discovered that this means rice is the perfect food in a humid tropical climate — a siesta in the afternoon is a much better idea than rushing around in the heat.

To Steam Rice

The Balinese are passionate about their rice and an entire meal can be spoiled by inferior quality or by incorrect cooking. A fluffy, separate grain is essential, and this requires steaming. I find that the concept of steaming rice is often new to the people who attend my cooking classes but it really is the only way to achieve a perfect grain. When rice is boiled, even with the absorption method, it becomes what the Balinese call *bubur*, or rice porridge.

Generally, Balinese rice needs to be cleaned of small stones and dust and this requires winnowing. The next step is to wash it and soak it for maybe half an hour.

After straining the rice, it is then steamed either in a traditional steamer or an aluminium pot, above boiling water. A funnel is made in the centre of the rice for the steam to escape and then the process begins. After approximately 30 minutes of steaming, the rice and remaining water from the rice steamer are mixed together in a separate container for the rice to absorb all the liquid and its goodness. The rice is then steamed again for another 20–30 minutes, or until it is cooked and fluffy.

Electric Rice Cooker Method

Electric rice cookers are worth their weight in gold as they can cook an amazing amount of rice in a relatively short time. I have a wonderful relationship with my rice cooker, resulting in perfect rice every time. Mine also has a heat setting allowing the rice to be reheated at mealtimes.

1. First, select your rice. Ketut says it is not necessary to wash Australian rice as it's already sparkling clean. I always use short-grain Australian rice because I prefer its soft, rounded belly, but any other variety will do. It is good standard rice with a subtle fragrance, making it suitable for dishes ranging from *nasi goreng* to yellow rice and *bubur*.

2. Place the amount of rice you want to use in the cooker. Generally 50 g–75 g (1½ oz–2½ oz) per person is enough.

3. Top with fresh water up to the first finger joint, although I always add a little less so it remains dry. The last thing you want is soggy rice. Then turn on the cooker. Against instructions, I always take the lid off quickly after 10 minutes (don't do this if your model turns off automatically at this point) and give the rice a little stir to let it know I haven't forgotten it. Then I replace the lid and wait for it to continue cooking. If the rice is too dry and the machine has turned off, I add extra boiling water, replace the lid and leave it to be absorbed. The only thing you can do wrong with these cookers is to add too much water, but you'll soon

identify how much is needed. Become friends with your rice cooker and you'll never fail.

Nasi Kuning
Fragrant yellow rice

The first time I saw *nasi kuning* was when I was living on Monkey Forest Road in 1985 with my friend Jo. It was her birthday and I decided to surprise her with something special as we had been away from home for four months. So I visited my brother-in-law the day before and asked if he could make a large cake for the day. I explained that I wanted something grand and colourful and left it up to him. The next day I returned to pick up the cake I had ordered. There, perched on a painted wooden pedestal, was a huge cone of yellow rice. Its peak was covered with a banana leaf and its base was decorated with bright red chillies that looked like spidery flowers, carved tomatoes in the shape of luscious red roses, sprigs of lemon basil and fried peanuts. 'This is a Balinese birthday cake,' said my brother-in-law proudly. I looked at the colourful mountain of rice and felt a little nervous that Jo might not share his excitement. Somehow, I'd been expecting a chocolate birthday cake with candles and writing on top. I hadn't realised that the Balinese don't actually celebrate their birthdays. But when I presented the golden offering to Jo at dinnertime, she was ecstatic. 'How beautiful,' she cried. I was so relieved.

Nasi kuning is my favourite rice dish and much of its magic relies on the combination of fragrant gingers and aromatic leaves. Flecked with fried shallots, fresh lemon basil, heavenly torch ginger and chilli, the clean fresh flavours of this golden-yellow rice make it food for the gods. *Nasi kuning* is part of the ceremonial menu enjoyed on the day after *Hari Saraswati*, called *Banyu Pinaruh*. Smoked duck and a variety of side dishes make up the complete menu.

FOR SOAKING THE RICE
>   *1 heaped tablespoon chopped turmeric*
>   *1/2 cup water*
>   *1 1/2 cups white rice*

FOR STEAMING WITH THE RICE

    4 kaffir lime leaves
    1 pandan leaf, tied in a knot
    2 stalks lemongrass, bruised
    5 salam leaves

SUNA-CEKOH

    3 tablespoons chopped turmeric
    4 candlenuts
    10 cloves garlic
    2 tablespoons chopped kencur
    3 tablespoons cooking oil

TO MIX WITH THE STEAMED RICE

    3 teaspoons sambal goreng (see recipe, page 200)
    7 kaffir lime leaves, shredded
    3 tablespoons fried shallots
    2 tablespoons suna-cekoh
    3 calamondin limes, halved
    2 tablespoons shredded lemon basil
    2 tablespoons torch ginger petals, finely sliced
    1/4 teaspoon salt

Place the fresh turmeric and 1/2 cup of water in a blender and blend on high speed or blend 1/2 teaspoon powdered turmeric with the water.

Place the rice and turmeric water in a large bowl and add extra water to cover the rice. Set aside for 10 minutes or until the rice is golden yellow in colour.

Place water and rice in a steamer and bring to the boil. Drain the soaking rice and mix with the lime leaves, pandan leaves, bruised lemongrass and salam leaves. Place in the rice steamer and cook until dry and fluffy. Otherwise, place the rice and leaves in a rice cooker and cover with less than a thumb of water (to account for the earlier soaking).

For the *suna-cekoh*, grind the turmeric, candlenuts, garlic and *kencur* into a paste. Otherwise, place these ingredients in the bowl of a food processor and blend on a high speed until it becomes a fragrant, golden-yellow paste. Add water if necessary.

(Note: If you have trouble getting *kencur*, I have successfully replaced it with galangal in this recipe.)

Heat the oil in a wok and fry the *suna-cekoh* paste on a low–medium heat, stirring the spice paste vigorously to prevent burning. Add water if necessary. Fry the paste for at least 3 minutes or until it appears curdled. It should be glossy and fragrant. Set aside to cool.

Place the steamed yellow rice in a large bowl and remove the pandan leaves, lime leaves, lemongrass and salam. Mix the steamed rice with the final seasonings: *sambal goreng*, kaffir lime, fried shallots, *suna-cekoh*, lemon basil, torch ginger and sea salt.

Check seasonings, remembering to balance sweet, sour, salty and spicy.

Garnish with extra fried shallots.

Serves 4–6.

Nasi Goreng
Fried rice

Nasi goreng is served in just about every restaurant in Indonesia but its ingredients vary from island to island. In Bali, *nasi goreng* is tossed in a vivid, almost iridescent red sauce. It's a nourishing way of using up yesterday's rice and even the kids love it!

2 tablespoons oil
100 g (3½ oz) chicken, finely chopped
3 small red shallots, finely chopped
5 cloves garlic, finely chopped
¼ leek, finely chopped
½ large red chilli, trimmed, de-seeded and chopped
1 cup steamed rice
½ cup finely chopped cabbage
½ cup choi sum chopped into 3 cm (1 in) pieces
1 tablespoon tomato sauce
½ teaspoon vinegar
2 teaspoons soy sauce
2 teaspoons kecap manis
½ teaspoon fish sauce
salt and black pepper, to taste
1 tablespoon fried shallots

Heat the oil in a wok over a medium flame. Fry the chicken in the oil until it shrinks or for about 2 minutes. If there is too much water from the chicken, remove the chicken, drain the liquid, wipe the wok and add the same amount of oil again. Reheat, add the chicken then the finely chopped shallots and garlic. Toss around for 20 seconds. Add the leek and chilli. Mix thoroughly, keeping the food moving to prevent it sticking to the wok. Add the steamed rice with the vegetables, followed by the sauces and vinegar. Mix and toss. Keep tossing until the vegetables are wilted and the rice is thoroughly heated. Check seasonings.

Serve topped with fried shallots or chopped spring onion.

Makes one serve.

Bubur Ayam
Chicken porridge

This is a very simple nourishing rice porridge that we always eat at home when we're sick. The epitome of comfort food, *bubur* soothes a delicate tummy, helps fight off colds or flu and generally makes you feel better. When the children were babies, I fed them *bubur* every day, adding seasonal vegetables, tofu or meat. Similar in texture to risotto, it makes a wonderful creamy, hearty and sustaining breakfast, lunch or dinner. It's also delicious served plain with a curry sauce and *urab*, a warm salad of cooked greens, roasted coconut, sambal and lime.

100 gm (3½ oz) chicken or half a chicken thigh
1 cup white rice
1 stalk lemongrass, bruised and tied into a knot
2 salam leaves
1 large slice of turmeric
3 cups water
1 teaspoon sea salt or to taste
½ cup carrot, julienne
1 cup spinach or choi sum, washed and chopped coarsely into bite-size lengths
1 tablespoon fried shallots

Chop the chicken into small pieces. Otherwise, if using chicken thigh, leave it whole.

Put the rice, chicken thigh, lemongrass, salam leaves, turmeric, water and salt in a medium-sized saucepan and bring to the boil. Lower the heat and simmer for about 10 minutes or until the rice is soft and creamy, stirring occasionally.

Add the carrot and simmer for 1 minute. Stir in the spinach and turn off after 30 seconds. Set aside for 1 minute and then serve.

Garnish with fried shallots.

Serves 2–4.

Precious jewels

THE MAIN INGREDIENTS IN
BALINESE COOKING

Why, it is just like taking betel — the first time, it is hot to the lips,
But there is no doubt that the next time it, instead, becomes delightful . . .

PARTHAYANA, THE JOURNEYING OF PARTHA

The Spices

If rice is the heart of Balinese cooking, then spices are its soul. Steeped in their own fascinating history, they are the foundation upon which the local cuisine is built. Purple-red shallots, delicate miniature garlic, fragrant earthy gingers, sunripe chillies, dried aromatic seeds and nuts are the essential spices in every Balinese kitchen. They hold a silent grace that speaks of power and vitality and, like precious jewels, are stored in a special place: in the dark in an aerated container.

Every morning, the deliberate rhythm of the mortar and pestle grinding fresh spices can be heard coming from the depths of the kitchen. Body, mind and soul are energised as we pound the luscious red of chilli, the sweet scent of coriander seeds, the warm orange glow of turmeric, musky nutmeg and aromatic peppercorns into a delicious paste. The refreshing citrus fragrance of lemongrass always makes me smile and the subtle note of torch ginger warms my heart. The root spices such as turmeric, galangal, resurrection lily and ginger are like a grandma's hands, wise and well worn. They are ancient seasonings that have blessed many cultures and carry with them a thousand years of memories and magic. They firmly embrace other spices with their flavour, colour and texture, to create a magic sensation that transcends language.

Just as fire ignites offerings, so it is the same for spices. The volcanic stone is the essential element that brings these vibrant ingredients to life: through gentle bruising and grinding, hard seeds, herbs and fibrous spices are transformed into a powerful paste. Hot oil then releases their fragrance and flavour and water develops their intensity. Like a favourite tonic, a perfectly balanced spice paste nourishes the entire being.

For the making of spice pastes and ceremonial food, piles of spices are chopped with handcrafted knives to a deliberate rhythm that echoes an ancient beat. This primal paste relies on a balance of aromatic pungent spices which represent all that grows from the soil to the sky, the magic that lies beneath and above. Carefully selected and blended, the bitter, sweet, salty, sour, spicy and astringent flavours meet in dynamic harmony to form the basis of these sacred dishes. The success of the communal meal that follows lies in this balance, for the spirit of the preparation is ingested with each bite.

The careful cooking of spices is necessary not only for the complete development of flavours but also for easier digestion. In my cooking classes I always suggest students keep frying the spices to a point after the fragrance is released and the paste appears curdled or separated on the surface. This can often take longer than you might imagine, but be patient as correct cooking will result in a heavenly fullness of flavour that makes all the difference to your food. Spices are raw organic matter and contact with the hot oil brings them to life.

I watch my children sitting beside their father as he carefully chops spices for ceremonies and marvel at this opportunity for them to absorb this ancient art. From an early age, the Balinese learn about spices, and my children already understand that turmeric heals cuts and bruises, that ginger soothes a sore throat, onion cools the body, and that all these ingredients put together create the food they love. A fragrant golden curry, or Asian spinach with a handful of chillies, is their favourite food and so the learning process continues as their palates are fine-tuned. Their education in the subtlety of taste, colour and texture develops constantly in a culture where food is an expression of religion.

Spices have healing powers that restore body and soul, powers that are magically released as soon as they are ground into a paste. Used in herbal tonics, spices purify the blood, cleanse the liver, assist circulation and help maintain good health. For the Balinese, their food is their medicine, and eating sensibly and moderately is of paramount importance. Their preference for fresh natural flavours demands that all ingredients are bought only in small quantities, to get maximum flavour. Spices are bought throughout the week and seasonal produce is bought daily. In addition to their healing properties, spices are also powerful food preservatives. This explains why a Balinese curry can be kept outside the fridge all day without spoiling. A jackfruit curry will taste more delicious the next day, even after sitting in a warm kitchen all night.

Most of the spices used in Balinese cooking are now available in other countries fresh throughout the year. For maximum flavour, always buy these ingredients in small quantities as they deteriorate quickly. Pay homage to your spices by storing them in clean jars, or in the fridge. That little extra effort is always worth it. If you find that you have overdone the spices and your mouth is on fire, a good way to cool it down is to eat some plain steamed rice, drink a mouthful of sweet tea, or even swallow a teaspoon of sugar.

Base Wangen: The Fragrant Seeds and Nuts

Candlenut: Kemiri
Aleurites moluccana
Obtained from the candleberry tree, this creamy-coloured nut is related to the macadamia and similar in appearance. Used as a

thickening agent to hold spices together, it is soft, oily and easy to work into a paste. It is one of the few nuts that should not be eaten raw, as its high oil content renders it a natural laxative. Some people also say it is poisonous if taken in large quantities. Candlenut is rich in proteins, calories and fats and has a pleasant mild flavour.

Mixed with cotton and copra, these nuts are still used to make candles in certain parts of Java, hence the name. Australian Aborigines used to thread the nuts onto sharp sticks, tie them to trees and light them.

Substitute: Macadamias, almonds, cashews.

Cloves: Cengkeh
Eugenia caryophyllata

Clove trees generally grow in the cooler mountain areas of Bali, near the coffee plantations. These beautiful slim trees have bright green and pink leaves studded with clusters of clove buds, which are dried out for further use. Cloves are not used frequently in Balinese cooking; in fact, their intense camphor-like fragrance and powerful flavour is more prized in the Indonesian cigarettes known as *kretek*. Smoking these crackling cigarettes leaves your mouth tingling with a sweet freshness that softens the tobacco flavour. A Balinese told me that a clove cigarette smoked while drinking a strong cup of *kopi Bali* or Balinese coffee supposedly has no damaging effect on the health, as one counteracts the other.

Coriander Seeds: Ketumbar
Coriandrum sativum

Related to parsley, the refreshing orange flavour of coriander is a main ingredient in curries and may even be used as a substitute for pepper. The whole seeds, freshly ground, are far superior to the powdered variety and should be bought only in small quantities. Coriander is one of the ingredients used in *boreh*, a Balinese herbal paste that warms the body and helps alleviate congestion.

Coriander leaves are not used in Balinese cooking.

Nutmeg: Pala
Myristica fragrens

A native of Indonesia, nutmeg has a powerful bittersweet flavour that cools the tongue, aids digestion and liver function, prevents discoloration of the skin and scar formation. I read somewhere that it also cures madness; on the other hand, nutmeg is also said to be highly poisonous because it contains myristicin and elemicin, both toxic narcotic substances — all of which makes you wonder if an untimely death is the cure for insanity. When taken in large quantities, nutmeg is a powerful hallucinogenic; when taken in small quantities, it helps you sleep, and in Ayurvedic medicine is prescribed for insomnia. In Bali, fresh nutmeg is available at the market, either loose or still in its shell. It is mainly used with beef and pork and in curries. The Monkey Forest in Sangeh in north-west Bali is made up of tall leafy nutmeg trees.

Substitute: Dried nutmeg.

Pepper: Merica
Piper nigrum

Pepper was one of the first spices ever used in cooking. It was an important article of trade in early times, and spurred Christopher Columbus to make his journey to India, although he ended up in the New World by mistake. Prized as a food preservative, pepper enhances any food, stimulates the appetite, and alleviates digestive ailments and colds as well as constipation. The Balinese ceremonial dish of lawar is a powerful pungent explosion of black, white, sometimes fresh green and long pepper. It's a great example of how ancient Balinese food probably tasted, before the introduction of the chilli in the sixteenth century.

In everyday cooking, white pepper is more commonly used. White pepper is obtained by removing the matured outer layer of the peppercorn. Many people say white pepper is hotter than black pepper, but black pepper is prized for its unmistakable aroma. Fresh green pepper has a refreshing pungency similar to fresh chilli and green capsicum. All these peppers come from the same tropical vine. In general, the pepper in Indonesia is sweeter and more fragrant than that available in Australian supermarkets. When I smell the bags of black and white pepper in my cupboard, their cinnamon–clove scent always overwhelms me. It's as if all these spices are related somehow.

Long Pepper: Tabiabun Lenge
Piper retrofractum
This is another favourite in traditional Balinese cooking. In the Balinese language, *tabia* translates as chilli and *bun* means vine. This tropical climbing plant is usually seen in the villages and even grows on our stone fence at home. The fresh long pepper is similar to a small chilli in appearance, with a bubbly texture which, when dried, looks like a miniature long black pine-cone. Long pepper is hotter, sweeter and more aromatic than black pepper, with a musky pungency that is redolent of cinnamon, cloves and nutmeg.

Sesame Seeds: Wijen
Sesamum indicum
Sesame is a native to Indonesia, India and tropical Africa and is one of the world's oldest seeds. When ground, it works as a thickening agent while adding that subtle sweet sesame flavour. It is a key ingredient in *base wangen* and seldom used on its own. For Balinese cooking, the organic unhulled seeds are preferred. Sesame is high in calcium.

Substitute: Tahini paste.

Base Bebungkilan: The Rhizomes and Roots

Galangal: Laos
Alpinia galanga
A member of the ginger family and native to Java, this aromatic rose-coloured root has a eucalyptus–lemon fragrance reminiscent of pine needles. Its main purpose is to mask strong flavours and aromas, and it is considered the natural partner to seafood. When we make fresh seaweed salad, we always add grated roasted galangal to tone down the bite of the ocean. It also gives meat and vegetables a cleaner, more delicate flavour and fragrance. When

fully matured, the root is woodier and becomes stronger in flavour, so buy small quantities and use it as soon as possible.

Fresh galangal is readily available in most Asian food stores and many supermarkets.

Substitute: Frozen, dried or powdered galangal.

Ginger: Jahe
Zingiber officinale
Possibly originating in China, ginger is one of the world's most wonderful spices. Its clean spicy lemon flavour adds a refreshing pungency to just about all Asian cuisines. Praised for its medicinal properties, ginger aids digestion and alleviates stomach disorders and sore throats. Its warming soothing calmative qualities help ease nausea caused by morning sickness and motion sickness.

Substitute: ginger powder.

Resurrection Lily: Kencur
Kaempferia galanga
Resurrection lily is a highly fragrant plant root or rhizome which is much smaller than galangal and reminiscent of camphor. Its perfumed musky vigour adds a distinctive taste to Balinese food; when combined with garlic, turmeric and candlenut, it makes a delicious seasoning known as *suna-cekoh*. The fresh root has a thin brown skin, similar to a potato, with a creamy white flesh. The small dark green glossy leaves are a popular dish when blanched and combined with grated coconut and chilli. Resurrection lily is known as *pro hom* in Thai cooking, and otherwise called aromatic ginger, white turmeric or zeodary. Throughout this book, I refer to it as *kencur*. Store fresh resurrection lily in a cool dark place, otherwise buy dried or powdered *kencur* in small quantities only.

Substitute: Frozen, dried or powdered *kencur*.

Turmeric: Kunyit
Curcuma domestica
Turmeric is a bright yellow root obtained from the rhizome of a plant from the lily family. Native to Southeast Asia, it is a mild warm spice that gives curries a dazzling orange colour, and also

your clothes if you are not careful! The flavour is earthy, but similar to mustard with a clean lemony fragrance. Powdered turmeric cannot match the full flavour and vibrant colour of fresh turmeric. The round central body of the root is affectionately known as the mother because it has the strongest flavour and most intense colour — required characteristics for any mother. This part of the root is prized for herbal tonics. The shoots are called the children, and both these and the mother are used for everyday cooking. Turmeric is used in medicines for skin disorders, and cosmetics, and is also one of the principal ingredients in *jamu*, due to its magical health-giving properties.

Substitute: frozen or dried turmeric.

The Shoots

Torch Ginger Shoot/Torch Ginger Flower:
Bongkot/Kecicang
Nicolaia elatior

Torch ginger is an especially tall wild ginger with long green leaves and glorious rosy-pink flowers that look similar to waratahs when in bloom. Both the young shoot and bud are used in cooking. The juicy young shoot can be easily ground into a paste, or bruised and added whole like lemongrass. The bud is eaten raw like a herb in certain sambals or fragrant rice, or added as an aromatic to curries and soups. It has an intriguing flavour which is redolent of rose petals and shallots combined, and is particularly delicious with seafood, liver and rice-field eels.

Lemongrass: Sereh
Cymbopogon citratus

Native to Southeast Asia, lemongrass is a tropical grass with a bulbous root and thin blade-like leaves. Related to citronella, it has a distinctive lemon flavour that blends magically with all the other spices, especially when added to soups, curries, rice puddings and sambals. The white part or stalk is mainly used, up to 10 centimetres (4 inches) from the base. It can be ground with a multitude of spices or chopped with a cleaver for certain sambals; or it can be used purely as an aromatic by bruising a 20-

centimetre piece with the back of a knife and tying it into a loose knot. This helps to release the fragrant essential oils contained in the juicy bulb and inner stalk of this most precious ingredient, and can be easily removed before serving. I call lemongrass the 'happy herb' as its refreshing uplifting aroma always makes me smile. It is naturally sweet and makes a delicious tea. Lemongrass cools the body and alleviates a hot tummy or Bali belly, as well as candida and eczema, and makes a wonderful tonic against colds and flus. It is also excellent for the complexion and a good source of vitamins A and D.

Substitute: Lemon peel.

The Sour Flavours

Calamondin/Musk Lime: Limau Kesturi
Citrofortunella micrcarpa

In Bali, the musk lime is smaller than a golf ball and has an exceptionally fragrant lime–tangerine flavour. It is known as calamondin, or kalamansi, and is sweeter and juicier than its Thai counterpart. The skin is smooth like a Tahitian lime and used mainly when it is still green.

Substitute: Cumquats.

Kaffir Lime
Citrus hystrix

Kaffir lime leaves, known as *daun jeruk purut* or *daun lemu,* are dark green and glossy and are added whole like bay leaves to soups and curries, to give the same distinctive refreshing flavour as the fruit. In sambals, salads and satay, the leaves are finely shredded to evenly disperse their wonderful flavour. I always say, 'When in doubt, add more kaffir lime,' because of the luscious uplifting flavour of these tiny leaves and fruit. Ketut always grumbles that I add too much. When I first found frozen kaffir lime leaves in Melbourne several years ago, I thought I was halfway to heaven. Nowadays, you can even find them fresh in greengrocers and supermarkets. The leaves are also available in dried or frozen form. Both leaves and fruit are very high in vitamin C.

Tamarind: Lunak/Asam
Tamarindus indica

Tamarind is the soft brown pulp extracted from the pods of the tamarind tree and sold in blocks. Known as the 'date of the East', its aroma is not unlike that of a date but the flavour is like a tangy apricot. In Singaraja, North Bali, the main avenue is lined with tall shady tamarind trees and in the afternoon, you'll often see the locals clambering into the branches for these sweet-sour treats. My children love to eat them by breaking open the small suede-like brown pods and sucking out the tangy soft pulp inside.

The delightfully sour and refreshing taste of tamarind transforms curries and soups, but is most popular in the snack called *rujak*. Tamarind is said to disguise the strong odour of fish and duck, while also tenderising strong meats. My sister-in-law always adds a sizeable chunk to her famous porcupine curry to disguise the gamey flavour of the dark meat. It can be soaked in water and then strained, so only the juice is used, although in our household we tend to just throw it in, seeds and all. When buying tamarind, choose the soft wet variety with seeds intact.

Tamarind is very high in vitamin C, iron and fibre. It is said to purify the blood and is used in tonics in Indonesia for women after they have given birth. It cools the body, therefore is an antidote to heat stroke, and is effective against mouth and throat infections.

Substitute: Cooked rhubarb stalks, dried apricots, lemon juice, tomatoes.

The Sweet and Salty Flavours

Shrimp Paste: Terasi/Belacan

Shrimp paste, or *terasi*, is what I call the parmesan cheese of Balinese cooking! This pungent seasoning is essential to Southeast Asian cooking and is made mainly of fermented crustaceans. Shrimp paste blends miraculously with all the other local spices and has a richer, mellower flavour than fish sauce. And, of course, where there is shrimp paste there will always be chilli. These two dynamic ingredients are culinary partners and go hand in hand in every dish; they are what I call the Romeo and Juliet or Rama and Sita of Balinese cooking.

It's important to remember that shrimp paste is considered raw when you buy it and is either fried or, if incorporated as a raw ingredient, grilled first over an open flame like a satay. The Balinese version is muddy brown in colour and particularly intense, unlike the milder pink Javanese version. It is used like salt and often mixed together with salt. Store it wrapped in foil in a glass jar and keep it in the refrigerator. Don't forget to open the windows while cooking!

Shrimp paste is rich in calcium, protein and B vitamins.

Substitute: fish sauce, anchovy paste.

Soy Sauce: Kecap Asin/Kecap Manis

Soy sauce was introduced to Indonesia by the Chinese and there are two types used in Balinese cooking to give added life to famous dishes, such as *nasi goreng, mie goreng* and a whole host of sautéed vegetable dishes. *Kecap asin* — *asin* meaning salty — is a dark soy sauce. *Kecap manis* — *manis* meaning sweet — is a dark rich sweet soy sauce with a distinctive molasses-like flavour and thick pouring consistency. It is perhaps more popular than *kecap asin* and is certainly delicious in marinades, stir-fried vegetables and sambals. It's what I call the balsamic vinegar of Indonesian cuisine.

Substitute: For *kecap manis*, mix soy sauce with brown sugar.

Palm Sugar: Gula Bali, Gula Merah

This delicious caramel-flavoured natural sugar is prepared in people's backyards all over Bali; it is made by extracting the nectar from the flower bud of the same palm tree from which *arak*, the local palm wine, is made. It is an amazing process to watch, and a labour of love as the return for the immense hard work is very low. Once the nectar has been collected from the lofty heights of the wavering tree, it is boiled down to make a thick golden syrup. To taste this warm freshly brewed fudge-like sugar on a smooth banana leaf is my idea of nirvana. I always laugh at the all-too-familiar Western query of 'Isn't it bad for you?' 'Nothing's bad for you here!' I reply.

Palm sugar comes in varying colours, depending on what is added to it. In Bali, it is mixed with jackfruit wood and lime powder: the wood adds a deep yellow colour and the lime kills any bitterness while also adding calcium. It is sold in solid lumps, the size and shape depending on whether it has been set in halved coconut shells or pieces of bamboo. Even a strong dose of chilli will lose its intensity with the addition of palm sugar, and with sour ingredients it forms a perfect marriage that is the basis of many Asian dishes. In fact, palm sugar is what I call the magic ingredient. How many times have you made a curry to find something is missing? Nine times out of ten, a teaspoon of palm sugar is all you need to make the difference. Palm sugar is an important balancing agent because of its capacity to heighten and harmonise a multitude of flavours.

In Ayurvedic medicine it is hailed as the complete vitamin tablet as it contains all sorts of minerals, some of the B vitamins, iron and calcium. Palm sugar is lower in calories than white sugar and not as sweet.

Substitute: Brown sugar, golden syrup.

Sea Salt: Garam

Undeniably the world's first seasoning, fresh sea salt is the only salt used in Balinese cooking. White, flaky and tasting like the ocean, it is produced in coastal areas around Bali. In Goa Lawah, East Bali, you can see the small salt-making huts and coconut-trunk drying pans from the road. There, in the morning sun, black salt is hand-raked and processed in what is known as the 'agricultural technique'. This is where I like to buy my sea salt. Its gentle quality means that up to three times more sea salt is necessary for cooking than table salt; because of its coarse nature, the larger quantities also assist the grinding of spices. Sea salt is prized not only for its natural, almost sweet flavour but also for the minerals it provides. It is said that fresh sea salt contains up to eighty-four minerals, all of which the body requires. We add sea salt to sweet dishes as well as savoury, like black rice pudding, to enhance flavour, and even coconut milk is bland without it. As Ian Hemphill states in his book, *Spice Notes*: 'Salt performs the essential function of maintaining the equilibrium of body fluids, a balance so critical that one can be at greater risk from dehydration from the lack of salt than from a shortage of water.'

The Hottest Flavour

Chilli: Cabe
Capsicum annum

Mexican Indians had been cultivating chillies for thousands of years before Columbus discovered them in the New World while on his quest for black pepper. But it was the Portuguese who introduced the chilli to India around 1560, where it was received as affectionately as an embrace from a Bollywood heart-throb. And from there it worked its way eastwards across the oceans and eventually into Balinese cuisine. Prior to the arrival of the chilli, gingers and pepper were the main heating elements in Balinese cooking. Now, these vibrant bursts of almost citrus-lime flavour transform any dish, while adding a shot of intense heat, fragrance and heart-warming colour, making them a vital ingredient. I heard my five-year-old nephew protest one day that his lunch at our house wasn't delicious because it wasn't spicy enough.

The chilli has an overall liveliness and harmony that forms the basis of Asian food. The ripe red chillies are rich in carotene and vitamin A, and both the fresh red and green varieties are rich in vitamin C. Chilli also contains a natural chemical known as capsaicin, which is responsible for releasing endorphins in the brain — our body's natural painkillers — and is the basis for claims that the chilli is addictive. Eating a spicy meal gives you a natural high, which in turn relaxes the body and reduces stress levels. Chilli is also a powerful anti-oxidant, stimulating the palate and appetite. It thins the blood, therefore enhancing blood circulation, and aids digestion. It is said that chilli speeds up the metabolism, which is why Deepak Chopra states that eating chilli can actually help you lose weight. It seems that chilli provides something like an inner body workout, and when eaten in large quantities, an inner cleansing too. Capsaicin is also used for sinus treatment.

The heat of the sun determines the intensity of the chilli and it is said that the fruit growing on the north side of the shrub will be hotter than those on the south side. Chillies cause you to sweat profusely by opening up the pores of the skin, which in turn cools you down, explaining why people in hotter climates enjoy hot food. This is another example of Mother Nature's ingenuity. In fact, I've decided that Mother Nature must surely be Balinese as she seems to have thought of all that's necessary to maintain good health here.

Three types of chilli are eaten in Bali: *tabia Lombok*, *tabia biasa* or *cabe* and *tabia kerinyi*. *Tabia Lombok* is my all-time favourite chilli; I adore its sweet red capsicum flavour and glorious red colour. Nowadays, I add it to just about everything, from homemade mayonnaise to pasta sauces. The seeds of the *Lombok* chilli must be discarded, as they are large and hard to digest. Some people even say they are poisonous and can cause appendicitis. To remove the seeds, roll the whole chilli between the palms of your hands; you will feel them loosening instantly. Then all you need to do is slice off the top and tip them out. Otherwise, slit the chilli lengthwise and scrape out the seeds with the tip of a small knife, or wash them away under a cold tap. *Tabia biasa* or *cabe* is a medium-sized chilli with a wonderful flavour and moderate heat. For the sweetest, most satisfying flavour, I combine *Lombok* with *tabia biasa*. The smallest variety of chilli, known as *tabia kerinyi* or bird's-eye chilli, is the hottest, and vital for powerful sambals. Unlike *tabia Lombok*, the smaller chillies do not require seeding, although if you remove the seeds the effect will be milder. In general, the smaller the chilli, the bigger the bite. Red chillies are always sweeter than green ones and often hotter, and it is said that the long pointy chillies are usually hotter than the round ones.

Always wash your hands thoroughly after use and avoid touching your face and eyes. If you happen to get a chilli sting, rub oil onto the inflamed area.

Substitute: Dried chillies, chilli sauce such as *sambal oeleck* or *sambal bajak*.

Additional Flavours: Herbs and Leaves

Hoary Basil/Lemon Basil: Kemangi
Ocimum citriadorum

Kemangi, hoary basil or lemon basil, is a sweet minty lime-scented herb redolent of lemongrass. It adds the finishing touch to fragrant yellow rice and seafood, and completes the arrangement of accompaniments for the smoked duck feast on the day after Saraswati Day. It also makes a very refreshing herbal tea.

Substitute: Lemon balm.

Pandan Leaf/Screwpine Leaf: Daun pandan harum
Pandanus odorus

Called the 'vanilla of the East', this rich green blade-like leaf adds a subtle flavour and distinctive fragrance to all sweet dishes and is the perfect culinary partner to palm sugar. For many people, the sweet leafy aroma of pandan is the scent of Bali. Finely shredded, it adorns the daily offerings that are placed everywhere, even on the dashboards of taxis or handlebars of bicycles for hire. Left whole and tied into loose bundles, these long dark green spear-shaped leaves add a distinctive flavour and fragrance to desserts such as black rice pudding. Rice steamed with pandan leaves has a similar redolence to jasmine rice. In the villages, a soothing aromatic tea is made by boiling pandan leaves with water. I remember becoming addicted to the coffee at one of our previous restaurants, and found out later that it was the addition of pandan leaf to the water that made it extra delicious and intriguing. Pandan is a cooling ingredient that assists in the treatment of internal inflammations, urinary infections, bleeding gums and skin disease.

Substitute: Pandan essence.

Salam Leaf: Daun Salam
Eugenia polyantha

This deep green leaf is a favourite in Indonesian cooking. Added to just about everything, it has a clean citrusy forest-scented flavour and aroma that marries delicately with all other ingredients. We generally use the fresh leaf, but I've noticed in other homes that the leaf is hung in bundles in the kitchen to dry until it turns a silvery black colour. In our household, the rice is steamed with salam leaves every day, giving it a herby freshness and fragrance. When the children are sick, we always make them rice boiled with salam leaves. Sometimes we add a little chopped spinach to the simmering brew for extra flavour, all topped with a handful of fried shallots.

The salam leaf has a similar flavour to the Indian curry leaf, although is larger in size. It is usually available in dried form at Asian grocers, but if you can't find it, leave it out rather than using bay leaves as a substitute, because these are too strong in flavour.

Basa Genep
Traditional spice paste

Basa genep is a sacred combination of spices and other select ingredients ground together to create a unique aroma, taste and colour. This lively multi-flavoured paste is the essence of many traditional dishes such as Balinese satay, smoked duck and suckling pig. It is simple to make and can be stored in the refrigerator for up to one week.

3 small red shallots, chopped
1 tablespoon chopped ginger
1¹/₂ tablespoons chopped galangal
1 tablespoon chopped turmeric
2 teaspoons chopped kencur
1 teaspoon coriander seeds
1 teaspoon whole black pepper
3 candlenuts
1 teaspoon sesame seeds
3 cloves garlic
2 large red chillies, trimmed and de-seeded
3 red bird's-eye chillies
¹/₄ teaspoon white pepper
¹/₄ teaspoon ground nutmeg
¹/₃ teaspoon shrimp paste (optional)
2 tablespoons oil
2 tablespoons water

Pound the red shallots, ginger, galangal, turmeric and *kencur* with the other ingredients in a mortar and pestle until paste-like and juicy. Otherwise, place the coriander, black pepper, candlenuts and sesame seeds into the container of a coffee grinder and grind until fine. Add these to all the remaining spice ingredients and place in the bowl of an electric blender or food processor and process on high speed until puréed, adding water and oil if necessary. You might need to stop and start the machine to push the spices down around the blade.

Basa genep should be fragrant, deep golden-yellow and of a thick moist paste-like consistency.

To store, cover with a thin film of oil and plastic wrap and store in the refrigerator.

Makes approximately ⅓ cup.

Base Wangen
The fragrant seeds and nuts

This combination of fragrant seeds and nuts is used in all ceremonial foods and many other everyday dishes. This combination is unique to Bali and varies slightly from region to region.

1 teaspoon black peppercorns
¹/₂ teaspoon white peppercorns
4 candlenuts
5 long peppers (or 1 teaspoon black peppercorns extra)
¹/₂ teaspoon ground nutmeg
¹/₄ teaspoon sesame seeds
1 clove
1 teaspoon coriander seeds

Grind all the spices in the container of a coffee-grinder or dry spice grinder to a paste. Otherwise, grind in a mortar and pestle. Store in an airtight jar in the refrigerator.

Makes approximately 3 tablespoons.

Suna-Cekoh
Garlic and aromatic ginger seasoning

This is a very popular seasoning in Bali and works particularly well with chicken. It has an earthy flavour and fragrance that can be overpowering, so needs to be balanced with fried shallots, lime and fresh herbs.

6—7 cloves garlic, peeled
3—4 tablespoons chopped fresh turmeric
2 tablespoons chopped fresh kencur
4 candlenuts
3 tablespoons cooking oil

Place the garlic, turmeric, *kencur*, candlenuts and oil in the container of a food processor and blend to a smooth paste. Alternatively, grind in a mortar and pestle until fine. The paste should be a warm golden colour; if not, add more fresh turmeric. Cover and store in the refrigerator. If *kencur* is not available, use fresh galangal instead.

Makes approximately 4 tablespoons.

Gula Merah Cair

Palm sugar syrup

Every couple of days we make a large jug of palm sugar syrup, which is used to drench the coconut crepes that we serve to our guests for breakfast, and also added to just about everything we cook. Syrup is a very effective way of storing palm sugar, as it tends to get too soft in a tropical climate or become too hard in a temperate climate. Try the syrup drizzled on ice-cream or blended in a milkshake.

500 g brown palm sugar
2 cups water
1 pandan leaf or 1 vanilla bean

Put the palm sugar, pandan leaf tied in a knot or vanilla bean and water in a saucepan. Bring to the boil and simmer for approximately 15 minutes, without stirring, until the liquid has reduced by nearly half. The syrup is ready when large bubbles appear on the surface, as when making toffee. While warm, strain into a jug and leave to cool. It will thicken up at this point. The flavour of your syrup will depend on the quality of your palm sugar. Store in the refrigerator.

Makes 1¹/₂ cups.

The Coconut

The ivory coconuts were like uncovered breasts
in the fullness of their beauty.

PARTHAYANA, THE JOURNEYING OF PARTHA

A key element in wedding ceremonies and all offerings, the coconut is a symbol of life and fertility. In the *Bhagavad-Gita*, Krishna explained to Arjuna that the supreme offering to God must consist of leaves, flowers, fruit and water. The coconut represents all of these elements and provides the Balinese with the basis for the blessings of each day's existence. The Balinese say a coconut will never fall on your head because it has three eyes, a testimony of its human quality! Coconut is always one of the ingredients in ceremonial food and is used extensively in Balinese cooking. When roasted and grated, it adds an alluring smoky sweetness to many of my favourite vegetable dishes, and when mixed with water it becomes the creamy gentle coconut milk that adds such a luscious finishing touch to curries, desserts and drinks.

High in proteins, minerals and vitamins, all coconut products contain potassium and natural lecithin while also being an excellent source of fibre. Almost equivalent to a dairy product, the coconut provides the Balinese with milk, oil and cream, as well as nutritious water and the hard flesh of the meat. Assisting in the growth and development of bones and teeth, it contains natural chemicals that protect the immune system. The water or juice of the young green or yellow coconut is especially high in potassium and is a complete dehydration drink which also helps to cool the body, thereby assisting in reducing fevers.

In Bali, newborn babies used to be given young coconut juice as its properties are similar to mother's milk. In isolated tropical areas, young coconuts have been used effectively for intravenous feeding. I always imagine this would be a more pleasing sight for patients in hospital than a plastic bag hanging from its stand.

Substitute for fresh grated coconut: Desiccated or shredded coconut steamed for 10 minutes or mixed with warm water.

Coconut Milk: Santen

The milk is obtained from the grated flesh of the coconut, mixed with warm water and then strained. Freshly pressed coconut milk has a fragrant, delicately sweet and slightly nutty flavour that is far superior to packaged coconut milks. A light coconut milk is generally used in Balinese cooking, as opposed to the coconut creams used in Thai cooking.

When choosing a fresh coconut, make sure it is heavy with juice and that no cracks or wet spots are apparent. The older coconuts usually available in supermarkets are ideal for making coconut milk as they yield the creamiest liquid. To open a fresh coconut, hold it in the palm of your hand and hit it in the centre with the back of a kitchen cleaver. Rotate the coconut and hit it again in the centre. Keep doing this until it cracks open. Discard the old coconut water and place the coconut in a low oven for about 15 minutes; this will help to separate the flesh from the skin. And a pinch of salt is always added to coconut milk to enhance the flavour.

To make fresh coconut milk

1 1/4 cups fresh, grated coconut, tightly packed
1 cup water
1/2 teaspoon sea salt

This recipe makes a lovely creamy milk. If you would like it lighter, just add more water. By hand or in a blender, mix the coconut meat with the water and blend at high speed for about 30 seconds. Strain and squeeze out the milk from the residue. For maximum flavour, knead the meat with 1/3 of the water first and then add the remaining amount. Strain thoroughly. For a vastly superior coconut milk that will be used like fresh cream and not cooked, roast the outer, brown skin of the coconut before grating. You can do this by placing pieces of coconut on a barbecue or under a grill (skin side up) or over an open flame. Cook the coconut until it is black and blistered and then clean the skin as you would burnt toast. Then follow the method for making fresh coconut milk.

Substitute with canned coconut milk, packaged coconut milk and instant coconut milk powder.

Makes 1 cup.

Cooking oil

Coconut Oil: *Minyak*

Coconut oil is the favoured cooking oil in Bali and is often made at home by boiling down coconut milk. It is an unrefined oil that adds a sweet coconut flavour and fragrance to their food, although for some this is not unlike the aroma of certain suntan lotions. Coconut oil is one of the few oils that can be heated to very high temperatures without burning or breaking down, and the hot oil sears food quickly without penetrating it. Smoked duck, suckling pig and sambals rely on the distinctive flavour of coconut oil and just don't taste the same without it. It is the most cooling of the oils and a favourite outside the kitchen too, as skin moisturiser, hair conditioner and to soothe nappy rash or mosquito bites.

Substitute: Canola, sunflower or safflower oil. (Olive oil is not suitable as it has a Mediterranean flavour and a low smoking point.)

Garlic, Onion and Shallots

Garlic: *Bawang Putih*
Allium sativum

In most households, the tiny organic local garlic is used. This purple-tinged bulb is sweeter and gentler than its Western counterpart, with a distinctive fragrance and mellow flavour. Garlic cloves are usually smashed and chopped up with a cleaver or ground into a paste with other spices. It is not necessary to remove the skin from each clove. Garlic is also sometimes deep-fried and added to a dish with deep-fried coconut or other cooked seasonings to give extra flavour.

Garlic is a powerful natural antibiotic which is believed to boost the body's immune system.

Onion: *Bawang Merah*
Allium ascolonicum

The delicate glossy reddish-purple Balinese shallot is a joy to behold. It has a sweet clear flavour and is as delicious raw as it is cooked. Drier in texture than the larger onions, they are more suitable for spice pastes and also for the deep-fried shallots used to garnish most dishes. The smallest of the red shallots are prized by the Balinese as they are the sweetest and driest, and consequently the most expensive. Peeled and finely sliced or ground with other ingredients, they are a vital ingredient in this cuisine. You can make a delicious sambal just by mixing red shallots with chilli, roasted shrimp paste and fresh coconut oil.

Fried Shallots: Bawang Goreng

These crispy golden slivers of shallot are valued for their distinctive sweet flavour and heart-warming fragrance. A handle of fried shallots improves the taste of just about anything, often balancing other ingredients. A serving of steamed rice is usually topped with a few slivers of fried shallots. It is said that they represent the crown of the rice and are placed on top to pay homage to this revered life force. Fried shallots are sold in Asian food stores in sealed bags and plastic jars.

Under the banyan tree

HOME COOKING

For in Bali in those days, people were frank
about life and death,
and they ate meat gracefully,
with an intimate knowledge of where it had come from.

THE PAINTED ALPHABET

Any Balinese will tell you that the most delicious Balinese food is found in a Balinese kitchen, within the cosy walls of the family compound. Second to the home is the *warung*. These casual restaurants can be as basic as a table and bench set up in a bamboo lean-to where simple food is available, or they can be more sophisticated. The system is the same, though, with most of the food being ready prepared. You can choose what you want, or enjoy a freshly cooked *gado-gado* or *rujak* in minutes. The Balinese love to see Westerners eating in these humble establishments. They're always very curious to see if we can tolerate the fire of a sambal or the pungent flavours of a *lawar*.

Under the village banyan tree is usually a culinary hot spot. This huge shady tree, the symbol of Siwa, is often the communal meeting place and centre of town. Here, the older women set up shop and sell steamed rice or rice pudding with assorted seasonings in the mornings or late afternoons. All the food is prepared at home and tastes as good as a Balinese grandma's, sometimes even better. The freshly cooked fare is carried to and from the site on a small wooden table balanced on the head; the homeward run is much easier because all the pots are empty. Trading begins when the small table appears under the banyan tree and is set with old aluminium pots of cooked rice, coconut vegetables, spicy fish, steamed meats and a pungent sambal. A couple of cheap dinner spoons and a dozen chipped bowls are provided for those who want to use them. Otherwise, take away in a plastic bag or a waxy banana leaf is the most popular way to eat.

Bubur, or boiled rice, is an afternoon favourite. When we feel like a special treat we drive to a nearby village to buy *bubur ayam*: soft fragrant boiled rice topped with barbecued chicken mixed with roasted coconut milk. Similar to risotto, it is a gentle creamy dish that gives you energy in the afternoon. The extra depth and aroma provided by the shrimp paste, balanced with just the right amount of turmeric, *kencur* and fresh coconut oil, is more than delicious.

Then there are the food-sellers with the three-wheeled carts. Generally from Java, their speciality is *bakso*, boiled meatballs served in a gentle stock. The Balinese love to snack, so when they hear the sound of spoon tinkling on glass from these mobile food stalls, they rush out with their bowls for an early dinner.

Fragrant soups, roasted sambals, simmered curries and steamed seasonings are the essence of a lively peasant fare that has been shaped by nature's abundant surroundings. For my husband and earlier generations, embodied in this cuisine are memories of happy carefree childhoods and, at times, great hardship. Deep-fried dragonflies is a food that holds the spirit of boyhood and adventure in the rice fields. Peasant food such as steamed rice studded with hard yellow corn, *nasi jagung*, or sweet potato, *nasi sela*, carries with it the memory of the hungry years during the rice famine and the communist coup in the early 1960s. One Balinese woman told me how the sight of *nasi sela* brings tears to her eyes, as it revives painful memories of hardship and suffering at that time. Ketut said that he remembers as a child how agonising it was to eat *nasi jagung*, because the hard corn made his gums bleed where his milk teeth had fallen out. *Nasi sela* is still a favoured rice in Ubud homes and is also sold in the market.

A simple everyday meal is based on rice, the precious grain that feeds body and soul. Vegetables, meat, fish and chilli seasonings are served merely as enhancements. Curries simmered with lemongrass and tamarind, sardines tossed in fiery tomato sauces, spiced corn fritters and crunchy deep-fried baby eel exemplify the rustic style of the local cuisine. Sambal, or chilli sauce, accompanies every meal. Grilled chicken or fish is delicious served with fresh sambal made from red shallots, chilli, glossy lime leaves and lemongrass, and tomato sambal with roasted eggplant is both luscious and appetising.

In my experience, all young Balinese can cook. I marvel at the way every one of them has the chopping and slicing technique of a professional chef. This is such a contrast to my own upbringing in Australia, where most teenagers' cooking skills go no further than opening cans.

The staff who help me with my cooking classes are amazed not only that tourists want to learn about their food, but that they need to be shown such simple things as how to make coconut milk. For them, preparing food is an integral part of their lives, and skills and recipes are learnt from childhood. They also think of the West as being more sophisticated and knowledgeable, and are therefore surprised at the continuing interest in Balinese cuisine. In the beginning, I had to keep reminding my staff that the tourists really would arrive for the class each week.

Balinese food can be easily adapted for vegetarians. Shrimp paste is vital for the authentic taste, but the dishes will still be delicious without it. In general, people here eat very little meat so there is a wide choice of recipes that use only fresh leaves and legumes. One of the main sources of protein for Balinese people is soy products, such as tofu and tempe. This makes their food ideal for vegetarians.

In general, Balinese cooking can be a simple blending of a few ingredients, or a more extensive combination, especially for ceremonial foods and certain curries. Flavours are clean and fresh, utilising seasonal produce selected daily. Central to this cuisine is the careful blending of spices and flavours that reflects the Balinese ideal of harmony and balance in every aspect of life. The preparation of each meal is performed with the same ceremony and care as the making of offerings.

Nasi Campur

Nasi campur is Bali's most famous and treasured dish. The Balinese eat it for every single meal; in fact, the English translation could be said to mean 'breakfast, lunch and dinner', for *nasi campur* is simply rice with a number of side dishes, eaten together from one plate. *Nasi* means steamed rice and *campur* means mixture, so it describes a style of eating rather than an individual dish. There's no official recipe for *nasi campur*: what appears on the plate is determined purely by the seasons and the whim of the individual — whatever's cooked in the kitchen on that particular day. It might include one or two vegetable dishes, sometimes egg, something soupy like jackfruit curry, spicy meat or fish, and of course a sambal. The rice takes centre stage, occupying most of the plate, with a small amount of the other dishes sitting alongside. A spoonful of a spicy sauce over the top makes it even more delicious. The essence of a great *nasi campur* is in the surprise of wonderful flavours that burst forth from each combination. And it is always exciting, as each day presents a different choice.

Any local review of *nasi campur* should really begin at Kedewatan, near Ubud, the home of two famous *warungs* that have been serving *nasi campur* for many years. They are located before the Kupu-kupu Barong Hotel, on the opposite side of the road. Every now and then, my husband goes to the second *warung* on the right for a breakfast of spicy free-range chicken, coconut vegetables, salted egg and sambal. At this quaint little place, the line-up of vehicles outside is as exciting as the food offered: BMWs, Harley-Davidsons, brightly coloured Vespas and Cherokee Jeeps are amongst the holy chariots parked there. While eating with his mates, my husband loves to listen to conversations about rice fields sold, hotels built and business deals gone sour.

A full *nasi campur* here will cost around Rp 10,000 and you can select a drink from the zillions of bottles perched on the thick red and white plastic-covered benches. A selection of crackers and other assorted fare can also be bought and munched on while waiting for the tasty meal. Service is meek, mild and typically Balinese. When I went recently, I chose to sit near the open doorway on a bright red plastic stool and delighted in watching village life saunter past. What a nice way to start the day!

Tum Hati Ayam

Spiced steamed chicken liver in banana leaves

This is a dish that we always make for special occasions at home. Torch ginger ground together with the spices adds a lovely freshness and delicate fragrance.

500 g chicken liver
2 tablespoons sambal goreng (see recipe, page 200)
2 tablespoons suna-cekoh (see recipe, page 180)
2 tablespoons fried shallots
2 kaffir lime leaves shredded
3 salam leaves, chopped
banana leaves
salam leaves for each package

SPICE PASTE

2 stalks lemongrass
1 small torch ginger shoot
1 teaspoon palm sugar
1/2 teaspoon salt

Rinse the liver under cold running water and pat dry with kitchen paper. Pull away any sinews and chop into rough dice. Grind the spices in a mortar and pestle or place in the bowl of a food processor and blend to a paste. Add a tablespoon of water or a little oil from the *sambal goreng* if the mixture is too dry. Otherwise, chop the lemongrass and ginger shoot finely with a cleaver and mix with the palm sugar and salt.

In a large bowl, mix the chopped liver with the spices, *sambal goreng, suna-cekoh,* fried shallots, lime leaves and salam leaves.

Cut the banana leaves into squares approximately 15 cm x 12 cm (6 in x 5 in).

Place a salam leaf on top of the banana leaf and a spoonful of the chopped liver on top of this.

Wrap like an envelope and secure with a toothpick or tie with string. Steam above water for 10 minutes

Serve with steamed rice and *timun mesantan* (see recipe, page 73).

Makes 10 packages.

Urab Pakis

Fern coconut salad

This is the sort of dish you dream about when you're away from Bali. In our household, we eat *urab* nearly every day. This simple combination of seasonal greens, roasted coconut and fried sambal is as common as a summer salad and has the same fresh lively energy. You can use just about any green vegetable or leaf, and we often add legumes such as adzuki or kidney beans and sprouts for an extra nutty flavour and texture.

2 cups boiled or steamed fern leaves (see Note)
1 1/2 cups roasted, grated coconut (see recipe, page 121)
2 tablespoons sambal goreng (see recipe, page 200)
3 kaffir lime leaves, shredded
1 calamondin fruit or kaffir lime
1 tablespoon fried shallots
sea salt, to taste
2—4 tablespoons water

Chop the fern leaves finely. Mix the *sambal goreng*, shredded lime leaves, sliced lime fruit and fried shallots thoroughly with the roasted coconut, bruising the ingredients heartily.

Mix in the leaves.

Add sea salt to taste and a little water to make it juicier if necessary.

Check seasonings and garnish with fried shallots.

Note: This is an edible fern, sometimes known as marsh fern. Spinach is a good substitute.

Serves 4–6.

Ayam Gecok

Grilled chicken with roasted coconut

This is a lovely mellow soupy dish of grilled chicken, subtle spices and roasted coconut milk. Sometimes we buy this in the afternoon under the banyan tree at a neighbouring village and eat it with soft boiled rice porridge. You can simmer large, stew-sized chunks of chicken with the spices as an alternative to pulling the meat into strips.

¹/₂ chicken breast

2 tablespoons oil

1 cup shredded roasted coconut, roasted in the shell for five minutes (optional)

2 kaffir lime leaves

1 kaffir lime fruit

2 tablespoons sambal goreng (see recipe, page 200)

1 tablespoon suna–cekoh (see recipe, page 180)

1¹/₂ teaspoons palm sugar

1 teaspoon sea salt

1 cup roasted coconut milk

salt to taste

¹/₄ teaspoon white pepper

1 tablespoon fried shallots

Grill the chicken until cooked. Set aside to cool.

Heat the oil in a wok over a medium flame. Fry the *suna-cekoh* for 2–3 minutes or until fragrant and the oil sits on the top.

Finely slice the lime leaves by rolling them in a bundle like a cigarette and shredding with a knife. Slice the lime fruit in half.

Mix the shredded coconut with the lime leaves, sambal, *suna-cekoh*, palm sugar and salt, bruising the ingredients to release more flavour.

Pull the cooled chicken into thin pieces and mix with the shredded coconut and spices.

Add the roasted coconut milk and juice of the lime, tossing the fruit into the mixture.

Check seasonings.

Garnish with fried shallots and serve with steamed or soft, boiled rice.

Note: You can also add finely sliced cucumber and mung beans.

Makes 1 cup.

Urab Bulung
Seaweed salad

Just one mouthful of this deep green bubbly squeaky seaweed will take you straight back to your childhood and that sensation of being dumped by a wave at the beach. Sometimes my sister-in-law buys this salad from a *warung* in Denpasar where they grind red chillies into the roasted coconut. Our version is slightly different. It's amazing how a handful of sweet coconut, fragrant galangal, lime leaves, sambal and shallots can weaken the intense ocean flavour of this fresh sea plant.

1 cup fresh seaweed
2 teaspoons roasted, grated galangal (see method below for instructions)
1¹/₂ cups roasted coconut, grated (see instructions, page 121)
2 teaspoons sambal goreng (see recipe, page 200)
1 tablespoon fried shallots
2–3 kaffir lime leaves, shredded
1 calamondin lime, sliced in half
extra shallots for garnish

Wash the seaweed under cold running water and strain. Roast the galangal, skin still on, by sitting it on a piece of foil and grilling it under a pre-heated griller until slightly charred or for 30 seconds. You can also barbecue the galangal over hot coals. Scrape the charred bits off with the back of a knife and grate. Mix the roasted coconut with the *sambal goreng*, fried shallots and shredded lime leaves. Squeeze the fruit and toss it in, leaving it to flavour the coconut. Add the seaweed, taking care not to squash the seaweed bubbles. Check seasonings.

Garnish with extra fried shallots.

Serves 2–4.

Seafood at Goa Lawah

One of my favourite adventures is to drive to Karangasem, East Bali, to eat fresh spicy fish. I fill the car up with children and Balinese friends and we travel for two hours through Klungkung, past quarries, rice fields and salt-making districts, to enjoy a meal in this authentic and charmingly simple Balinese setting. Bapak Sade and his wife serve an array of fragrant fish dishes at their *warung*, Mertha Sari, in Jalan Kresna, just before Goa Lawah, including steamed fish parcels, fish satay, spicy fish soup, beans in spices and homemade sambal. They're used to catering only to Balinese, so you have to prepare yourself for a powerful dose of chilli, but it's always worth it.

I particularly love the old *warungs* in this area. Painted in faded pinks, greens and lavender, their low cool verandahs shelter a hive of activity, especially in the afternoons when the last batch of fresh fish rolls in. Piles of grilled fish in banana leaves are displayed at the front, and at the side fish satays are energetically fanned over coconut coals. Underneath the main bench, you'll see large pots of fish curry simmering over kerosene flames, and of course fresh sambal and rice are always plentiful. Sometimes I stop to buy a selection of these delicious treats, but the queues are often too long, so I end up driving past and have to satisfy myself with breathing in the sweet fragrance of lemongrass and lime leaves as the aroma of freshly cooked satay drifts across the road.

Ikan Mekuah
Fish soup

This is a refreshing piquant soup usually served with seafood dishes in the Kusamba region, East Bali.

1 large fish head of tuna, mackerel or sword fish
250 g (8 oz) tuna, mackerel or sword fish
2–3 tablespoons oil
4 kaffir lime leaves
2 stalks of lemongrass, bruised and tied in a knot

3 salam leaves
10 cups water
sea salt, to taste
fried shallots, to garnish

SPICE MIXTURE
¼ teaspoon shrimp paste
2–3 teaspoons tamarind pulp, seeds removed
6 cloves garlic
¼ teaspoon pepper
2 red shallots
1 tomato
3 small chillies
1 mild large chilli
1 stalk lemongrass
2 teaspoons palm sugar
2 teaspoons chopped turmeric
1 teaspoon chopped kencur
2 teaspoons chopped ginger
2 candlenuts
1 tablespoon chopped galangal
pinch of fresh nutmeg
½ teaspoon coriander seeds
¼ teaspoon black pepper
¼ teaspoon sesame seeds

Rinse the fish head under cold running water and pat dry with a kitchen towel. Chop the fish into small chunks.

Chop all the spices with a cleaver or place in the bowl of a food processor and blend until you have a coarse paste. If the spice mixture is too dry add some oil. It is not necessary for the spices to be a smooth paste.

Find a large pot that will easily hold 10 cups of water. Place the oil in the pot and heat over a medium flame.

Add the spice paste, lime leaves, lemongrass and salam leaves. Toss for about 20 seconds in the oil, until the spices are fragrant and glossy.

Add all the water with the fish head and meat.

Bring to the boil. Simmer, covered for at least 1 hour.

Check seasonings. Garnish with fried shallots. Serve with steamed rice and wedges of lime or lemon.

Serves 6–8.

Satay Lilit

Seafood satay

This is one of the most popular dishes at Casa Luna. In our recipe, we pound chunks of fresh mackerel together with shrimp paste to make the spice paste. The golden mixture is moulded onto fresh juicy skewers of delicious lemongrass and grilled. This is one of those dishes that's guaranteed to impress your friends. You can also use this mixture for Thai-style fish patties (serves 4–8).

300 g (10 oz) tuna, mackerel or sword fish
4 kaffir lime leaves
¹/₄ cup coconut milk
3 teaspoons palm sugar
sea salt, to taste
lemongrass stalks or bamboo skewers, soaked in water, for grilling

SPICE MIXTURE
¹/₄ teaspoon shrimp paste
2 teaspoons tamarind, seeds removed
6 cloves garlic
¹/₄ teaspoon pepper
2 small red shallots
1 tomato
2 stalks chopped lemongrass
3 large mild chillies, seeds removed
3 small chillies (only if you want hotter flavour)
2 teaspoons palm sugar
2 teaspoons chopped turmeric
2 teaspoons chopped ginger
2 candlenuts
1 tablespoon chopped galangal
pinch of fresh nutmeg
¹/₂ teaspoon coriander seeds
¹/₄ teaspoon black pepper
¹/₄ teaspoon sesame seeds

Place the spices in the container of a food processor and blend to a paste or grind with a mortar and pestle. Remove and set aside. Slice the fish into chunks. Place in the container of the food processor and blend until ground like sausage mince, or chop finely with a cleaver. In a large bowl, mix the ground fish with the spices, lime leaves, coconut milk, palm sugar and salt thoroughly until it forms a strong dough.

Take a tablespoon of the mixture and wrap onto a stalk of lemongrass. The end should be slightly thicker, like a drumstick. Grill under a pre-heated griller or barbecue over hot coals. Rotate the stick as it cooks so that it browns evenly. Brush the satay with coconut milk if they brown too quickly.

Garnish with fried shallots and serve with steamed rice and *kangkung pelecing* (see recipe, page 62).

Serves 2–4.

Cumi-Cumi Panggang
Grilled squid

One of our most exciting outings is to go for dinner at Jimbaran. Many *warungs* are now set up along the bay and serve grilled seafood that you can select fresh from small ice-chests. As the sun slowly sets, we sit on the sand and eat succulent seafood treats which have been basted and grilled over smoky coconut husks. I often wonder if heaven provides such meals!

150 g (5 oz) squid
2 cloves garlic
2 tablespoons oil
3 teaspoons kecap manis
1/4 teaspoon white or black pepper
2 kaffir lime leaves, shredded
1 teaspoon fish sauce
1 teaspoon soy sauce
1 teaspoon lemon juice

Clean squid and remove head. Gently pull the cartilage and ink sac from the squid tube. By passing the finger under the flaps where they join the body, lift the flaps away from the central body. Rub the purple-coloured membrane from the flesh and rinse the squid under cold running water. With a sharp knife cut squid into rings. Smash the garlic with the back of a cleaver and then chop finely.

Put the chopped garlic, oil, *kecap manis*, pepper, lime leaves, fish sauce, soy sauce and lemon juice into a bowl and stir. Add the squid and marinate for 10 minutes.

Heat the grill or barbecue. Remove the squid from the marinade and place under a heated grill or on a hot barbecue. Cook for a minute or until lightly charred and still tender. Baste with the marinade during the cooking process. I always flick a little oil onto the barbecue to encourage flames, which adds to the smoky flavour.

Serve hot with steamed rice and wedges of lemon.

Serves 2.

Bregedel Tempe
Tempe fritters

There are many tempe stalls at the Ubud market that sell this fermented soy cake as large slabs wrapped in banana leaves or as small packages sealed in plastic. In the West, tempe is available from health food stores. These small light fritters resemble Middle Eastern falafels and are equally at home served with rice or Mediterranean fare.

150 g (5 oz) tempe
2 tablespoons fried shallots
3 kaffir lime leaves, shredded
1 tablespoon flour
1 egg
1 cup oil for frying

SPICE PASTE
3 large chillies, seeds removed
3 small chillies
2 red shallots
2 cloves garlic
1/2 teaspoon chopped turmeric

2 teaspoons chopped galangal
1 candlenut
¹/₂ teaspoon coriander seeds
¹/₂ teaspoon sea salt
¹/₄ teaspoon shrimp paste

Mash the tempe with a fork or place in the bowl of a food processor and blend until it resembles coarse breadcrumbs.

Grind the spices in a mortar and pestle or place in the bowl of a food processor and blend to a smooth paste.

Put the mashed tempe in a bowl and mix with the spice paste, fried shallots and lime leaves.

Stir in the flour, followed by the egg.

Shape the tempe into fritters the size of a golf ball and flatten a little with a fork.

Heat the oil in a wok over a medium flame. When the oil is hot, drop the fritters into the oil, five or six at a time.

Fry until golden brown on both sides, drain on absorbent paper and serve hot.

Serve with steamed rice.

Serves 2–4.

Sambals — Rice's Little Helper

Not a meal goes past without some sort of sambal or fiery chilli condiment served on the side. A handful of vibrant red chillies mixed with sweet purple shallots, tiny white garlic cloves and brick-red shrimp paste are all you need to make a great Balinese sambal. Valued not only for its heating properties, a sambal also stimulates the tastebuds and clears the mind and palate. The Balinese consider Western food flat and tasteless because of its lack of spices. Over the years, my senses have been slowly awakened to the brilliant reds, oranges and greens, intoxicating aroma and addictive bite of chilli and I've developed the ability to identify many layers of subtle flavours, like a luminary. Sometimes my thrill-seeking spirit can be more like torture as I try increasingly hotter sambals.

Sambal makes the heart sing and warms the soul, comforting the weariest spirit. There is nothing more pleasing than a colourful freshly cooked sambal in which chilli, onion and garlic dance to the gentle hum of shrimp paste. An essential component of every meal, like salt and pepper for a Western meal, sambal is served on the side and added according to your preference. There are countless variations but all are an explosion of colour, flavour and luscious texture. A sambal can be as simple as sliced green chilli with sweet soy or as elaborate as chilli stir-fried with shrimp paste, onion, garlic, bitter melon and egg. The essential combination is chilli and shrimp paste; I call them the perfect partners, like husband and wife — you can draw your own conclusions as to which is which.

I have listened to many heated and passionate discussions about sambal, such as colour and texture versus flavour and aroma, whether you add extra tomato, anchovies or ginger. Every Balinese wife knows that hot steamed rice and a delicious sambal are the key to marital bliss, and even my husband, Ketut, is happy when these basic requirements are met!

Mastering the art of cooking sambals is of paramount importance. Oil is the essential starting point, with the type, amount used and temperature being crucial: skimping on the oil will create a tired sambal that lacks life and depth of flavour. Of course, the juiciest, freshest, brightest chillies are also vital. Try adding roasted eel and the petals of pink torch ginger to a sambal — the effect is wondrous.

Sambals make a handy seasoning for many dishes and a little goes a long way. *Urab*, a coconut salad, and *sager*, dried anchovies with coconut, both rely on a fried sambal to give them their characteristic flavour. Sambal provides the crescendo to a good meal and its addictive burning sensation keeps you coming back for more and more.

Sambal Goreng
Fried chilli seasoning

This would have to be the quintessential sambal for most of Bali and the vital seasoning in so many Balinese dishes. It has a deep mellow flavour punctuated by the bite of spicy chilli, pungent shrimp paste and sweet shallots and when freshly cooked glows with the warmth of all these ingredients. The recipe following is a simple way to make *sambal goreng*, but purists, like my sister-in-law, will fry the shallots and garlic separately to obtain perfect results. I remember watching her cook this seasoning every day and her attention to timing that yielded the crispest garlic and sweetest shallots to create the ultimate sambal.

Take a walk along any village street in the mornings and you will be enveloped by the aroma of sizzling fried shallots and shrimp paste as the sambal gets cooked for the main meal. It is one of those fragrances that tells you you're in Bali.

6 red shallots
10–11 cloves garlic
5 large red chillies, trimmed and de-seeded
2–5 small chillies, finely sliced
2 teaspoons shrimp paste
1 teaspoon sea salt
¹/₃–¹/₂ cup oil

Slice the red shallots and garlic very finely. They should be paper thin and even, so that they all brown together.

Chop all the chillies finely.

Mix the shrimp paste with the salt until it resembles breadcrumbs.

Heat the oil slowly in a wok, over a medium flame.

Fry the sliced shallots and garlic for at least 30 seconds moving the ingredients back and forth continually, so that the ingredients brown evenly. This will depend on the moisture content of your shallots and could take up to 1 minute.

When the shallots and garlic are a pale, golden-brown colour, throw in all the chilli and shrimp paste. Fry for another minute mixing the ingredients quickly and squashing the shrimp paste with the back of the spoon on the base of the wok. Then turn off the flame.

Strain the sambal and transfer to a small bowl. Reserve the chilli oil for further use.

Sambal is a seasoning to be eaten in small quantities only. It is best eaten fresh as the crunchy fried shallots soon soften but, if you don't mind that, you can store it in a plastic container in the refrigerator for 5 days.

Note: Packaged fried shallots can be added to the sambal as an alternative to frying the shallots.

Makes 1 small bowl.

Sambal Matah
Raw chilli seasoning

This is one of the most popular sambals eaten in Bali and is usually served at the *warungs* selling fresh grilled fish that have sprung up along Bali's coastline. Its clean, crisp flavour goes perfectly with seafood and it's also a wonderful accompaniment to summer salads, grilled chicken and chunks of avocado. It's even more delicious when mixed with freshly made coconut oil. You can make a simpler version by mixing together shallots, roasted shrimp paste and fresh chilli.

3 small red shallots
1 teaspoon sea salt
3 tablespoons oil
3 large chillies, trimmed and de-seeded
2–3 small chillies
3 teaspoons finely chopped lemongrass
1 teaspoon finely chopped or grated ginger
5 kaffir lime leaves, shredded
1/2 teaspoon shrimp paste, grilled (see Note)
2 teaspoons torch ginger bud, finely chopped
sea salt, to taste

With a sharp knife, slice the shallots as finely as possible. Using your hands, mix robustly with a teaspoon of salt until the shallots feel soft and the bitterness is extracted. Wash, strain and set aside on absorbent paper.

If you want a mild sambal, also remove the seeds of the smaller chilli and discard. Slice all chillies finely.

Put all the ingredients in a bowl and mix thoroughly, making sure the shrimp paste is blended in.

Add sea salt to taste.

Wash hands thoroughly after handling these ingredients.

Note: To grill the shrimp paste, place it on a small piece of foil in the oven or under a griller for 30 seconds until slightly browned.

Makes a small bowl.

Sambal Goreng Hati

Liver sambal with sweet chilli and potatoes

This is a gentle sweet dish that my children love. My sister-in-law, Nyoman, always prepares this for family gatherings and it's such a joy to eat it all together in her spacious pavilion on the edge of the rice fields.

500 g (1 lb) chicken liver
250 g (8 oz) potato
2 stalks lemongrass
3 kaffir lime leaves
6 small red shallots
5 cloves garlic
4 large red chillies, trimmed and de-seeded
3 small chillies
2 thick slices galangal
2 tablespoons oil for frying
1/4 teaspoon shrimp paste
2 salam leaves
2 teaspoons kecap manis
1/2 teaspoon palm sugar
sea salt, to taste
2 tablespoons fried shallots, to garnish

Boil the liver in water to cover for 10 minutes. Strain and pat dry with kitchen paper. Slice liver thinly.

Rinse or wipe the potatoes. Skin and slice into julienne.

Bruise and tie the lemongrass into a knot. With a sharp knife, slice the shallots and garlic into paper-thin slices. Slice the chilli into long neat thin strips. Bruise the slices of galangal by smashing them with the back of a cleaver.

Heat the oil in a wok over a medium flame. Fry the potatoes in two batches until golden brown, adding more oil if necessary. Alternatively, these can be roasted in the oven until golden brown.

Fry the liver in the same oil until browned outside. Lift out of the wok and set aside on absorbent paper.

Fry the shallots and garlic in the oil until golden brown for 3 minutes over a medium flame, moving constantly around the base of the wok.

Lower the heat and add the sliced chilli and shrimp paste. Throw in the bruised galangal, salam leaves, lemongrass and lime leaves, mixing constantly.

Add the cooked liver chunks. Stir in the *kecap manis*, palm sugar, sea salt and cooked potatoes. Cook together until the potatoes are heated through.

Check seasonings.

Serve topped with extra fried shallots.

Serves 4–8.

Tuwung Goreng
Stir-fried eggplant

This is one of Krishna's favourite dishes and we eat it nearly every week for breakfast, lunch or dinner. We generally use white eggplant, but black eggplant can be used instead. Chilli, red shallots, garlic and shrimp paste are the main seasonings of this simple stir-fry, with the optional addition of Indonesian soy sauces. Sometimes we add tomato for variety, and you can also make it with any vegetable or even meat. I love the flavour of shrimp paste with eggplant so I always add more than the specified amount. You can substitute fish sauce instead.

2 small white eggplants

2 red shallots

4 garlic cloves

2 large red chillies

2 small chillies

$1/2$ tomato, finely sliced (optional)

3 tablespoons oil

$1/2$ teaspoon shrimp paste or 1 teaspoon fish sauce

2 kaffir lime leaves

2 salam leaves

¹/₄ cup water
1 teaspoon light soy sauce
¹/₂ teaspoon kecap manis
sea salt, to taste

Slice the eggplant in half lengthwise and then finely crosswise, like thin discs. Sprinkle with salt and rub it on the eggplant. Wash the eggplant with water and set aside. Slice the red shallots, garlic, chilli and tomato finely. Heat the oil in a wok over a medium flame. Fry the shallots and garlic for approximately 30 seconds. Stir the ingredients constantly and try not to burn them. Add the chilli, optional shrimp paste and optional tomato. Toss around for a few seconds until slightly wilted. Add the sliced eggplant, lime leaves, salam leaves and water if necessary. Bring to the boil and simmer for at least 2 minutes or until the eggplant is wilted. Finish off with soy sauce, *kecap manis* and sea salt to taste.

Alternatively, fry the eggplant in oil, then add *sambal goreng* and other ingredients.

Serves 4.

Sambal Tuwung

Roasted eggplant sambal

Late one afternoon I happened to be walking past the bakery kitchen while my staff were preparing dinner. The scent of smoky chilli, roasted tomatoes, shrimp paste and garlic filled the air and stopped me in my tracks. I could hear the rhythmic grinding of the mortar and pestle rocking back and forth, blending these almost Mediterranean flavours into a rich red mass to be mixed with roasted eggplant. When I peeked into the kitchen, I saw one of the girls sitting on the back step, carefully pulling cooked eggplant into thin strips. I stayed and watched her finish the dish, which has since become a favourite at home. Try it with crusty Italian bread or with an antipasto platter.

2 small white or black eggplant
2 tablespoons oil
2 teaspoons grated palm sugar
1–2 teaspoons kecap manis

2 kaffir lime leaves, shredded
sea salt, to taste
fried shallots, to garnish

SAMBAL

3 large red chillies, trimmed and de-seeded
2 medium tomatoes
3 small red chillies
5 cloves garlic
$^{1}/_{2}$ teaspoon shrimp paste
3–4 tablespoons oil for frying sambal

Slice the eggplant in half lengthwise, place on a baking tray and drizzle with the oil. Roast in a medium oven for at least 20 minutes or until gently browned and soft. Alternatively, barbecue, grill or fry the eggplant.

Halve the tomatoes. Chop the large chillies into small pieces. You can also remove the seeds from the small chillies if you prefer it milder.

Heat the oil in a wok over a low flame. Fry the chillies, garlic and shrimp paste for a minute or two until lightly browned. Add the tomato and continue to fry until they are cooked but not burnt. Strain and set aside.

Grind the cooked chilli, tomatoes, garlic, shrimp paste and palm sugar in a mortar and pestle. Alternatively, place the ingredients in the bowl of a food processor and blend to a paste, making sure not to over-blend it. Add some oil if it is too dry.

Remove the skin of the eggplant and pull the soft flesh into long strips. Mix the sambal thoroughly with the eggplant. Add the *kecap manis*, shredded lime leaves and sea salt. Garnish with fried shallots.

Serves 4–6.

Sambal Tomat Ditunuh

Roasted tomato sambal

We often eat this sambal with grilled fish, tofu and roasted vegetables. It has a wonderful smoky flavour that also works with feta cheese and Middle Eastern dishes.

3 large red chillies or small red capsicum, trimmed and de-seeded
3 small red chillies
¹/₂ teaspoon shrimp paste
4 cloves garlic
4 tomatoes, halved
2 tablespoons oil
1 calamondin lime, halved or ¹/₂ teaspoon lime juice
2 teaspoons palm sugar
4 kaffir lime leaves
sea salt, to taste

You can remove the seeds of the smaller chilli if you prefer it milder. Place the chilli, shrimp paste, garlic and tomatoes in a small baking dish, drizzle with the oil and roast in a medium oven until slightly charred or for about 20 minutes. If the large chilli cooks quickly, remove it first and set aside to cool.

Place the roasted ingredients in a mortar and pestle or in the bowl of a food processor and blend to a paste.

Squeeze the calamondin lime into the dish and throw it in. Otherwise, add the lime juice. Then add the palm sugar, shredded lime leaves and sea salt to taste.

Serves 2–4.

Sambal Khukus Bongkot
Steamed torch ginger sambal

One of my most valued garden plants is the torch ginger. Apart from sharing its glorious waxy pink flowers with us, it also provides us with culinary blessings. This gentle sambal is delightful with steamed or grilled fish, eel, liver and even salad ingredients such as rocket and avocado.

7 cloves garlic
5 red shallots
2 small chillies
2–3 large red chillies
1 torch ginger shoot or 1 stalk lemongrass
1 tomato
¹/₂ teaspoon shrimp paste
1 tablespoon oil

Steam all the ingredients, except for the oil and salt, until soft.

Grind to a paste or place the ingredients in the bowl of a food processor and blend to a paste with the oil. Add sea salt to taste.

Makes 1 cup.

Sambal Goreng Jepung
Choko in coconut milk

Choko features regularly on our home menu as it is a cheap vegetable that is available most of the year. The children love to eat this soupy dish with compressed rice and chicken. The choko can be replaced with potatoes or green papaya.

600 g (20 oz) choko, or 1 large choko
1 teaspoon sea salt
2 tablespoons oil, for frying
3 salam leaves
3 kaffir lime leaves
2 large chunks galangal, bruised
1 lemongrass stalk, bruised and tied in a knot
250 ml (8 fl oz) water
250 ml (8 fl oz) coconut milk
sea salt, to taste
3 tablespoons fried shallots

SPICE PASTE
4 cloves garlic
3 small red shallots
3 large red chillies, trimmed and de-seeded
1/4 of a tomato
2 teaspoons palm sugar
1/2 teaspoon shrimp paste

Peel the choko and slice into matchsticks. Knead with a teaspoon of salt. Set aside for 10 minutes, wash and strain.

Grind the spices in a mortar and pestle or place in the bowl of a food processor and blend to a paste.

Heat the oil in a wok over a medium flame.

Add the spice paste and fry for about 30 seconds or until fragrant and glossy. Throw in the salam leaves, lime leaves, galangal and lemongrass. Fry for 1 minute, moving quickly around the base of the wok. Lower the flame if they burn.

Add the water and bring to the boil. Add the washed choko and simmer until the choko is soft. Slowly pour in the coconut milk and bring to the boil for a minute to thicken.

Add sea salt to taste and garnish with fried shallots.

Serves 4.

Sweet Things

In general, milk and butter are not used in Balinese cakes and desserts, in accordance with Hindu dietary restrictions, but, as in most things, the Balinese are flexible and do use dairy products from time to time. Their way of honouring the sacred cow is to avoid using dairy produce in offerings, whereas in India it is the opposite for ceremonial foods.

Temple cakes come in all shapes and sizes. A simple mix of duck eggs, cane sugar and wheat flour makes the brightly coloured steamed cupcakes that we all love at our house. Larger caramel-coloured cakes are made with palm sugar syrup, coconut milk, vanilla and flour. Other temple cakes mix steamed sticky rice with grated coconut, fresh fruits, sugar and fragrant pandan leaves. These cakes are made primarily for God, who adores bright colours, and are eaten only on special occasions such as temple ceremonies, tooth-filings and weddings.

The tradition in Bali is to buy cakes from the experts rather than to make them at home. Large temple cakes are often ordered in town or bought from the cake-seller at the market. This share system lends support to those who are trying to earn a living and also saves a lot of time when there are offerings to be made and other duties to be performed. The delicate construction of the pyramid-shaped offerings can take up to an hour, and the time spent on them is part of the ritual.

You will find the best selection of cakes and desserts at the village markets. Little sticky rice 'pillow' cakes, cleverly wrapped in young coconut leaves, small green balls filled with palm sugar syrup that squirts out when you bite into them, diamond-shaped golden-coloured sweet rice cakes and toasted coconut bread are available every day. Brilliant green pancakes filled with grated coconut and palm sugar are one of my favourites.

Aside from cakes, there is a whole range of *buburs* or porridge-like dishes, which are eaten mainly as a sweet breakfast or as snack foods throughout the day. In the marketplace, or under the local banyan tree, you'll see women serving all sorts of colourful sticky-rice mixtures. Palm sugar syrup is usually drizzled on top and, if you're lucky, a handful of freshly grated coconut provides the finishing touch. The ominous-looking black rice pudding is surprisingly delicious and these days is often served to tourists for breakfast. *Kolak*, fruits poached in coconut milk and palm sugar, is another one of my favourites, and to my taste is even more delicious with fresh cream or ice-cream!

The preferred dessert in Bali is fresh fruit. A wedge of juicy red watermelon or slices of small sweet banana are the usual end to a lavish feast. Mango is my children's favourite fruit and when it is in season we always eat it in the steamy afternoons to revive and replenish us, letting the juices run down our chins. There is something so sensual about the shape and flavour of this brilliant orange luscious fruit: the symbol of joy and eternal life in India, it must be one of the world's most divine bites. Known for its cooling properties, a slice of ripe mango is said to contain just about every nutrient the body needs and will instantly ease dehydration. Green mango is also popular in Bali and is eaten with lashings of chilli, palm sugar and roasted shrimp paste. Mangosteen is probably the most spectacular of the tropical fruits: perfectly packaged, they are as beautiful to behold as they are to eat. This small crimson fruit is crowned with a frilled stem and the base is sealed with a stamp that indicates the number of tender white segments inside. It reminds me of a delicate Japanese-style wood-block print, perfect on a kimono, and I feel elated every time I eat one. *Salak* or snakefruit is an interesting combination of apple and pineapple in flavour and has a beautiful smooth brown covering, like snakeskin. In the West we say that an apple a day keeps the doctor away; in Bali it is said that a *salak* a day does the same. *Salak* aids digestion and is a good source of vitamin C. Papaya is another popular fruit — in Bali, the red variety is mainly grown. Loaded with goodness, it is said to be full of vitamins A and C and is excellent for the digestion. My children love to eat chunks of plain fresh papaya, whereas I prefer it with a squeeze of lime. Banana would have to be the most venerated fruit in Bali and there are countless varieties. The sweet ladyfingers are popular for offerings and have a sweet, almost lemony flavour. The fatter bananas are perfect for frying or boiling into snacks and the large *pisang raja* are the ideal first baby food.

Bubur Injin
Black rice pudding

We decided to make black rice pudding at a recent family gathering at our house, part of a monthly event called *Arisan*, when family members get together to pool their money and generally strengthen family ties. One of our cooks, Ketut, was in charge of cooking the black rice and Nyoman was in charge of the coconut milk. For at least an hour, Ketut stirred the black grains as they simmered in a huge pot on the stove, checking the texture and making sure the rice didn't stick to the bottom of the pan. A thick knot of fresh pandan leaves had been added for extra fragrance. When the black rice was cooked, we added a generous lashing of palm sugar syrup and a dash of vanilla.

In the meantime, Nyoman and I started to prepare the coconut milk. I was excited and a little nervous because I wanted to show all the mothers that I could cook as well as any Balinese woman. Nyoman cracked open the coconut and prised the white meat out of the shell. She then roasted the pieces by sitting them on an open flame. The skin crackled and blistered under the heat and after about two minutes the heavenly scent of roasted coconut filled the air. We took it off the flame and scraped off the flesh — a bit like scraping burnt toast! — then mixed the grated flesh with water and strained it. Now we had a jugful of delicious creamy roasted coconut milk.

Finally the task was finished. We laid out lots of small bowls on the kitchen bench in preparation; we'd also made small coconut-leaf spoons with which to eat the pudding. As the guests arrived, we went into action. The black rice, topped with a swirl of white coconut milk, looked so beautiful served in the simple white bowls. I couldn't wait to see the expression on our guests' faces.

We passed the dessert around and waited for the response. As soon as each person had taken a few mouthfuls, the chatter started. We could see looks of disappointment on the women's faces and I quickly realised something was wrong.

'Nyoman, didn't you put salt in the coconut milk?' asked my sister-in-law.

The entire gathering looked disapprovingly at Nyoman, who blushed, laughed, mumbled something and raced into the kitchen to add a pinch of sea salt to the remainder of the freshly made coconut milk. I couldn't believe that we'd overlooked such a crucial ingredient. We then had to add another layer of coconut milk to all the puddings. I tried to add a little humour to the situation by saying, 'Well, you know these young village girls don't always know how to cook nowadays!'

Highly nutritious, this famous pudding is eaten by the Balinese mainly as an afternoon snack. It's great topped with fresh fruit, toasted coconut and, of course, a liberal serve of coconut milk.

Serves 4–6.

PUDDING
  1/2 cup black rice
  2 tablespoons sticky white rice or plain white rice
  4 cups water
  2/3 cup palm sugar syrup
  1 pandan leaf or essence
  1 vanilla bean or 1/2 teaspoon vanilla essence
  1/2 teaspoon sea salt
  2 cups roasted coconut milk

Put the black rice in a large saucepan with the water and leave to soak for about 8 hours. Add the white rice for the last 2 hours.

Boil the rice with the pandan leaf, salt and vanilla bean (not the essence) for at least an hour or until the water has evaporated and the rice is soft enough to eat. This is very important, as the rice will not cook any further once the sugar is added. (I always turn the rice off at this point and set it aside to absorb all the liquid.)

Stir in the palm sugar and vanilla essence. Simmer over a low flame, and cook for another minute or two, making sure the sugar is thoroughly mixed in. The pudding should be thick and glossy. Check the sweetness adding more palm sugar syrup if necessary.

To serve: Spoon the pudding into small bowls and top with roasted coconut milk. You can garnish the pudding with grated coconut or sliced banana.

Bubur Sagu
Sago pudding

In the early days, I used to spend much of my time in the kitchen at the Pantheon with Wayan, the cook. She usually had some spare time after she'd cooked lunch for the workers, so for afternoon tea she would make sweet snacks such as *bubur sagu*. This is one of my favourite desserts: the mellow sweetness of palm sugar and creamy coconut milk are perfect partners to the soft pearly sago. You can often buy *bubur sagu* at the market in the morning or in the late afternoon under the banyan tree. We also make this at home for special dinners or for a sweet treat.

100 g (3¹/₂ oz) pearl sago
3 cups water
2 pandan leaves, tied in a knot
1 heaped teaspoon sea salt
vanilla essence
²/₃ cup palm sugar syrup
1 cup coconut milk

Put the sago pearls and pandan leaves in a medium-sized saucepan and cover with the water. Soak for 10 minutes or until the sago has fully expanded. Add the salt and vanilla. Gently heat the sago over a low flame and stir continuously with a wooden spoon until it becomes a gluey, transparent mass. Stir in ¹/₃ cup of the coconut milk and the palm sugar and stir over low heat until thoroughly mixed in. Set aside and leave to settle for a minute or two.

Spoon into small bowls and swirl a layer of coconut milk or even ice-cream on top.

Serves 8–12.

Kolak

Fruits in coconut milk

The alluring fragrance of cinnamon makes this dish as pleasurable to cook as it is to eat. It can be made with a variety of ingredients, including banana, ripe jackfruit, sweet potato and tapioca. It is equally suitable for cool winter evenings or balmy summer nights. It can be made several hours before serving and then reheated or served chilled.

250 g (8 oz) palm sugar or brown sugar
3 cups water
2 pandan leaves or 1 teaspoon pandan essence
1 teaspoon vanilla essence
100 g (3¹/₂ oz) sweet potato
100g (3¹/₂ oz) pineapple
6 bananas
1 cup coconut milk
¹/₂ teaspoon sea salt
1 heaped tablespoon tapioca flour or cornflour

In a large pot, boil the palm sugar in the water with the pandan leaves until the sugar has dissolved and reduced by half. If using pandan essence, add with the vanilla essence. Strain the sugar water and return to the pot.

Slice the sweet potato, pineapple and banana into chunks. Return the sugar-water to the boil and add the sweet potato. Simmer for 5 minutes or until half-cooked. Add the pineapple and banana and simmer until the banana is soft but not mushy. Stir in the coconut milk and salt.

Mix the flour with a tablespoon or more of cold water. Stir until it has dissolved and is free of lumps. Bring to the boil again, and stir for a minute until the sauce has thickened. Add more cornflour if you would like it thicker. Check for sweetness and serve.

Serve with vanilla or coconut ice-cream.

Serves 6–8.

Pisang Goreng
Banana fritters

My mother-in-law used to sell banana fritters when Ketut was a little boy. In the early mornings, she'd fry up dozens of golden bananas smothered in creamy batter and then walk from door to door selling these warm sweet treats from a bamboo basket. Not long before her death, I remember sharing banana fritters with her on the steps of the eastern pavilion at the family home. We were approaching a temple ceremony and had spent the afternoon making offerings together. My sister-in-law was in charge of afternoon tea and presented us each with a small plate of hot vanilla-scented banana fritters, drizzled with palm sugar syrup and topped with freshly grated coconut. My mother-in-law was thrilled. They were obviously a favourite and I imagine each bite must have brought back a thousand memories. Whenever I eat banana fritters now I think of my mother-in-law.

6 large bananas
1¹/₂ cups flour
3 teaspoons caster sugar
3 teaspoons palm sugar
¹/₂ teaspoon sea salt
1 teaspoon vanilla essence
2 cups of water
3 tablespoons oil, for frying

Peel bananas. Slice down the centre and, if large, cut in half crossways.

Place the flour, caster sugar, palm sugar, sea salt, vanilla and water in the container of a blender. Blend until smooth and lump-free. The mixture should be like a pancake batter. Set aside for a few minutes.

Heat the oil in a frying pan over medium heat. When the oil is hot, dip the bananas into the batter and spoon into the hot oil. Fry two or three at a time until golden brown. Remove the cooked bananas with a slotted spoon and drain on absorbent paper.

Serve warm dusted with grated coconut and drizzled with palm sugar syrup (see recipe, page 181).

Makes up to 24.

Bubur Kacang Hijau
Mung-bean pudding

This popular Balinese snack is usually sold by the travelling vendors who push their little carts through the streets. This dish always takes me back to the premature birth of Krishna in hospital in Denpasar. Every day, we were given a small bowl of creamy warm *bubur kacang hijau* for morning tea. Soothing and nutritious, it gave me great comfort at a time when I needed to replenish my strength for both my tiny son and myself.

This unusual mixture of mung beans with sweet coconut-milk soup is punctuated with a hint of fresh ginger. It is perfect for cold wintry nights or as an instant energy-giver! Pour it into small plastic bags and freeze to make the popular iced version: *es bubur kacang hijau.*

250 g (8 oz) mung beans
60 g (2 oz) sticky white rice
1/4 teaspoon salt
30 g (1 oz) brown sugar
large chunk of ginger, crushed
1 vanilla bean or 1 teaspoon vanilla essence
2 cups coconut milk

Soak the mung beans for 2 hours. Drain.

Mix the beans with the sticky rice in a large saucepan. Add salt and sugar. Cover with 8 cm cold water. Add ginger to saucepan with the vanilla.

Bring the mixture to a simmer over medium heat and then simmer with the lid off until the beans and rice are cooked.

Pour in the coconut milk, stirring constantly.

Simmer for 5 minutes longer then serve.

Serves 6.

Bubur Sum-sum

Creamy rice porridge with palm sugar

Bubur sum-sum is like a rice-porridge creme caramel. The success of this dish will depend as much on the quality of your palm sugar as it will on the freshness of the rice flour. It's even more delicious topped with banana simmered in coconut milk.

125 g (4 oz) rice flour
2 heaped teaspoons grated coconut
1/2 teaspoon sea salt
1/2 teaspoon vanilla essence
2 heaped teaspoons white sugar
2 cups water
2 pandan leaves, tied in a knot
1/2 cup coconut milk
250 g (8 oz) palm sugar
250 ml (8 fl oz) water

In a small jug, mix the rice flour, grated coconut, sea salt, vanilla essence and white sugar.

In a saucepan, boil the 2 cups of water with the pandan leaves over a medium flame. Pour the rice-flour mixture into the boiling water in a slow stream, stirring robustly with a wooden spoon until all the mixture has been incorporated. (This is a little like making choux pastry.) Lower the heat and keep stirring until the mixture forms a solid mass. Add the coconut milk. If you would like a creamier texture, add even more coconut milk. Set aside.

To make the palm sugar syrup, boil the palm sugar in 250 ml of water until the sugar has dissolved and the liquid is thick and syrupy.

Spoon the porridge into a bowl and pour some syrup over the top. Serves 8.

Dadar Unti

Green coconut crepes with coconut filling

These thin green coconut crepes, delicately flavoured with coconut milk and pandan leaves, are a favourite breakfast for our guests at home. In the morning, we serve them filled with soft warm bananas, or as a sweet treat during the day with grated coconut and palm sugar. My children love them either way. At the market, the vendors add tapioca flour or a little rice flour to the batter to create a chewier texture, but I prefer the drier effect of wheat flour. For something different, try experimenting with savoury fillings.

BATTER

    1 cup plain flour
    1 large egg, lightly beaten
    1/4 teaspoon salt
    1 1/2 tablespoons sugar
    1/2 teaspoon vanilla
    1 cup coconut milk
    1/2 cup water
    1/2 teaspoon pandan essence for green colour
    1 teaspoon lemon juice (optional)
    oil, for frying pancakes

FILLING

    1 cup grated coconut
    1/4 cup palm sugar syrup (see recipe, page 181)
    1 pandan leaf, knotted or 1 teaspoon pandan essence
    1/2 teaspoon vanilla essence
    pinch of sea salt

Mix all the batter ingredients together in a blender. The mixture should be smooth and lump-free, like a crepe batter. Set aside for a few minutes and make the filling.

Mix all the filling ingredients together thoroughly and cook over a low flame in a saucepan for 3 minutes, until the coconut is soft.

Heat a small frypan or non-stick crepe pan over a low flame. Add a smear of oil and then 1/4 cup of the pancake mixture, tilting the pan so that the mixture reaches the edges. The pancake should be very thin.

When bubbles appear on top of the pancake, flip it over and cook for a few seconds on the other side. Add a smear of oil to the pan when necessary (I like to use a brush made of pandan leaves) and continue until the mixture is used.

Fill each pancake with 2–3 tablespoons of coconut filling and fold like a spring roll.

Makes approximately 10 pancakes.

A walk amongst the trees and flowers

HERBAL DRINKS AND REMEDIES

. . . bidding him welcome, warmly offering him every efficacious herb and medicine as well as delicious fruits . . .

PARTHAYANA, THE JOURNEYING OF PARTHA

For the Balinese, their food is their medicine. The lush gardens of this tropical paradise abound with herbs, leaves, seeds and roots that can be used to cool a heated body, aid digestion, purify the blood and relieve aches and pains. Spices, used to make a glorious curry, can also make a revitalising tonic or a poultice for colds and flus. Even my children know that for certain ailments, a walk amongst the trees and flowers will provide them with a medicine chest of cures. Plants breathe life into all beings: they are imbued with healing, as well as magical powers. In this land of nature worship, certain trees are considered sacred and are revered with offerings. They are wrapped in the protective black and white cloth that symbolises the eternal opposites of life and death, good and evil, and are considered as alive as we are. The same leaves and herbs that are used to cure ailments are also used to worship the deities. The garden island of Bali represents the natural balance of the cosmos, a world that regenerates and provides spiritual refuge free from worldly desires. And the interaction with its flora and fauna maintains balance and harmony in the lives of its people.

Jamu is the generic word for herbal tonics throughout Indonesia. A walk through the Jogjakarta market will reveal a sea of packaged herbal remedies with a cure for everything under the sun. *Jamu* can be an elaborate mixture of many fresh gingers, tree bark, herbs, seeds and nuts, or as simple as fresh turmeric juice mixed with lemon juice and honey. The latter is a simple effective energiser for just about everything. Whenever I'm feeling out of sorts, especially after having a baby, I perk myself up with drinks that combine these ingredients. If you can ignore the temporary yellowing effect it has on the teeth and tongue, the results are wondrous. Sometimes I've seen the girls in our compound dilute the mixture with warm water, so it becomes a reviving drink to be sipped during the day. Depending on the complaint, other gingers or spices might be added to the foundation recipe. When my husband needs an energy booster, he mixes turmeric juice with honey, orange juice, warm water and a dash of whisky, topped with a fresh egg yolk. My sister-in-law drinks basic *jamu* with an egg yolk nearly every day and I can only imagine this must be why she's hardly aged in ten years. Her skin is as soft and youthful as ever and she's rarely sick.

Turmeric forms the basis for many herbal tonics consumed throughout Indonesia. It is a natural antiseptic, when taken internally and externally. If my children cut themselves, I rush to the spice tray, grate some fresh turmeric and cover the wound with the vibrant yellow substance. When they complain of mosquito bites, I cover their scratches with coconut oil mixed with fresh turmeric. The turmeric kills the infection and reduces scarring while the coconut oil takes the itch away. Turmeric is a natural preservative, is used to treat skin diseases and fungi and is an ingredient in many skin cosmetics and medicines. It is also a powerful anti-oxidant and anti-inflammatory. Viewed as a modern-day miracle drug, turmeric is alleged to help prevent cancer, aids digestion and helps clear up respiratory infections. The list of its benefits goes on and on.

Once, when I was attending to Arjuna, I bent to lift him up and felt a sharp twinge in my back. I found I couldn't stand straight; in fact, I could hardly move and was in agony — even lying down provided only minimal relief. One of the workers saw my feeble condition and asked me if I would like the Balinese treatment; she said her grandma often had backache and this was how they dealt with it. I love Balinese remedies so I waited enthusiastically for the natural medicine. She returned with two small bowls, one filled with white lime paste often used in cooking, the other with what I identified as freshly cleaned knobs of turmeric. I was instructed to stand and reveal the painful area. She gently smeared my back with lime paste using the tip of her finger; it had a wonderful cooling sensation that instantly relieved the troubled spot. I was thrilled with the improvement. But there was more to follow. She slowly chewed up the chunks of turmeric and spat them onto my back. Tiny cannonballs of fragrant spice covered the area in question, one after the other. I looked in the mirror and decided that with the rich dark orange turmeric sprayed over the white pages, I resembled a piece of contemporary art. I was instructed to let the mixture dry out, which would take half a day. So I lay on my front and gradually felt the whole area cool right through to my bones. The lime paste turned into a thick crusty mass like coarse cement and the tightening effect slowly eased the pain, giving me more relief than any of the Western tablets I'd been provided with. After two days of the treatment, I was on my way to a speedy recovery.

The leaves from many other trees and shrubs are used to make all sorts of dangerous-looking herbal tonics, or what the Balinese call *loloh*. They are used to cool the body and act as a mineral supplement, liver cleanser and general preventative against ill health. In hot weather, the Balinese prefer the cooling properties of herbal tonics as opposed to drinks filled with ice. The workers at our house like to drink a tonic made with bitter leaves and water, which is prized for its medicinal benefits and guaranteed to stop the mosquitos biting.

Krishna loves *babi kecap* and one *Galungan* ate just a little too much of this luxurious pork stew. After praying in the temple, he disappeared to his room. From behind his closed door, I could hear his tears of agony and peeked in to see him rolling around on his bed, holding his bloated aching belly. His stomach was hot to touch and Dewi confirmed that it was over-eating that was causing the pain. So we went into the garden to gather some of the *dadap* leaves that grow around the temple. They help cool the body and also alleviate constipation. We cut off a dozen branches and stuck them into his underpants, front and back. The sight of Krishna lying on the bed with leaves and branches sprouting from his underwear was a comical one and I tried to imagine his Australian cousins enjoying the same treatment. After five minutes, the leaves had created the necessary chemistry and all was relieved and restored to normal. Krishna still loves *babi kecap* but only has one helping at a time now.

Dalumen is a herbal tonic made from a green vine leaf which, when mixed with water, becomes dark green and gelatinous and is full of natural chlorophyll and anti-cancer properties. I affectionately call it 'green slime'. In my early days in Bali, I remember waiting each morning for the *dalumen* lady to stroll through the gates of Ketut's woodcarving gallery, carrying effortlessly on her head a small wooden table laden with *dalumen*, coconut milk, palm sugar and other assorted ingredients. After setting up shop on the steps of the gallery, she would mix a little of the *dalumen* in a glass, top it with a drizzle of palm sugar, add a few spoonfuls of roasted coconut milk and then stir it proudly, the spoon tinkling confidently against the glass. As I drank her precious potion, delighting in the aroma of roasted coconut milk, she would eye me with curiosity. At this time in 1985, she had never sold this drink to a Western person before. In time, we grew fond of each other and I became very attached to this delicious, sinister-looking drink that cooled my entire being. I enjoyed the sensation of it working its way down to my stomach, creating a path of calm and satisfaction. The *dalumen* lady loved to tell me the virtues of this popular drink. 'It's good for pregnant women,' she would say, 'it helps the baby pop out.' She told me that it cools a hot stomach, is full of vitamins and maintains a youthful complexion. The list grew longer with every passing month.

Now when I feel like drinking *dalumen*, Nyoman, the children's nanny, goes home to her village to collect a bagful of leaves and we make it together. Even my children love this dark green drink with its mellow flavour and jelly-like texture, although the palm sugar probably adds to the appeal.

Friends sometimes drop in from faraway parts of Indonesia, bringing gifts of homemade herbal tonics which are always received with great enthusiasm by Ketut. Probably the most delicious to date is the one we mixed with Australian honey and whisky: the resulting taste was reminiscent of a luscious aromatic port and it was great to know that the lovely calming warm sensation we felt after drinking it was all in the name of good health.

Years ago, when I sprained my ankle, the massage man from a neighbouring village was called to treat me. As I sat on the step in front of our little bungalow, grimacing with pain, he gently examined my swollen ankle, slowly rotating it. I watched him concentrating on my foot and noticed how he gathered so much information through his sturdy hands. With a final gentle tilt of my foot, he smiled and pronounced that the bone inside was already home. After a gentle massage, I felt almost like new again. To prevent bruising and to warm the bones, I was instructed to make a paste of rice and fresh galangal and spread it on the injury twice a day. I expected to see shades of grey and yellow on the injured spot the next morning, but not a trace of a bruise ever appeared. By the next day, I was walking around as if nothing had happened.

Farmers often grind fresh galangal into a paste with grains of rice to make a poultice to warm up their cold legs after hours of standing in muddy rice fields. Similar to ginger, galangal curbs flatulence and nausea, helps reduce swelling, and assists in healing bruises, respiratory ailments and skin disease.

Coriander cools the body, aids digestion and settles the stomach, and is a favourite in herbal tonics and poultices throughout Indonesia. When my staff get the flu, they grind coriander, cloves, nutmeg and rice into a gritty paste and smear it onto the chest to relieve the congestion. *Kencur* ground with grains of rice will help cure headaches and, made into a simple tonic, aids in the treatment of persistent coughs. It is also believed to be a body-strengthening ingredient that purifies the blood and warms the body, aiding circulation. It stimulates the appetite of young folk and is a favourite spice for many.

Ginger is a powerful herbal medicine used to settle a common complaint in Indonesia known as *masuk-angin*, which can be a cold, a fever, the flu or just about anything. It translates as 'the wind entering', and once that happens you have to push it out again. After the birth of Laksmi, I complained to Ketut one morning that I was feeling listless and generally unwell. My energy reserves seemed to have come to an almighty halt; I lay on the bed longing for some power to flow through my veins. Ketut was concerned and decided to solve the problem by giving me a massage. He instructed me to lie on my back. I melted into the mattress, awaiting the divine pleasure of gentle healing, but instead felt something sharp, cold and metallic being scraped along my back.

'What on earth are you doing?' I asked, distressed by the unpleasant treatment.

'I'm testing you for *masuk-angin*,' he replied confidently, 'and that is exactly what you have, *masuk-angin*.'

He was delighted with his prognosis, proved when my skin instantly flashed red. Ketut continued the treatment by running the metallic instrument, a Rp 100 coin, across my back with short swift strokes. '*Masuk-angin*, I should have known,' I mumbled under the pressure of his heavy hand, all the while thinking this wasn't the treatment I'd been expecting. By the time he was finished, my back was scarlet red. Ketut then softened the treatment by giving me a luscious head-to-toe massage using soothing sandalwood oil. The prescribed medicine was homemade ginger tea to keep the body settled, made by infusing fresh bruised chunks of ginger with boiling water, weak tea and a teaspoon of sugar. What a lovely service! The following day I was back on my toes, full of happiness and energy. All that air had been pushed out of my tired limbs under the caring hands of my husband.

Every night after the birth of Arjuna, my youngest child, I drank a large mug of hot milk with ginger and honey. This gentle beverage relaxed my body and sent me to the land of sweet dreams, if only for three or four hours at a time. Ginger warms the body, aids circulation, soothes a sore throat and relaxes the muscles. Ginger tea with honey is a marvellous tonic for a cold or flu and will help fight off motion sickness.

The Balinese red shallot is also surrounded by myths and magic and is believed to protect small children from black magic. It is believed that the reincarnated spirit enters through the fontanelle of a newly born baby, so this delicate spot is smeared with rice paste and topped with a sliver of red shallot to guard the baby against unwelcome intruders. Applied topically with coconut oil, red shallot cools the body and helps heal skin irritations and infections. Each morning after the baby has been bathed, he or she is massaged with an aromatic mixture of fresh coconut oil and roasted red shallots. The shallot is pierced with a satay stick and roasted over a flame, a gesture that invites Brahma, the god of fire, to infuse the tiny seasoning with added power. Red is the sacred colour of Brahma, and in every child's offering box, there will be a red shallot or two for good luck.

The Balinese will apply red shallots to the chakra points of an unsettled baby's body for extra strength and protection. When Krishna cried at night, Ketut placed red shallots around his bed to help him sleep again; it was as if he thought some evil energy was disturbing the baby and the shallots held the power to ward them off. In the evenings, I'd check on Krishna as he slept in his tiny cot beside our bed and also inspected under the mattress. Over the weeks, a couple of red shallots grew into more than a dozen, at the corners of the cot, around the edges and in the middle. I remembered wondering to myself if the pile of shallots could be the cause of his broken sleep. As Krishna grew and became more settled, the red shallots slowly disappeared.

Sometimes people place red shallots around the bedroom, particularly in doorways or on windowsills — places where evil spirits might enter.

Like olive oil for the Italians, golden coconut oil is a popular Balinese remedy for just about everything. When mixed with grated turmeric it heals wounds, with grated galangal it alleviates muscular pain and with onion cures nappy rash. Prized for its luxurious moisturising properties, it rehydrates sun-drenched skin and is the perfect conditioner for dry hair. It also takes the itch out of all sorts of insect bites.

For a refreshing herbal tea, infuse a stalk of bruised lemongrass with boiling water and steep for a few minutes before serving. This tea cools the stomach and helps ease cramps, menstrual pain and indigestion. It is also great to drink when suffering from colds and flus and is excellent for the complexion. When my children have an upset stomach, I make them rice porridge boiled with a single knot of lemongrass and salam leaves. The wondrous fragrance of fresh lemongrass combined with the soft creamy rice instantly cools and revives the troubled area.

Tamarind is another favourite ingredient in herbal tonics. It is high in vitamin C, folic acid and fibre and has a mild laxative effect. It cools the body thus being an antidote to heat stroke and is effective against mouth and throat infections. Tamarind and palm sugar boiled together is said to be a great tonic for purifying the blood after childbirth. One of my workers recently approached me with tears streaming down her face; she had terrible menstrual cramps and was desperate to find some sort of relief. When she asked me what she could take to feel better, I blankly replied, 'Panadol?' This was not the solution she was looking for and she disappeared outside. Five minutes later, she had made a miraculous recovery and was back in the house, sweeping the floor.

I stared at her in disbelief. 'Did you take some painkillers?' I asked.

'Absolutely not,' she answered. 'I made a tonic of tamarind and palm sugar and now the pain has gone.'

The staff often expect me to have miraculous Western cures for minor health problems, but their own natural methods are usually the most effective.

Basic Jamu Recipe

4 tablespoons fresh turmeric juice (see method)
1 tablespoon calamondin lime or lemon juice
2 teaspoons honey

Select the mother or central body of the turmeric. Wash thoroughly, peel and grate. Strain into a glass. Alternatively, push down the shoot of a juice extractor and collect the resulting liquid. Mix with the lime juice and honey. Add extra honey or lime juice if necessary.

Ginger Tea

1 large chunk of ginger
favourite tea leaves or tea bags
hot water
sugar or honey

Clean the ginger and bruise it with the back of a knife.

Place in a teapot and pour boiling water over it. Add some of your favourite tea and let it steep for a few minutes. Add honey to taste.

Pandan Tea

2 fresh pandan leaves
1 L (32 fl oz) water

Boil together for 5–10 minutes and either use for making your favourite hot tea or coffee, or cool and serve with ice.

Glossary

Ari-Ari: The placenta and symbol of the four guardians of a newborn child. The Balinese believe that a baby is born with four brothers, *kanda empat*, represented by the blood accompanying the foetus, the placenta, amniotic fluid and coating skin of the newborn. The placenta is the most tangible aspect of the four brothers, so great effort is made to ensure its well-being — after birth, it is collected and buried ceremonially, and is considered sacred.

Arjuna: The princely bowman and hero of the *Mahabarata* and one of the five Pandawa brothers. The Balinese see Arjuna as the eternal playboy, always surrounded by beautiful women, fast chariots and palm wine.

Atman: The soul, the venerated essence of the individual, the unseen and untouchable everlasting spirit.

Bale: A Balinese-style pavilion used for a variety of purposes.

Balinese calendar: Known as Pawukon, it is a 210-day calendar brought to Bali in the seventeenth century by the Hindu Majapahits who fled Java at this time. It governs almost all ceremonies, anniversaries and auspicious days. The other Balinese calendar system is known as *Saka*, from South India. This is a lunar calendar and each of the 12 months ends on a new moon, called *Tilem*.

Banjar: Local community or neighbourhood organisation, which takes part in and helps with all village festivities.

Bhagavad-Gita: Meaning 'the divine song', it contains the sacred dialogues between Arjuna and Krishna. It is part of the *Mahabarata* and one of the foundation books of Hindu philosophy.

Bird's-eye chilli: The smallest chilli with the hottest flavour, the bird's-eye chilli is used in many spice pastes in Indonesian cooking.

Brahma: The supreme being, the creator. The first deity of the Hindu trinity or Trimurthi.

Barong: A mythical creature reminiscent of a Chinese lion that is seen as the protector of the village and is always present at temple ceremonies.

Bhutas and kalas: Evil spirits or negative forces that can upset the balance of life.

Candlenut: Candlenuts come from the candleberry tree. They are used as a thickening agent to hold spices together.

Choi-sum: Choi-sum is a flowering cabbage. It originated in Asia but is now regularly available in supermarkets, greengrocers and Asian supermarkets.

Coconut milk: Milk made from fresh coconuts is far superior to that found in tins in the supermarket, although the tinned product is suitable as a substitute ingredient. The milk is made from the flesh of the coconut and is creamy in texture.

Coriander seeds: The seeds of the coriander plant are dried and used in spice mixes. The whole seeds should be freshly ground for use in spice pastes.

Dewi: A goddess.

Dewi Saraswati: The wife of Brahma and the gracious goddess of learning, literature and fine arts, who glides through the heavens on a swan, strumming a guitar. She is the essence of intelligence and accomplishment.

Dewi Sri: The legendary goddess of rice and fertility.

Fish sauce: Don't be put off by the strong smell of fish sauce. The flavour it imparts is quite unique and omitting it from recipes leaves an obvious hole in the balance of tastes. Made from salted and fermented fish, it is an essential ingredient.

Galangal: Galangal is a member of the ginger family but with a woodier texture when mature. The galangal root is pinker skinned than ginger and is available in fruit and vegetable stores and Asian grocers.

Galungan: The most important Balinese Hindu festival that celebrates the victory of truth over evil and occurs every six months, the dates being determined by the phases of the moon and the Balinese calendar.

Gamelan: A Balinese orchestra. None of the music is written down, everything is learnt from the old folk in the compound or by chatting with friends and neighbours.

Ganesha: Brother of Kumara, the son of Siwa.

'Hello': Balinese word for a tourist.

Joged: A flirtatious and erotic Balinese dance performed at family ceremonies, particularly weddings. The woman dancer claims a partner from the audience by lassoing him with the silky belt.

Kanda empat: The four brothers or guardians that a baby is born with to protect them throughout life.

Kangkung: *Kangkung* is a water spinach. It grows in water but some varieties can also tolerate soil with plenty of water. The slim, pointed leaves form on a hollow stem. Both the leaves and the stems can be used in stir-fries and salads. It is available in Asian grocery stores and markets and is easily grown at home.

Kecap manis: *Kecap manis* is a sweet, thick soy sauce used in Balinese cooking.

Kencur: This is the name for the resurrection lily. The highly fragrant root is the part that is used in cooking.

Komara and Kumari: The celestial twin brothers responsible for the traditional three-holed design of the Balinese kitchen oven. It is believed that bad fortune will fall upon those who build a stove with only two holes.

Krishna: The most celebrated hero in Hindu mythology, and the 'master of all mystics' of the *Bhagavad-Gita*.

Kumara: Was saved from death at the hand of his brother Ganesha by his father, Siwa, but in exchange Kumara was ordered to be the guardian of all small children until the time they lose their first milk teeth. Also the name of a small ornate throne often painted in bright red and gold which usually sits beside the parents' bed where baby sleeps.

Laksmi: The Hindu goddess of prosperity and general voluptuousness, and consort of Wisnu.

Lemongrass: As the name implies, lemongrass is a grass-like plant that imparts a strong lemon flavour and fragrance to food. The stalk can be quite tough and is often bruised before cooking to release its flavours. It is readily available in supermarkets and greengrocers.

Long pepper: Long pepper is a tropical climbing plant that yields a long pepper, similar to a chilli in appearance with a bubbly texture.

Lontar: A sacred book of inscriptions, often in old Javanese or Kawi and based on Sanskrit, where the text is written on the leaves of the lontar palm.

Mahabarata: The celebrated Hindu epic.

Manusia yadnya: The five rituals of mankind, rites of passage ceremonies that every Balinese must complete before he or she dies.

Mesangih: The tooth-filing ceremony. One of the *manusia yadnya* rituals, it symbolises maturity and becoming civilised. It is believed that the filing of the teeth is a way of balancing the evils within and obtaining inner peace.

Nyepi: Balinese New Year, occurring at the end of the ninth month on the Balinese calendar. *Nyepi* is the celebration of Surya, the sun, who gives life to all beings, and the moon, who influences the oceans and the human spirit.

Ogoh-ogoh: Monsters or 'ogres' made for the New Year's Eve procession. These demons help chase the evil spirits away in order to begin the New Year in peace and harmony.

Otonan: An elaborate Balinese birthday ceremony that begins 210 days after birth and might continue throughout life. Small ceremonies called *oton* are performed every month for the baby until he or she loses their first tooth.

Palm sugar: As the name suggests, palm sugar comes from palm trees. It is a caramel-flavoured sugar used to balance the flavours of Balinese cooking. It is sold in solid form in Australia.

Pandan leaves and essence: A rich green blade-like leaf that adds a subtle flavour and distinctive fragrance to sweet and spicy dishes.

Perada: Brightly coloured fabric painted with gold Balinese patterns, always used for ceremonies and dance costumes.

Pusing: Confused, dizzy, loss of orientation, not knowing which direction is north and which south — which can induce a state of absolute panic.

Ramayana: The famous Hindu epic of the quest of Rama.

Sago: Pearls of sago are made from the starch of a palm that grows in Asia. It is available in supermarkets.

Salam leaf: A citrus and forest scent comes from these deep green leaves used in Indonesian cooking.

Semara Ratih: The god of beauty.

Shrimp paste: A highly pungent paste made of fermented crustaceans. It is available in supermarkets and Asian grocers. The strong smell of the paste dissipates when it is mixed with other ingredients.

Siwa: The third god of the Hindu trinity, who deals with death and destruction.

Snake beans: Snake beans are long, thin, round, strong beans used in Asian cooking. They are sold in bunches at Asian grocers and supermarkets.

Tamarind: The pulp of the pod of the tamarind tree is used in cooking. It has a flavour similar to dates. If buying the fresh pods, peel the hard skin away and eat the fleshy pulp, discarding the string-like fibres that run up the side of the flesh. The seeds are a lovely mahogany colour and are quite decorative. The ready-prepared pulp is available in supermarkets and Asian grocers.

Tempe: Tempe is fermented soya bean cake. It is similar to tofu in both its properties and uses but, unlike tofu, it is fermented. Available in supermarkets and health food stores.

Torch ginger: Torch ginger is a very tall, wild ginger. Both the young shoots and the bud are used in cooking.

Turmeric: The root of a plant in the lily family, turmeric lends its rich golden hue to many spice pastes in Indonesian cooking. Its earthy flavour is quite distinctive. Fresh turmeric is available in supermarkets and Asian grocers. The dried turmeric is an alternative, although its flavour will not be as superior.

Wisnu: The second deity of the Hindu trinity, entrusted with the preservation of the world and the protector and symbol of male fertility.

Recipe index

Bibliography

Ayurveda: A Life of Balance, Maya Tiwari, Inner Traditions International Ltd, 1995.

Bali, Sekala and Niskala, Volume I, Essays on Religion, Ritual and Art, Fred B. Eiseman, Jr, Periplus Editions, 1989.

Bali, Sekala and Niskala, Volume II, Essays on Society, Tradition and Craft, Fred B. Eiseman, Jr, Periplus Editions, 1989.

Island of Bali, Miguel Covarrubias, Periplus Editions, 1999.

Parthayana, The Journeying of Partha, An eighteenth-century Balinese kakawin, Helen Creese (editor and translator), KITLV Press, The Netherlands, 1998.

Spice Notes: A cook's compendium of herbs and spices, Ian Hemphill, Macmillan, Sydney, 2002.

The Painted Alphabet, Diana Darling, Tuttle Publishing, 2001.

Acknowledgements

This book has been a journey of love, passion and growth. Several years ago, I realised that *Fragrant Rice* had a life of its own. I wrapped it in *poleng*, the sacred black and white cloth of Bali, blessed it with offerings, wished it well and sent it across the waters. From there it took its own course and ended up in the hands of some earthly goddesses at HarperCollins. The angels of serendipity took charge and the book transpired.

Wonderful people from all over the world have nurtured *Fragrant Rice*. My deepest thanks goes to my husband, Ketut, and my beautiful children, Dewi, Krishna, Laksmi and Arjuna, for providing me with a story of love and understanding. I also have to thank my parents, John and Joan in Australia, for their patience and support for my somewhat alternative lifestyle, my sister Sue for creative advice and my brother Tim for the beautiful photographs. Thanks to: my dear friends Annee Lawrence, Lorraine Bacchus, Ian and Lynda Burke, who provided literary assistance when I needed it most; Ross and Sandra Heaven for their humour and never-ending devotion; Ann Whalin for her meticulous typing; Sid Jacobsen, Ted Gannan, Sabine de Lisle, Julia, Margaret and David Burke for their encouragement and corrections; and Sarita Newson for being an expert on all things Balinese.

Many thanks to Louisa Dear and Judy and Jessie Chapman, the angels of serendipity who blew the book into the hands of the HarperCollins goddesses — Katie Mitchell, Helen Littleton and especially Nicola O'Shea, my talented editor. And finally, my thanks to the people of Ubud for their kindness and generosity in sharing a precious way of life.

Conversion table

Conversion measurements have been rounded up or down slightly to make measuring easier.

	metric	imperial	US
liquid	5 ml	1 teaspoon	1 teaspoon
	15 ml	1 tablespoon	1 tablespoon
	60 ml	2 fl oz	$^1/_4$ cup
	125 ml	4 fl oz	$^1/_2$ cup
	250 ml	8 fl oz	1 cup
	500 ml	16 fl oz	2 cups
	1 litre	1$^3/_4$ pints	4 cups
dry	7 g	$^1/_4$ oz	
	10 g	$^1/_3$ oz	
	15 g	$^1/_2$ oz	
	25–30 g	1 oz	
	50 g	2 oz	
	125 g	4 oz	
	150 g	5 oz	
	200 g	7 oz	
	250 g	8 oz	
	450 g	1 lb	
	1 kg	2 lb 2 oz	

	metric	imperial
linear	3 mm	$^1/_8$ inch
	5 mm	$^1/_4$ inch
	10 mm (1 cm)	$^1/_2$ inch
	2 cm	$^3/_4$ inch
	2.5 cm	1 inch
	5 cm	2 inches

oven	°C	°F	gas mark
very cool	130	250–275	
cool	150	300	2
warm	170	325	3
medium	180	350	4
medium hot	190	375	5
	200	400	6
hot	220	425	7
very hot	230	450	8
	250	475	9

For more information on
the Honeymoon Guesthouse or
the Casa Luna Cooking School, go to
www.casalunabali.com